Psychological Interventions

Psychological Interventions

A GUIDE TO STRATEGIES

Edited by Mary Ballou

Westport, Connecticut
London

Library of Congress Cataloging-in-Publication Data

Psychological interventions : a guide to strategies / edited by Mary
    Ballou.
        p.   cm.
    Includes bibliographical references and index.
    ISBN 0–275–94851–X (alk. paper)
    1. Psychotherapy. 2. Ballou, Mary B.
    RC480.P783   1995
    616.89'14—dc20   95–6939

British Library Cataloguing in Publication Data is available.

Library of Congress Catalog Card Number: 95–6939
ISBN: 0–275–94851–X

First published in 1995

Praeger Publishers, 88 Post Road West, Westport, CT 06881
An imprint of Greenwood Publishing Group, Inc.

Printed in the United States of America

∞™

The paper used in this book complies with the
Permanent Paper Standard issued by the National
Information Standards Organization (Z39.48–1984).

10 9 8 7 6 5 4 3 2 1

Contents

Preface   vii
Introduction   ix

1   Paradoxical Intention   1
    Roueida Ghadban

2   Modeling and Role-Playing   21
    Suzanne St Onge

3   Cognitive Restructuring   37
    Lucia Matthews and Lawrence Litwack

4   Bibliotherapy   55
    Mary Ballou

5   Expressive Therapies   67
    Mary Ballou

6   Imagery   83
    Mary Ballou

7   Systematic Desensitization   95
    Suzanne St Onge

8   Focusing   117
      Mary Ballou

9   Assertiveness Training   125
      Mary Ballou

10 Journal Writing   137
      Jan Youga

11 Divorce Mediation   153
      Mary Ballou

12 Feminist Community   163
      Elaine Leeder

13 Ecological Strategies   175
      Jane Fried

14 Conclusion   195
      Mary Ballou

Index   207
About the Contributors   215

Preface

I would like to take this opportunity to tell a bit about how and why this book was written. I am both an academic and a practitioner of counseling psychology. As an academic, I teach graduate students to become therapists and also teach about this discipline and profession of counseling psychology. Standing with a foot in both the academic and practice worlds often lends a perspective to both, which is enriched by the other. However, it also imposes the knowledge that neither world has the answers. In fact, humbling questions reside in both the domains of practice/profession and academic/discipline. Some of these questions are discussed in the first chapter.

I need this book both as a practitioner and as a teacher of therapists in training. I truly hope it will be helpful to those who use it and, through them, to their clients and students. As an academic, I read student papers, and although I react to the presentation and reasoning of those papers, I also am informed by them. Over the past years, I have taught courses in which graduate students have written papers about a variety of topics, including intervention strategies. Students write papers to learn and to be evaluated; they sometimes hope for reactions to their ideas and questions. These students' papers, however, rarely migrate beyond school walls.

This book contains some chapters based on student papers that I have collected over the years. As I began planning this book, I shared my intentions with the students in appropriate classes. I asked generally for papers and specifically for exceptionally good or unique papers for eventual use in this book. As the plan became a reality, I asked some students with whom I still had contact if they would like to rewrite their papers to become chapters in this book. In other cases, I shared old student papers with current students who recently had written similar papers. In still other cases, I asked students who wanted to learn about writing for publication to write chapters for this book.

So, in a variety of ways, this text presents a new writing form. It is neither a single-authored text nor merely an edited volume. Rather, it contains all sorts of authorship arrangements and categories. Moreover, it shares with its readers the value and enthusiasm of student learning, something usually reserved for academics. Finally, the text also contains chapters written, singly or jointly, by experienced professionals, sometimes from other disciplines. In all cases, the chapters have been structured, discussed, and edited by me. Contributing authors are designated in the table of contents. Students whose work informed the development of chapters are Gary Ralph, Kathleen Biebel, Beth Ruehle, Pam Harris, Mary Watson, Theresa Costello, Lucia Matthews, Linda Rhodes, Bruce La Flamme, Jill Lack, Mary Clancy, Susan Brennan, Jonathan Locke, Anne Stuart, Beth Darrell, Sherri Damon, Steve Robinson, Karen Freeman, Troy Evertt, Mary Gaynor, Linda Birney, Joelle Dobkin, Pam Grasso, Stacey Green, Nancy Wells, Beth Ann Zdinak, Liz Gottman, Jerry Bolnick, Christian Mitchell, and Pam Kerouack. I have learned from them, and I thank them.

The present book is needed for training and for in-service provision. Its delineation of particular strategies for specific change joined with evaluation of appropriate use and effectiveness is judicious and sage in both training and clinical practice. This book is intended for use in university and professional schools and by therapists in practice.

Introduction

This is a book of diverse psychological strategies, interventions used in counseling and therapy to bring about a particular kind of change. It is a handbook of strategies that attends to wide-ranging forms of interventions, reviews research evidence of effectiveness, and escapes theoretical boundaries. The goal of this book is to provide a source of interventions that counselors or therapists might consult to increase their knowledge of interventions and to assist their clients.

In this era of limited therapeutic sessions, the need for interventions that hasten (when possible) the therapeutic process is critical. Yet, the demands for brief or episodic therapy are not easily met with professional training being so theory bound. Often, one finds handbooks of similar kinds of interventions all guided by the same theoretical underpinning, for example, cognitive-behavioral. Alternatively, books exist of treatments for the same malady, for example, trauma, depression, or personality disorders. This book, in contrast, offers interventions identified by their goal of change rather than by a particular theoretical orientation or the kind of difficulty. Finally, the book reviews research findings regarding the appropriate use and effectiveness of each strategy. Where inadequate research and evaluation exist, the questions that must be addressed before effectiveness can be assessed are raised.

Several contemporary conditions inform the text. An overarching position is that mental health theory, research, and practice is not adequate to the task of mental health promotion. Indeed, controversy about the causes and the definition of mental illness is far-reaching. Yet, even among those who agree with the medical model and its individ- ualistic mental illness construction, disagreement exists about effective treatment for each named disease. Treatment is often theory driven, rather than stemming from professional consensus. A psychodynamic therapist seeks uncovering, catharsis, and insight; a behaviorist strives for changed behavior; and a cognitivist, changed thoughts.

Research efforts seeking to demonstrate the efficacy of one approach over another are able to do so only with small, carefully circumscribed units. For example, although systematic desensitization is often more effective for more people with simple phobias, behaviorism generally has not been demonstrated to be any more effective than other theoretical orientations.

Additionally, there are those models and views that look outside the individual for influences in people's distress. These views may or may not accept the medical model for individual factors involved with mental health, but they certainly do point to a wide range of systemic factors and sociocultural influences, external to but impacting on the individual. From these viewpoints, analysis of the interaction between the person and the environment should be the focus of mental health in theory, practice, and research.

Most mental health training encourages individualistic views. Thera- pists are trained to look at, interact with, or treat the individual, rather than the larger group cultural, social, and economic forces that influence individuals. Most treatments are geared toward changing the individual, rather than changing the broader environmental conditions. For example, some therapists would use stress management to reduce a client's stress. Often, a more appropriate action is careful analysis of the stress-causing conditions in the individual's work and social life, followed by efforts to change the stressors in those environments. It is, then, always important to consider the context in which a person lives and consider the influ- ences of that context upon the individual. Sometimes, applying change efforts to the environment instead of at the individual level is the warranted course. Indeed, some contemporary approaches for improving mental health suggest, with some frequency, social and structural change vastly important to mental health. Their calls are for social change, prevention, policy recommendation, and systemic planned change. Among the important areas developing these understandings are com- munity approaches in psychology, psychiatry, and social work; preven- tion, psychoeducation, and social change; and feminist, multicultural, and ecological psychology.

This book contains one section on strategies aimed at broader than individual interventions. Jane Fried's chapter on ecological interventions and Elaine Leeder's chapter on feminist community interventions are both attempts to address our responsibility as therapists to consider sociocultural engendered forces and address the interaction of environment with individual in conceptualization and interventions. The two chapters in this section are only a small selection of the possible interventions. Psychoeducational and planned change efforts have fairly long histories in community work and progressive activism. Their overt combination with individual change strategies is unusual in therapy and counseling texts. Their placement here in a text of psychological interventions is important to the contemporary interactive dysfunction models and the health care changes brought by managed care. No longer is consideration of needed individual change without context enough, nor are only individual interventions satisfactory to treatment. The contemporary call is to understand individuals in context and to think broadly about multiple and many-leveled influences upon the individual. The treatment challenge is to expand beyond bounded theoretically driven interventions to interventions that aim at specific individual change and at sociostructural conditions.

The text presumes that therapists will have a thoughtful and planned approach to their treatment with individuals. Particular goals for change are most often identified early in therapy. Indeed, clients most often come to therapy because they (or some other person with control) seek change. Specifying the change goals is an essential part of today's mental health work. No longer is it general practice to engage in long-term therapy with the expectation that, at its outcome, clients will be better developed and healthier. Instead, overt and informed client agreements and insurance companies' managed benefits compel specification of therapy goals and delineation of interventions to be used in goal attainment. Further protocols of customary practice based on collected experience and evaluation have been and are being developed as standards of treatment practice within regulated mental health settings. Regardless of the practice setting and control issues, more highly developed research methods and resultant studies are providing some useful guidance in the selection of interventions for particular kinds of individuals with certain sorts of difficulties in specific contexts by distinct sorts of therapists. This book seeks to expand the scope and range of such interventions.

SPECIFICS ORGANIZATION

In addition to the section on community interventions, the text also includes chapters on more traditional individual change strategies. These chapters address some of the cognitive, affective, symbolic, nonverbal, and skill-building strategies for change. The book does not include all strategies in these areas; certain strategies have been selected. There are others that might have been included; in fact, the last chapter outlines some of the developing areas of strategies that also need careful attention. The range of existent strategies is huge, and volumes two and three could be written without difficulty.

Each chapter describes a strategy, presents clear instruction for how to use it, and, importantly, considers appropriate and inappropriate uses. Each chapter also addresses the research evidence underlying claims of effectiveness. Neither the appropriate use nor the effectiveness evaluations are simple; each chapter struggles with them. However, even though they are complex and difficult questions with few ready answers, they also are vital concerns demanded in competent practice. Theory-based professional habit and rule-based authority are no longer adequate criteria for intervention selection.

It is important to thoughtfully consider the appropriate uses of particular strategies, because there is no always-fitting intervention in counseling and therapy. Individuals differ in important ways. Although some generalizations might be drawn and some treatment strategies based upon them, the resulting treatment protocols are not helpful or fitting for all. Variation among individuals, differing life circumstances, and variable sociocultural factors, including culture, race, sex, and class assignments, exist and matter. Serious questions also exist about the correctness or singularity of the medical/scientific model for mental health practice, making the effectiveness evaluation and appropriate use questions central.

It seems more likely that a number of different phenomena, each fitting to different ways of understanding, and multiple factors and their interactions are involved in mental health. Careful, aware, and thoughtful selection of strategies for particular change is necessary in working with individuals toward mutually agreed-upon change goals.

Gone are the days when only a theoretical orientation determined one's activities of practice. Gone, too, are the days when the reigning ideology of the era set the therapy goals, as, for example, adaptation of the 1950s, human growth and potential of the 1960s, revolt of the 1970s, and treat the pathology of the 1980s. In the 1990s, diversity, awareness, and careful reasoning are the agenda.

The effectiveness of particular strategies (or, in the language of health maintenance organizations, treatment plans with specific goals and procedures to fulfill them) is an important issue. These chapters attempt to address this by attending to the research evidence about effectiveness. In some cases, little solid compelling research of the empirical, quasi laboratory sort exists. In others, conflicting results emerge. In still others, alternative means of substantiating effectiveness are used. Traditionally, it has been difficult to do research and to substantiate valid and reliable findings in clinical psychological practice (Bergin & Garfield, 1987; Harvey & Parks, 1984; VandenBos, 1986; Kazdin, 1992).

The philosophical and, as it turns out, political debates about positivism and the narrowly construed scientific research that support it (Harding, 1987; Unger, 1989) are not often a central interest of therapists; their implications ought to be. The implications are the stuff of effective strategies and how that claim is made. More traditionally, psychotherapy research has been difficult because of definition and measurement and control problems. For instance, the wide array of therapeutic approaches, the nature of the sort of change, linear and temporal obligations of quantitative methods, multiple and interactive causative influences, and the multifactored nature of the psychotherapy process (including such considerations as different affective intensities and the quality of human relationship between the client and the counselor) contribute to the difficulties.

Therefore, although some progress has been made in confirming the effectiveness of particular interventions for specific difficulties, psychotherapy's effectiveness is still problematic. In the 1990s, mental health practitioners and their guilds can no longer ignore these questions of effectiveness and how it is claimed.

UNDERLYING ASSUMPTIONS

Although this book does not stem from a particular theoretical orientation, it does stem from some assumptions and values. The first is that a therapeutic relationship must exist before the use of change strategies. These strategies are not intended to be employed in place of the time and effort of human connection between counselor and client, nor are they intended to be a set of instructions for therapeutic change.

A full therapeutic relationship at minimum would require: a competent therapist; a client(s) whose development, needs, and life experience match the therapist's competence; information about and understanding of the client's life experience and current concerns; knowledge of contextual factors, that is, gender, class, race, and culture, and their interactions and salience for that person; a mutual exploration of whether the particular therapist-client dyad is appropriate and useful; exploration and fit of values/worldview; agreement of goals and direction for therapy; and the development of effective, authentic, and mutual communication patterns. Another necessary requirement for the counselor before the use of these strategies would be an appreciation of the complexity of human nature and the person in context.

This text also makes the assumption that current personality theory is not yet able to describe and reflect the interactive complexity of human subsystems; the developmental course and full range of human nature; the complex and diverse sorts of interpersonal, kinship, and cultural relationships; relational essences and variable patterns; the consequences of various life experiences; and the structural and shaping influence of broader social, political, economic, and historical forces upon the individual. Although many theories and quasi theories of personality development and psychopathology exist, the whole picture does not fit in any specific frame. The six aspects identified above, among others, have not yet become the central focus for theory within personality and psychopathology. Until such inclusive and interactive theory is developed, practitioners will have to consider various and complex aspects of life and living as best they can, and they will have to aspire to mutual agreement between the changer and the changed about both the goals and the methods of that change.

Holistic, interdisciplinary, ecological, and interactive mindsets that acknowledge both the common ground and the differences among people will require a revised guide of evaluated strategies for change. Perhaps this guide will assist in the process of rethinking how and why therapy is done and in reinspecting the mindsets that support it.

REFERENCES

Bergin, A., & Garfield, S. (1987). *Handbook of psychotherapy and behavior change*. New York: Wiley.

Harding, S. (1987). *Feminist and methodology*. Bloomington: University of Indiana Press.

Harvey, J., & Parks, M. (Eds.). (1984). *Psychotherapy research and behavior change*. Washington, DC: American Psychological Association.

Kazdin, A. (Ed.). (1992). *Methodological issues & strategies in clinical research*. Hyattsville, MD: American Psychological Association.

Unger, R. (1989). Sex, gender and epistemology. In M. Crawford & M. Gentry (Eds.), *Gender and thought: Psychological perspectives.* New York: Springer-Verlag.
VandenBos, G. (Ed.). (1986). Psychotherapy research. *American Psychologist, 41,* 111–206.

1

Paradoxical Intention

Roueida Ghadban

Paradox: A statement that appears contradictory, unbelievable, absurd, or opposed to common sense but that may in fact be true. (Webster, 1975)

Paradoxical intention is a present-focused, short-term therapeutic strategy wherein the therapist recommends or encourages the continuation of maladaptive behaviors so as to ultimately undercut them. Symptomatic behaviors are thwarted by encouraging the client to view them as less adaptive options among a multitude of more adaptive behavioral choices. Paradoxical strategies are therapeutic tools that produce gradual change via a method that exaggerates and parallels processes that are common to most therapies: symptoms are accepted in order to reduce the client's resistance to change. Paradoxical intervention is most frequently used in therapeutic situations where clients have failed to respond to direct attempts at reducing their symptomatic behaviors. Such strategies typically are used to help clients establish distance between themselves and their symptoms, to place their symptoms into a more manageable perspective, and to break the pattern(s) of behavior and attitude that serve to maintain the symptom(s).

Paradoxical strategies are part of the larger therapeutic effort wherein the central paradox of therapy lies in the dual role that the therapist plays: simultaneously functioning as a follower (in an attempt to find the basic misperception[s] underlying the symptom) and as a leader (in an attempt to promote change in the client). Therapy is paradoxical because it purports, on one level, to eliminate symptoms while, on another level, to locate and unlock the resources that lie within the client. The client is almost always ambivalent about therapy because, even though the client wants to change, change is frightening. It is anxiety provoking to go from a known, albeit maladaptive, pattern of behavior to an unknown but more adaptive pattern of behavior. Therefore, regardless of whether or not the symptom is tied to an active fear, changing or removing it still evokes some resistance in the same way normal developmental changes evoke anxiety. It is when resistance is strong enough to retard an individual's development that clinical problems emerge.

Through the application of paradoxical techniques, the client is encouraged to gain control over the symptomatic behavior. Paradoxical interventions have been applied in the treatment of various symptomatic conditions, such as insomnia, depression, obsessions, compulsions, and phobias. They also have been used frequently with symptomatic behaviors that involve anxiety, such as performance anxiety or avoidance behavior. Furthermore, paradoxical strategies can be applied within a number of therapeutic frameworks: psychoanalytical, reality therapy, and systemic approaches. The effective application of paradoxical interventions depends largely on the skill and sensitivity of the therapist.

The aim of this chapter is to present an overview of the principal characteristics of paradoxical intention, its origin as a therapeutic technique, and its therapeutic applicability and effectiveness.

KEY CHARACTERISTICS

Paradoxical strategies possess several key characteristics. The first is their acceptance, or even encouragement, of the client's symptoms. For example, a therapist might encourage a depressed client to become even more depressed. This acceptance of the client's symptom confuses the client, who expects the therapist to thwart the symptomatic behavior. Instead of eliminating symptoms, the therapist accepts them, thereby placing the symptoms in the client's hands. In doing so, the therapist is saying in effect to the client, "You can keep the symptom(s) if you want."

A second key characteristic of paradoxical strategies is how they redefine symptoms. The therapist seeks to redefine the symptom by redefining its context. By accepting the symptom, the therapist implicitly redefines it as an optional behavior over which the client can exert control. The therapist may highlight the symptom further as only one option of a number of possible behaviors by reframing the symptom in terms of its context. For example, in a family where disputes are perceived as creating instability, the therapist may redefine the fighting as a mechanism through which the family maintains its stability. The therapist may say, "Your fighting is your way of showing one another that you care; it holds you together." In doing so, the therapist indicates to clients that their symptomatic pattern of behavior is accepted while simultaneously encouraging the family to consider other ways to maintain stability. However, if the therapist were to say, "You people shouldn't fight with one another because it shows how much you dislike each other," the family may band together against the therapist and refuse to consider the value of the conflict.

A third important characteristic of paradoxical strategies is that they are both present focused and short in duration. This means that behavioral changes may be achieved with very little time spent on the consideration of past causes and influences.

ORIGINS OF PARADOXICAL INTENTION

Paradoxical intention may be applied within a variety of therapeutic frameworks, but its origins are traceable to the logotherapy of Viktor Frankl. Logotherapy, initially used in treating phobics and obsessive compulsives, is based on an existential philosophy characterized by three basic assumptions: freedom of will, will to meaning, and the meaning of life. Existentialists emphasize that mental health involves taking responsibility for one's life. They contend that most individuals are out of touch with their ability to direct their lives and, as a result, fail to create a meaningful existence for themselves.

Existentialists argue that people tend to attribute their current situations to uncontrollable external events and that they downplay or fail to recognize their ability to make choices that would allow them to fulfill their potential. Therefore, existentialists see symptoms as problems that distract clients from engaging in issues of personal responsibility. Symptoms cause clients to be self-absorbed and to feel overwhelmed by their immediate problems. Existentialists recognize that a phobia may have originated as a result of early childhood experiences, but they emphasize that the symptom's current impact on a client is because of an overinvolvement with self. This is the opposite of self-transcendence, a major goal of existential therapy. According to Frankl (1967), "self-transcendence is one of the basic features of human existence. Only as man withdraws from himself in the sense of releasing self-centered interest and attention will he gain an authentic mode of existence. This rule finds clinical application and validation in the logotherapeutic techniques of deflection and paradoxical intention" (p. 46). It is this unique human capacity for self-detachment that is the basis for the logotherapeutic technique of paradoxical intention.

In addition to a capacity for self-detachment, paradoxical intervention requires another essential human attribute: a sense of humor. Frankl (1967) states that the purpose of paradoxical intervention is to "enable the patient to develop a sense of detachment toward his neurosis by laughing at it" (p. 147). It is assumed that those who can laugh about their symptoms have, on some level, overcome them (Lucas, 1982). Paradoxical intervention must be humorous in its application; otherwise, it becomes nothing more than a potentially dangerous autosuggestion.

The therapist's task, according to Frankl (1967), is to change the client's attitude toward the symptom(s) so as to detach himself or herself from the neurosis. In so doing, clients are encouraged in a supportive setting to place themselves at a distance, to alter their usual avoidant response, and to actually intend or wish for what they fear. It is the symptom's presumed function or intent on which they focus (Mahoney, 1986). Therefore, it is not just the symptom removal that the therapist seeks to achieve but also a change in attitude toward the symptom (Frankl, 1967).

How does paradoxical intention work? The explanations given depend largely on one's therapeutic orientation. According to psychoanalytic thinking, symptomatic behavior is viewed as the result of unconscious drives and needs, and paradoxical intention is a technique that attempts to cheat the punitive superego. In other words, psychoanalysts believe that, if clients become more aware of their unconscious drives and needs, their actions become less determined by them and they can be more responsible for their actions. According to this view, insight into the origin of the symptom itself is necessary for producing behavioral change, but understanding the paradoxical strategy is not necessary.

Reality therapists argue that "all behavior has a purpose: to control the world" (Wubbolding, 1984). Symptomatic behavior is the client's unsuccessful attempt at exerting control over the environment and the self. Therefore, paradoxical strategies give the client a sense of control over his or her symptom either through exaggeration of the symptom or by reframing.

On the other hand, systemic approaches, which recognize the symptom as a primarily interpersonal phenomenon, argue that it is the introduction of a new set of rules that replace the pathogenic rules binding the system that results in changes in the whole system.

Irrespective of the theoretical approach, there are as many varieties of paradoxical messages as there are varieties of clients: each paradoxical message must be tailored to the client's needs. Consequently, the therapeutic relationship must be a trusting and empathic one in order to effectively implement the paradoxical message. Regardless of orientation, therapists must be thoroughly familiar with the unique therapeutic needs of their clients and the effects that such a technique may have on the therapeutic relationship. If, after careful consideration, therapists decide that paradoxical intention is indicated, then they must choose an appropriate strategy that is consistent with the client's unique situation.

APPLICATION OF STRATEGIES

According to McKay, Davis, and Fanning (1981), paradoxical intention generally takes no more than ten sessions to be effective in bringing about change in the client's attitude toward his or her symptomatic behavior. It does so by replacing disruptive behavior patterns with more positive behavior patterns. This goal is achieved by helping clients realize that their own limitations as individuals are an integral part of the universal order of meaning (Lucas, 1982). To accomplish this, the therapist places the client in a very active role within the context of a supportive therapeutic relationship. The symptomatic pattern of behavior is presented in a more manageable form by framing it within a larger context. In effect, paradoxical intention tries to achieve a shift in the client's focus from the client's specific symptomatic behavior pattern to the universal forces affecting human behavior in general.

Paradoxical strategies are not, in themselves, powerful but serve to redirect the energy or power within the client that was previously used to maintain the symptom. The paradoxical message, on one level, is that clients are accepted as they are and, on another level, that they (not the therapist) are expected to be responsible for personal change. The client receives the message "don't change" as a result of the paradoxical intervention applied and the message "I'm here to help you change" as a consequence of the therapeutic relationship — that is, the paradoxical message "don't change" is overt or verbal, and the "change" message is expressed tacitly through the relationship.

According to McKay and others (1981), the implementation of paradoxical strategies generally involves 12 basic progressive principles:

The symptomatic behavior must be determined.

The symptom-solution cycle must be established.

Resistance is encouraged.

The goal behavior is defined.

The client is committed to change.

A time limit is established.

The symptom is prescribed.

Variations on symptomatic behavior are included.

Behavior is reframed in client's own language.

An agreement to follow instructions is secured from the client.

A relapse in behavior is predicted.

The process is demystified.

The number and order of principles used depend largely on the needs of the client; not all the principles are appropriate or necessary with every client. The application of these principles will now be examined more closely.

When using paradoxical intervention as a therapeutic tool, gaining insight is not important for behavioral change to occur. The tool itself acts directly on the undesirable behavior. For example, if a client complains of insomnia, the focus is on the client's inability to sleep at night, not on the underlying causes or motives of this problem. In effect, the therapist is concerned with the pattern of symptomatic behavior, not with why the symptomatic behavior is occurring.

Therapists using paradoxical strategies focus on a client's present behavior. The symptom-solution cycle is determined in order to arrive at the strategies that are most effective and appropriate. For example, if a client complains of insomnia, the therapist finds out the exact times and places, the events that led up to the symptom and what takes place afterward, and what a client says to himself or herself as it happens. In order to facilitate the effectiveness of paradoxical intention, it is best to describe the symptom, whenever possible, as an action. Rather than say to a client, "You have been feeling too anxious to sleep at night," it is more helpful to say, "You stay awake in bed at night." The more specific the description of the symptom, the more effective is the strategy.

Once the problem is recognized, the symptom-solution cycle is examined by focusing on unsuccessful solutions to the problem(s). Using as an example the client who complained of being unable to sleep, unsuccessful solutions might be trying unsuccessfully to fall asleep, worrying about not falling asleep, expecting to stay awake all night, and not wanting to stay awake. As Frankl (1967) points out, the compulsion to observe oneself (not sleeping), the excessive attention (lack of sleep), and the forced intention (wanting to go to sleep) perpetuate the problem.

Successful use of paradoxical strategies require that the therapist (and client, although not necessarily) sees the symptom-solution cycle of a problem behavior. By establishing which unsuccessful solutions have been attempted, one can better understand the undesirable behavior pattern.

CHANGE, RESISTANCE, AND CONTROL

Therapists may also encourage clients to resist the therapeutic process. As stated earlier, clients tend to be ambivalent about therapy. Even though they want to change, change is frightening. Why do clients resist change when therapy pushes directly for change? According to Freud, clients typically bring with them to therapy a symptom, an inability to change (opting for stability), and a desire for change (to lose the symptom). This ambivalence toward change is not abnormal in itself; all people resist change while also seeking it. Regardless of people's desire to change, they are constantly in the process of changing and growing while simultaneously maintaining a sense of continuity. Change and resistance to change counterbalance each other, creating gradual adaptive change. Eventually, people learn better ways of coping with their needs and with the environment, and they incorporate the coping skills into their self-structure.

Depending on the specific needs of the client, when applying paradoxical strategies, the therapist may choose to use the complaint-based directive, the defiance-based directive, or the joining/mirroring technique. Paradoxical techniques work differently with compliant clients than with defiant clients. Defiant clients are described as having voluntary symptoms and much resistance toward the therapist, whereas compliant clients are described as having involuntary symptoms and low resistance (Haley, 1963).

Haley (1963) explains how paradoxical strategies work with defiant clients by assuming that, in all relationships, there is some homeostatic tendency or a tendency on the part of the changee to resist any attempts by others to induce change. So, according to Haley, in order to create change, one must never push for it directly, or the changee will resist. Rather, one must appear to accept the changee, complete with symptomatic behavior. The client's resistance is used to create change: when the therapist pushes for more symptomatic behavior, the client's homeostatic tendency resists by pushing the client to reduce the behavior. On another level, Haley explains that paradoxical directives reduce symptomatic behavior because the client wants to maintain control in the relationship.

Adler (1925) describes the desire to control as flowing from a "depreciation tendency" on the part of the client. He believes that neurotic clients, because of their childhood frustration with authority figures, tend as adults to belittle authority figures. They hold onto their symptoms in order to spite the therapist and will probably regress if the therapist tells them that they are getting better. In such therapeutic situations, therapists must renounce their authority and say to the client, "You are in charge" and that the client will most likely (in the therapist's professional opinion) never improve. At this point, it is worth reemphasizing that paradoxical strategies must be carefully timed and targeted. If resistance is high, then telling a client that she or he cannot improve will influence the client to spite the therapist and improve. However, with other clients it might ruin the relationship, especially if it is delivered too seriously or too early in treatment.

By prescribing the symptom, the therapist prevents clients from using it as a power lever in the relationship and enables clients to see the symptom as what it is, a coping device. No longer offering any tactical advantage to the client, the symptom itself stands to be reevaluated and, perhaps, discarded. After it is prescribed, the only possible way the client can resist using the symptom is to go against the prescription and reduce the symptom. The effectiveness of a paradoxical directive depends on proper delivery. If a therapist redefines a symptom as desirable, he or she must present a believable explanation for why the symptom is desirable in order to increase the likelihood that clients will accept the directive. In effect, defiance-based directives work by placing clients in a double bind: if the clients increase the symptom, then they cooperate with the directive; if the clients decrease the symptom, they cooperate with the larger understanding that therapy aims to reduce symptoms. In effect, the double bind results in therapeutic change regardless of the client's response.

Complaint-based directives are presented in the same way as defiance-based directives, but because the client tends to be compliant, the dynamics set in motion are different. Presented with a directive, the compliant client, whose symptom is involuntary and whose resistance is low, will follow it and will gain control over the symptom. For example, compulsive clients, by following a directive to be more compulsive, will gain a sense that they can decide to be more or less compulsive. They see that control over compulsive behavior is possible. The symptom becomes voluntary and subject to elimination. Complaint-based directives are used mainly with symptoms such as anxiety attacks or compulsions that are maintained by clients who attempt to evade them.

With the joining/mirroring technique, the therapist, instead of interpreting the client's defensive maneuvers, actively plays them out with clients. For example, the therapist might travel with clients through their depressing inner world and say, "I see why you're depressed, I feel hopeless with you," rather than interpreting the client's depression as a cover for repressed anger. This active mirroring of the client's defensive maneuvers/resistance differs from standard interpretations of client resistance in that it is less abstract and more concrete. Clients can actually see themselves in the therapist.

Joining with resistance is an effective prelude to therapy because it reduces intrapsychic and interpersonal resistance. Intrapsychic resistance is reduced as a result of the therapist's participation and "implied" endorsement of the client's resistance. Clients receive no verbally expressed directive to change their symptomatic behavior. Joining serves to bolster the client's confidence in the therapeutic relationship as nonthreatening. Clients feel that they have gained a powerful new ally who is willing to befriend their symptomatic behavior and who is not out to impose change. Feeling safer, the client is more likely to ventilate repressed feelings directly and acknowledge defensive strategies, now embodied in the therapist, rather than resist therapeutic intervention. By joining with resistance, the therapist reduces the client's anxiety, which in turn undercuts the client's resistance to behavioral change. Joining reduces interpersonal resistance by making resistance more costly for the client. The therapist makes resistance difficult by taking on the client's defensive functions: clients can oppose the therapist only by opposing themselves. The therapist, in effect, undercuts the client's usual pattern of behavior by behaving "crazier" than the client, which will, it is hoped, compel the client to renounce her or his defensive stance.

In order for paradoxical strategies to be successful, it is necessary for therapists to determine the amount of ambivalence that the client feels toward change. If the client presents a paradoxical message to the therapist (I want to change/I don't), then the therapist must meet this ambivalence with a paradoxical message (change/don't). Sending only a change message will either damage the client's sense of self-empowerment or set up a power struggle in which symptom and resistance become even more tightly enmeshed.

Therapist and client must arrive together at a specifically defined goal in terms of a desirable change in behavior. This must be done in a way that is easily understood by the client. The goal behavior must be some kind of action that the client can do or experience. It may simply involve ceasing an undesirable behavior, such as not compulsively counting things, or the goal may be more subtle in nature, such as feeling relaxed or being more assertive. The goal(s) decided upon may be used as a means of measuring success or improvement.

Although accepting the client's ambivalent feelings toward change, therapists still may want to establish whether the client is sufficiently motivated to change an undesirable behavior. The nature of the symptom may make this difficult, and the risks involved also may interfere. Whatever the client's difficulties, the therapist may secure her or his commitment to change through the use of a written contract or a verbal expression of commitment to change.

Therapists may also encourage clients to set their own deadlines for the desired change to occur. In this way, the therapist shifts the focus away from skepticism of change to a question of time, thereby underscoring the assumption that change will occur. It also serves to secure the client's commitment to change by placing the expected deadline for change in the client's hands, giving the client a sense of control over symptom behavior.

PRESCRIBING THE SYMPTOM

One of the most essential elements, however, in the use of paradoxical strategies is prescribing the symptom. In order to understand why prescribing the symptom works, therapists must realize that the target for change is not the symptom itself but the unsuccessful solution(s) that the client applies to relieve the symptom. In cases where the therapist recommends that the client continue having the symptom (a compliance-based prescription), the client, having been told to have the symptom, ceases the effort to stop the symptom. The anxiety diminishes, and the symptom disappears, for example, the therapist might suggest that an insomniac stay awake. The therapist, in effect, breaks the pattern that the client has been using (i.e., worrying about not sleeping). The therapist is attacking the unsuccessful solution to the symptom rather than the symptom itself.

In therapeutic situations where the client is encouraged to intensify the symptom (a defiance-based prescription), the therapist expects the client to rebel against the prescription because the recommendation violates her or his freedom to have the symptom on his or her own terms. For example, a therapist may tell a depressed woman to have three crying spells a week, rather than the usual one. When resistance is primary in maintaining the symptom, recommending the symptom can serve to alter the interpersonal (or, in some cases, the intrapsychic) context that increases resistance and maintains the symptom. Recommending the symptom, in effect, creates a conflict between the resistance and the symptom whereby the resistance no longer serves to maintain the symptom. Rather, the prescribed symptom counteracts the resistance and results in undercutting the symptom. In this way, paradoxical techniques may be used to create contextual changes that indirectly result in intrapsychic changes.

In addition, the therapist, when prescribing the symptom, should include a variation on the client's usual behavior. This may be achieved by controlling the duration, intensity, location, or timing of the symptom itself. For example, the depressed client who typically engages in crying spells three times a week during the evening is instructed to have five crying spells in the morning (varying duration and timing).

However, in instances where a client's symptom is physically harmful or illegal, the therapist should introduce a variation of the presenting symptom so that its essential qualities are retained but it is safer and not illegal in nature. For example, an adolescent who is in treatment for stealing may be instructed, rather than stealing, to withhold positive information about progress in school from his or her parents. The client is still concealing information from his or her parents, but the behavior is safe and not illegal.

REFRAMING

Another aspect that is vital to the successful implementation of paradoxical strategies and that occurs at all stages of paradoxical intervention is the therapist's ability to reframe the situation in the client's own language — that is, therapists must ensure that the tone, word choice, and level of abstraction match the client's sex, age, education, and socioeconomic background to be sure that the client obtains optimal benefits from the technique(s) used.

The purpose of reframing in paradoxical intervention is not to supply the client with a more realistic, less distorted frame of reference but to break the hold of the old frame and to persuade the client to follow the therapist's instructions. It aims to alter the client's beliefs or perceptions underlying the symptom, especially the belief that the symptom is the only possible basis for the system maintaining stability. For example, in the previously mentioned family that engages in constant fighting, its members may believe that conflict is proof of their negative feelings for one another. The therapist may reframe the symptom (fighting) as an indication of caring by saying, "You fight to show each other you care; it keeps you close." In effect, reframing serves to loosen the tight frame that clients have around their symptom, yet it also agrees closely enough with the client's system and its language to compel clients to follow directions. As in the example of the family that defined the fighting as the source of the problem, the therapist may reframe a solution to the problem, rather than the actual problem. Reframing, then, is a key to lowering or raising clients' resistance in preparation for the directive (s) to follow. The family then may begin to behave in ways more in line with caring, and a healthier cycle may be established. Often, however, reframing alone is not sufficient to create behavioral change (e.g., reduction of fighting). It aims for cognitive change that will incline the client toward behavioral change.

It is recommended that the therapist conclude each session with a summary of the desired action and a clear understanding that the client has agreed to follow instructions. Whether or not the client actually accomplishes the tasks set up by the therapist, it is more important that the client understand the instructions given and that she or he sincerely agrees to follow them.

It is also recommended, especially in therapeutic instances where the client is making rapid progress and is at risk of relapsing, that the therapist predict a relapse. If the client does relapse, not only is the therapist perceived as being able to predict correctly, thereby increasing the client's confidence in the therapist's skills, but, more importantly, the client is given the assurance that the treatment is proceeding as planned. If the client does not have a relapse, it indicates to the client that she or he is healthier than the therapist thought. When a client experiences very slow progress, therapists are advised to persuade him or her to slow down as a means of encouraging resistance and resulting in the paradoxical effect of speeding up change.

When the problem behavior has been eliminated, the therapist may choose to demystify the process of paradoxical intention by explaining to the client what is involved. However, the therapist must establish whether such a move would undermine the results and whether or not the client would be able to apply the techniques in the future, independent of the therapist. Because understanding is not necessary for paradoxical intervention to work effectively, it may be more prudent for the therapist not to explain the process (McKay, Davis, & Fanning, 1981).

The ultimate goal of psychotherapy (with the exception of strict behaviorism) is to facilitate change in clients' attitude as well as to eliminate symptoms by increasing clients' sense of control over their behavior. This is also the primary aim of paradoxical intervention.

Consequently, all therapies may incorporate paradoxical strategies, because all therapies must deal with resistance. Such techniques are, whether the therapist is aware of it or not, inevitably incorporated into conventional therapy. In essence, whenever therapists accept clients' symptom(s), they are using a paradoxical technique.

RESEARCH AND EFFECTIVENESS

Much of the research that is currently available on the effectiveness of paradoxical intervention is based on case studies and anecdotal reports. Leon Seltzer (1986) states that studies reported fall short of reflecting the systematic use of paradox — especially as it is (and must be) tailored to fit the biases and needs of individual clients. He further states that such an admission is meant less as a negative judgment on the efforts to justify systematic paradoxical intervention than as a reminder of the immense practical difficulties involved in attempting, experimentally, to validate these complex therapeutic devices. Still, some conclusive results have been found on the effectiveness of paradoxical intention.

Numerous case studies have shown paradoxical intervention to be effective with symptoms such as impatience, blushing, bedwetting, fainting spells, eating disorders, and various phobias (McKay, Davis, & Fanning, 1981). Greenberg and Pie (1983) note that compulsions, schizophrenia, urinary retention, and Tourette's syndrome are among the many conditions described as responding to this technique. In a review of studies conducted by Rosenthal and Shoham-Salomon, Rosenfield (1988) cites the effectiveness of paradoxical strategies in treating depression, agoraphobia, stress, procrastination, and insomnia.

Two studies that look at the use of paradoxical intervention on procrastination in college students show it to be an efficacious technique. In one study by Lopez and Wombach (1982), 32 college students who complained of their excessive procrastination were placed in two treatment groups. Half of the subjects were told that the best way to fully observe and grasp the nature of their problem was to deliberately practice procrastination every day. The other group was instructed in a self-control treatment for practicing procrastination and actually decreased their level of procrastination more than the control group. These findings are consistent with the results of a replication of this experiment done by Wright and Strong in 1982.

In a study by Watzlawick, Weakland, and Fisch (1974), data were obtained during a six-year period of developing and testing at the Brief Therapy Center. The case studies cited deal with people from 5 years old to 60 years old and involve a variety of clinical problems, chronic as well as acute. Overall, they report to have a general improvement rate of 72 percent. This is more impressive when it is realized that most of the clients had less than seven counseling sessions.

Another study, entitled "Paradoxical Intention in the Treatment of Chronic Anorexia Nervosa" (Hsu & Lieberman, 1982), tells of therapists permissively "allowing" the symptom wherein the client counteracts a previously held eating disorder by maintaining a normal body weight. The follow-up study shows that 90 percent of the clients were able to maintain healthy body weight following treatment.

However, despite the positive claims, a closer look at the literature reveals reason for skepticism regarding paradoxical intervention's efficacy as a "risk-free" psychological counseling technique. In a more recent study, Martinez-Taboas (1990) found no convincing data to show paradoxical intervention to be more effective than placebo or other treatments. Accordingly, the following factors were cited as contributing to the findings: participants in the studies were typically students with mild or subclinical levels of dysfunction; the paradoxical intervention used was of atypical duration (less than three hours); most of the studies concentrated on a narrow field of problems; and the follow-ups, when done at all, often were conducted too soon, making it impossible to assess the long-term effects of paradoxical intervention. This study indicates that there is little in the form of well-controlled empirical studies investigating the efficacy of paradoxical strategies.

Most published reports appear to be either purely anecdotal or are contaminated by concurrent, antecedent techniques and interventions, therefore, making design soundness virtually impossible and rendering report reliability and validity highly questionable at best (Debord, 1989; Dowd & Milne, 1986; Mahoney, 1986; Greenberg & Pie, 1983). Another possible explanation for the inconsistent research findings may be the heterogeneous qualities of the clients included in these studies (Ascher, 1986). In numerous studies (Gomes-Schwartz, 1978; Garfield, 1978; Dowd & Milne, 1986; Ridley & Tan, 1986), it has been shown that the degree of client involvement in therapy as well as the perceptions of the client may be more valuable indicators of therapeutic progress than either counselor or technique variables. Given that therapeutic progress is greatly affected by these qualities in the client, future research needs to take such factors into consideration when assessing the effectiveness of paradoxical strategies.

Despite such difficulties in establishing the effectiveness of paradoxical intervention, it continues to be regarded as a highly effective counseling tool in its own right. It is often viewed as an integral component of a more comprehensive and complex treatment approach as opposed to being a unitary psychological counseling strategy. Consequently, it is difficult to ascertain if paradoxical techniques are efficacious in their own right or if they are being influenced by other psychological measures (Greenberg & Pie, 1983).

APPROPRIATE AND INAPPROPRIATE THERAPEUTIC USE

Paradoxical intention should be restricted to therapeutic situations where directly attacking the symptom will not result in behavior change. In such instances, the onus is on the therapist to ensure that the strategy is not being applied inappropriately as a result of the therapist's frustration, anger, or need to dominate.

Another consideration that needs to be addressed before implementing paradoxical intention is the symptom type. A symptom that is circumscribed and measurable is easier to change using paradoxical intervention than a generalized symptom pattern, such as free-floating anxiety. When the symptom is vague, it is hard to know what to prescribe. When the symptom is ongoing or always present, it is difficult to set up changes in duration and intensity. Consequently, the application of paradoxical interventions is limited to symptoms that are behaviorally observable and might be ineffective when dealing with issues that are more complex and intrapsychic in nature.

In addition, the therapist should consider the strength and nature of the therapeutic relationship. Because paradoxical intervention is really an exaggeration of conventional therapy, not a replacement for it, therapy must incorporate objectivity and empathy. In terms of objectivity, the therapist plays the role of a change agent who is external to the client's frame of reference. In order to be effective, as Haley (1963) has argued, the therapist should, on one level, become an ally to the client and empathically follow the client as he or she leads the therapist to an understanding of the client's worldview, irrespective of how distorted it may be. On another level, the therapist is looking for ways to impel the client to renounce distorted aspects of this worldview and the behaviors that these distortions engender. In this way, the therapist acts as both a follower and a leader in order for paradoxical intention to work most effectively.

Paradoxical strategies are said to be most appropriate in situations where clients have resisted conventional therapies that deal directly with the symptom. The therapeutic use of paradoxical strategies is most effective when it is in the context of a trusting therapeutic relationship where the symptomatic behavior is dealt with through the humorous interchange between therapist and client. Furthermore, the therapeutic effect of such techniques can be significantly enhanced when the therapist strives to match the client's word choice, level of abstraction, and education level.

Essentially, paradoxical intervention would be appropriate with any client who has enough ego strength to benefit from therapy but who uses symptoms in the following ways: as a means of avoiding responsibility, as a power tactic against the therapist, or as a way of avoiding the painful work involved in therapy. It is an appropriate intervention to use with neurotic clients, stress management, eating disorders, juvenile delin-quents, insomniacs, phobics, stutterers, and family therapy (McKay, Davis, & Fanning, 1981; Dowd & Milne, 1986; Rosenfield, 1988; Debord, 1989).

There are, however, according to Dowd and Milne (1986), instances in which paradoxical techniques should not be used. They would be inappropriate therapeutic tools, and should not be used, with the following types of clients: borderline, sociopathic, suicidal, paranoid, impulsive, aggressive, mentally retarded, and unmotivated. They also should not be used with victims of circumstance (e.g., rape) or with clients suffering from severe mental or affective disorders. Such strategies have been shown to be ineffective in instances of acute crisis. In addition, paradoxical strategies should not be used in situations where behavior is not voluntary but is due to physiological difficulties, for example, with clients whose inappropriate behavior is organic in nature.

DISCUSSION

Given the mixed research findings, the inherent difficulties in carrying out controlled empirical studies, and the ethical considerations that such techniques raise, there are significant questions that need to be addressed. One such question centers around the long-term effects of using such strategies, that is, accepting the assumption that one can achieve behavior change without the client gaining insight into the behavioral problem, can the client still acquire effective skills that are long lasting and generalizable to other related problem areas? Would the change in behavior simply result in symptom substitution, so that even though change is observed in the targeted behavior, another symptom may, in fact, replace the symptom that has been "treated"? Furthermore, what if the outcome of using paradoxical intervention backfires and results in reinforcing a symptomatic behavior? How would such an outcome be rectified without compromising the client's needs or the therapeutic alliance? Are certain behaviors or concerns more responsive to particular forms of paradoxical intervention (e.g., is reframing more effective with depression)? Also, the ethical and legal implications of using these techniques need to be examined closely.

An important question frequently asked is whether it is ethical to manipulate the client in the name of therapeutic intervention. Some therapists argue that the application of paradoxical strategies should be restricted to extreme cases, and only as a last resort. Others hold the view that no therapeutic intervention is completely free of some form of manipulation (Hill, Gruszkos, & Strong, 1985). Proponents of this view hold that minimizing the potential danger and ethical concerns depends more on the clinical competence of the therapist than on the specific technique used. Hill and others (1985) found that explaining the double-bind aspects of paradoxical intention resulted in clients viewing their therapists more favorably, but the effectiveness of the intervention was compromised. Debord (1989) poses the question, Do clients commit themselves to therapy so that their therapist will be seen in a favorable light or to seek help with changing certain behaviors and concerns? According to Dowd (1987), we rarely inform clients of the rationales for the techniques we use; therefore, this should not be an issue as long as counselors behave in a respectful, empathic, and genuine way toward the client. This concern appears to address the therapist's intent behind using such a strategy rather than whether or not such a strategy is used — that is, will paradoxical intention be misused by therapists as a quick-and-easy technique for dealing with complex psychological issues. It is in this respect that the therapist needs to be careful not to act out his or her own conflicts, frustrations, or hostilities on the client (Riebel, 1985).

Paradoxical intention often has been described as a last-ditch effort that employs deception and manipulation to deal with situations where traditional techniques have failed. However, these interventions are not magical tricks that produce instant changes. They tend to produce change gradually and should be regarded as a process that parallels the process that is common to most conventional therapies. The use of paradoxical intentions does not preclude the therapist from taking a personal history, helping the client to develop insight into his or her behavior, or providing interpretation. They are not discrete techniques but are intricately woven into the therapeutic process as a whole. In the attempts to scientifically prove the effectiveness of paradoxical intervention, what is often overlooked is that effectively implementing such a technique depends largely on how and when the directive is presented, rather than what the directive itself is, that is, words without context would have no meaning. This chapter's overview of paradoxical intention introduces some of the basic principles that are necessary for its application as a therapeutic strategy. In terms of where it falls on the affective-cognitive-behavioral continuum, paradoxical techniques depend on the therapist's individual style and therapeutic focus, whether it be intrapsychic, cognitive, affective, or behavioral. The therapist's frame of reference influences not only what is practiced but also how it is practiced. A paradoxical intervention may be presented to a client as truth, as an outrageous and absurd lie, or simply as a humorous gesture (Mozdzierz, Lisiecki, & Macchitelli, 1989). Whatever one's orientation, paradoxical intention generally is indicated when directly attacking the symptom results in increased resistance. It should be used cautiously by highly skilled therapists within a therapeutic relationship that is based on respect, empathic understanding, and therapeutic genuineness.

REFERENCES

Adler, A. (1925). *The practice and theory of individual psychology* (P. Radin, Trans.). Paterson, NJ: Littlefield, Adams.

Ascher, M. (1986). Several suggestions for the future of paradox in therapy. *The Counseling Psychologist, 14*(2), 291–296.

Debord, J. B. (1989). Paradoxical intervention: A review of the recent literature. *Journal of Counseling and Development, 67*, 394–398.

Dowd, E. T. (1987). Paradoxical intervention: Contextual and decontextualization. *The Counseling Psychologist, 15*(1), 159–163.

Dowd, E. T., & Milne, C. R. (1986). Paradoxical intervention in counseling psychology. *The Counseling Psychologist, 14*(2), 237–282.

Frankl, V. E. (Ed.). (1967). *Psychotherapy and existentialism.* New York: Simon and Schuster.

Garfield, S. J. (1978). Research on client variables in psychotherapy. In S. Garfield & A. Bergin (Eds.), *Handbook of psychotherapy and behavioral change* (pp. 191–232). New York: Wiley.

Gerz, H. (1967). Treatment of phobic and obsessive-compulsive patients using paradoxical intention. In V. E. Frankl, (Ed.), *Psychotherapy and existentialism* (pp. 199–220). New York: Simon and Schuster.

Gomes-Schwartz, B. (1978). Effective ingredients in psychotherapy: Prediction of outcomes from process variables. *Journal of Consulting and Clinical Psychology, 46*, 1023–1035.

Greenberg, R., & Pie, R. (1983). Is paradoxical intention risk-free? *Journal of Clinical Psychiatry, 44*(2), 66–69.

Haley, J. (1976). *Problem solving therapy.* San Francisco, CA: Jossey-Bass.

Haley, J. (1963). *Strategies of psychotherapy*. New York: Grune and Stratton.

Hill, H. J., Gruszkos, J. R., & Strong, S. R. (1985). Attribution and the double bind in paradoxical interventions. *Psychotherapy, 22*, 779–785.

Hsu, L. G., & Lieberman, S. (1982). Paradoxical intervention in the treatment of chronic anorexia nervosa. *The American Journal of Psychiatry, 139*(5), 650–653.

Lopez, G., & Wombach, C. A. (1982). Effects of paradoxical and self control directives in counseling. *Journal of Counseling Psychology, 29*, 115–125.

Lucas, E. (1982). The "birthmarks" of paradoxical intention. *The International Forum for Logotherapy, 5*(1), 20–24.

Mahoney, N. J. (1986). Paradoxical intention, symptom, prescription and principles of therapeutic change. *The Counseling Psychologist, 14*(2), 283–290.

Martinez-Taboas, A. (1990). Controlled outcome research with paradoxical interventions: A review for clinicians. *Psychotherapy, 27*, 468–472.

McKay, M., Davis, M., & Fanning, P. (1981). *Thoughts and feelings: The art of cognitive stress intervention* (pp. 179–201). New York: New Harbinger.

Mozdzierz, G., Lisiecki, J., & Macchitelli, F. (1989). The mandala of psychotherapy: The universal use of paradox — new understanding and more confusion. *Psychotherapy, 26*(3), 383–388.

Ridley, R., & Tan, S. (1986). Unintentional paradoxes and potential pitfalls in paradoxical psychotherapy. *The Counseling Psychologist, 14*(2), 303–308.

Riebel, L. (1985). Usurpation: Strategy and metaphor. *Psychotherapy, 22*(3), 595–602.

Rosenfield, A. (1988). When therapists talk crazy. *Psychology Today, 22*(12), 24–26.

Seltzer, L. (1986). *Paradoxical strategies in psychology: A comprehensive overview and guidebook*. New York: Wiley.

Shoham-Salomon, V., & Rosenthal, R. (1987). Paradoxical interventions: A meta-analysis. *Journal of Consulting and Clinical Psychology, 55*(1), 22–28.

Watzlawick, P., Weakland, J., & Fisch, R. (1974). *Change: Principles of problem formulation and problem resolution*. New York: W. W. Norton.

Webster's New Collegiate Dictionary (1975). Springfield, MA: Merriam Co.

Wright, R. M., & Strong, S. R. (1982). Stimulating therapeutic change with directives: An exploratory study. *Journal of Counseling Psychology, 29*, 199–202.

Wubbolding, R. (1984). Using paradox in reality therapy (part 1). *Journal of Reality Therapy, 4*(1), 3–9.

2

Modeling and Role-Playing

Suzanne St Onge

Imagine the difficulty in trying to speak, read, or write a foreign language, for example, Russian, without ever having witnessed a Russian conversation and hearing the various intonations and pronunciations and without ever having compared the Cyrillic alphabet with the Roman one. Such a task would be formidable if it were not for one important factor. We can learn new information by observing and imitating it and by comparing and integrating it with previously mastered knowledge. When we use modeling and role-playing to help clients implement change in their lives, this is exactly what we are doing: demonstrating, exploring, comparing, integrating, and enacting.

Modeling refers to the acquisitional stage of observational learning, during which the verbal and nonverbal behaviors of an individual or group (the model) are imitated or reproduced. Models can be simulated or real-life examples and can demonstrate, overtly or covertly, the effective behavioral components of an activity that a client wishes to master. Modeling may also be accomplished through using imagination, media, or interactions between models and observers. In the counseling relationship, one must come to terms with the counselor's being a very influential model in what he or she does or does not do.

Role-playing is the enactment phase or actual trying out of new ways of thinking, feeling, and doing. It can be done through simply repeating the model's behavior or by rehearsing what one imagines would be an effective solution to a problem situation. Quite often, role-playing is used in counselor training and in couples and group counseling to help participants understand different points of view. Role reversal is similar to role-playing with the exception that two or more persons exchange roles and each tries out the other's behavior. It can be useful in helping people explore previously hidden aspects of themselves.

ORIGINS OF MODELING AND ROLE-PLAYING

Early 1900s social scientists speculated that modeling was an innate phenomenon because they observed how easily infants and animals learned through imitation. In the 1920s, Gordon Allport (1937) used the principles of Pavlovian classical conditioning to explain how language was learned, that is, through the continuous pairing of the word (e.g., milk) with a neutral stimulus (e.g., the baby's bottle), eliciting the response (e.g., anticipation of hunger relief) formerly associated only with the neutral stimulus.

Miller and Dollard (1941) used principles of operant conditioning to explain modeling. They believed a motivated subject could learn the model's behaviors through the delight and positive reinforcement of having achieved correct responses. Albert Bandura (1961, 1963, 1977, 1986) is the one most commonly associated with the terms "modeling" and "social learning theory." His overall approach hypothesized that the development of personality is organized by the accumulation and integration of learned behaviors resulting from an individual's inter-actions in the environment. Observational learning, vicarious learning, and modeling are all influenced by environmental variables, but each individual brings to these factors their unique genetic and biochemical makeup.

According to Bandura (1986), the learning of new behavior depends on four factors: attention, retention, motor reproduction, and incentives. The client must be able to focus his or her attention on the model's target behavior. Learning can take place only to the extent that the client under-stands what is happening. Without comprehension, learning becomes a mere mechanical repetition.

Cognitive mediational processes underlie the ability to attend to and to retain the information that has been observed. The client must be able to symbolically understand and encode the behavior into memory in order to, first, retain it and, later, reproduce it.

According to Kazdin (1984), it is not merely model observation that fosters behavioral change. It is the modifying of the mental represen-tations that guide behavior that ultimately is responsible for behavioral transformations. The client also must be capable of physically enacting the behavior in order to further integrate the visual and cognitive information with the actual musculoskeletal performance. Ultimate mastery of the behavior relies on the client's motivation, the wish to acquire the behavior. If the model's enactments do not represent, for the client, a desirable goal, this behavior will never be totally learned. By 1982, Bandura had shifted to more vicarious modeling practices and had developed a self-efficacy theory. He theorized that the expectations of what one can do significantly colored the internalization of perceived rules and the organization and evaluation of how one performed and of how others rated it. A person's self-expectations affected how information was received — through overt or covert modeling and role rehearsal. His theory became more one of complete self-management (Okun, 1990).

By 1976, Albert Ellis (Ellis & Grieger, 1977; Ellis & Harper, 1975) instituted role-playing techniques in the behavioral rehearsal stage of his rational emotive therapy. He found that such concrete skill reenactments promulgated new ways of thinking and interacting. In the same vein, Donald Meichenbaum (1977) incorporated the modeling of how to monitor and stop injurious self-talk and how to develop and rehearse healthier coping stratagems.

Role-playing also has been used by nonverbal clinicians. In the 1920s, Jacob Moreno (1946) introduced the term "role-playing." As the literal meaning implies, he observed Viennese actors, or role-players, taking on roles. He then transferred this role-playing into the group and family interventions used in psychodrama. Clients act out roles they believe have been assigned to them or try on new roles.

The perceptually oriented, Gestalt psychologies were transformed into an experimental Gestalt psychotherapy by Fritz Peris (1969) beginning in the 1950s. Gestalt psychology assumes that individuals are continually forming meaningful wholes out of their experiences. Problems in living are thought to be related to conflicts within the self and the formation of externally imposed, binding, false self-images that disrupt using one's energies to meet the needs of both the self and the environment.

Gestalt techniques, like role-playing, are used to help individuals become aware of themselves and their conflicts and to resolve their impasses and integrate themselves by role-playing those denied aspects of self that had been projected to the outside. It was not intended to be a preoccupation with a self but, rather, a corroborative balance between the self and the environment.

TYPES OF MODELING

Modeling consists of a client observing, overtly or covertly, herself or himself or others carrying out or refraining from acting and consequently being either rewarded or punished. He or she can also role-play, or enact, wished for or hated roles in order to broaden his or her repertoire of skills. These interventions can be applied in individual, group, and family situations. The type of modeling and role-playing are live or direct, graduated, mastery and coping, participant, vicarious or symbolic/covert use of self, and others, as in multiple modeling.

Hergenhahn and Olson (1993) found live modeling more effective than abstract because it is more interesting and can facilitate problem-solving dialogue between observer and model. Graduated modeling invokes gradual presentation of increasingly difficult and increasingly anxiety-provoking behavior. Coping modeling is usually rated more effective than mastery modeling (Kazdin, 1984), because it utilizes problem solving and gradual overcoming of barriers by determined application of strategies. Contrarily, other controversial literal results may be because of the number of serviceable coping strategies conveyed by either of these formats.

Participant modeling (Ritter, 1968), or guided reinforced participation, is often rated especially effective because it provides a great deal of immediate feedback and nurturing guidance through the mastery of small steps. Symbolic or vicarious modeling is done by utilizing media: films, audiotapes, cartoons, written scripts. Its prime benefit is that recorded behavior can be controlled and replayed and can remain totally under the client's management.

Covert or imaginal modeling, promulgated by Kazdin (1984, 1975), involves clients imagining themselves or someone else performing target behaviors. The counselor consults with the client and describes with great detail and specificity the verbal and nonverbal actions, thoughts, and feelings wished for. It has been effective in treating phobia (Kazdin, 1984), lack of assertiveness (Kazdin, 1975), and alcoholism and obsessive-compulsive behavior (Hay, Hay, & Nelson, 1977). The literature suggests that covert modeling is quite promising because it can be easily tailored to client needs while offering pragmatic financial savings. The counselor must, however, assess whether the client is capable of visualizing mental pictures and what that process entails.

Every day, people learn many things through such vicarious imaginings. Many daydreams contain wished-for benefits that have not yet actualized, like visualizing ourselves performing more effectively.

Unfortunately, we are also inundated by unwanted, yet sensational, images of violence in our streets, television, and film. Our minds are continually creating and recreating images, both positive and negative.

However, the literature (Kazdin, 1984) has failed to identify the relationships between such varying factors as vividness, clarity, anxiety during visualization, the controllability of imagery, and the amount of material imagined in relation to what was presented and how all these correlate with therapeutic improvements. Controversies rage as to covert modeling's effectiveness (Anderson & Borkovec, 1980; Arnkoff & Stewart, 1973; Bailey & Sowder, 1970; Danet, 1968; and Griffith, 1974). Many practitioners indicate that imagery-based modeling is as effective as overt rehearsal. Yet, it has also been demonstrated that the addition of overt role-playing in treatment sessions and in homework assignments can greatly enhance therapeutic outcomes.

Multiple modeling techniques use models that are similar to and different from the observer. This can help demonstrate generality behavior and alternative ways to carry out actions. It is most effective with a group treatment modality, and, like graduated modeling, the skills can be presented and mastered sequentially.

GENERAL STEPS IN USING MODELING

Acquisition Phase

1. The helper should utilize the basic helping processes of clarifying client's concerns, setting goals, and making the learning environment psychologically secure. A warm collaborative relationship is essential to change. Therefore, facilitate a working rapport by providing support, minimizing distractions, and clarifying therapist and client roles.

2. The client can assume responsibility for change when she or he describes in detail the desirable behaviors, where and when they occur, who might be present, and what his or her fears are.

3. The helper might subdivide the desirable skills into manageable tasks that can be performed successfully. The helper must also be explicit and concrete about verbal and nonverbal behaviors.

4. While either doing or observing the modeling, the helper might point out which factors seem important and what their particular relevance might be for a certain client.

5. The model demonstrates thoughts, actions, and even feelings that accompany skills. The therapist and client can then comment on the general principles governing the model's performance, monitor the consequences

of actions, and engage in problem-solving dialogue if refinements are to be made.

Role-Playing or Performance Phase

1. This can be done either actively or imaginarily. The client must actually think, feel, and act the role in order for learning and changing of perceptions to occur.
2. Clear, specific, encouraging feedback must be given throughout the rehearsal. Concrete suggestions of what else might be tried could also be included.
3. Meichenbaum (1977) suggests ways of defusing intrusive negative "self-talk." This can first be done out loud, then more quietly, and, eventually, covertly.
4. The suitability of the new behavior for the client must be assessed, and modifications are to be carried out if necessary.
5. Clients may be given practice in visualizing scenes while the therapist describes the situation, how the model might think, behave, and feel, and the scene's total context. The client can remain with the imagery for at least 30 seconds.
6. Scenes or role-plays also can be arranged hierarchically and either contain some description of the role, with its resultant effects, or be left blank for the client's improvisations and associations of what the role would entail.
7. Encouragement by the therapist helps motivate the client to continue with the assignment. At other times, internal satisfaction with one's performance is all the client needs.
8. At the end of each session, the therapist should make time to review, summarize, clarify, discuss, and assign any relevant homework.
9. After the emotional, cognitive, and behavioral changes have begun to occur, the focus is on consolidating them and generalizing them for use in future situations.

CHARACTERISTICS OF THE MODEL
THAT ENHANCE LEARNING

1. The client can learn by modeling only if a suitable model exists who displays behaviors that the client really needs and wants. No learning will take place without cooperation between client and therapist.
2. Setting the stage and preparing an instructional set can facilitate learning. The helper discusses with the client risks and benefits of adopting the behaviors and ways to modify them. Timely and genuine positive

reinforcement is given (rather than waiting until later) to encourage the client during role-playing.

3. Similarity of expectations between helpers and clients and a mutual confidence that their working together will yield positive results all enhance modeling effects.

4. Sometimes it is useful for the model to resemble the client in age, sex, race, and attitudes. In multiple modeling, however, people of differing characteristics successfully handling feared events has more impact on the observer, because it allows opportunities for identification.

5. It might help to structure the situation by facilitating the client's positive feelings and esteem of the model when she or he sees others as benefiting from the model. Usually, those with status, competence, and prestige, rather than those of lower standing, are more effective in prompting imitation by others.

6. Competence can be demonstrated by having the model verbalize the general underlying principles and connecting them to concrete, real-life situations.

7. Quite often, the greater the helper's credibility, the greater will be the client's respect. Credibility usually consists of the perceived ability to know useful information and to be able to communicate this knowledge without bias.

8. The helper's warm, nurturant, and empathic stance is critical. The client must be certain that his or her interests are of prime concern.

9. If clients believe that mastering the behavior will positively affect their social power or earn them the recognition of significant others, they are more likely to be motivated. Resolution of problem, painful behaviors is also highly reinforcing.

10. The effectiveness of modeling depends on whether the client can encode the model's activities. Complex behaviors must first be broken down into their component parts and then reorganized into a meaningful whole.

11. Learning increases through rehearsal and repetition.

12. For resistive clients, Kanfer and Goldstein (1986) suggest:

    a. a less authoritative structure,

    b. always obtaining the client's explicit permission,

    c. the helper respecting and acceding to the client's needs for autonomy and personal power,

    d. best obtaining initial compliance under conditions of low external pressure,

    e. reducing the effects of sabotage by acknowledging modeling in the client's presence,

    f. respecting the client's beliefs while challenging his or her ineffective behaviors,

    g. building upon a client's unique strengths.

CLIENT CHARACTERISTICS

1. According to Bandura (1986), skills are not apt to be learned when they have little functional value from the client's perspective.

2. The effectiveness of varying modeling stratagems correlates highly with the observer's developmental competence. Everything must be done more carefully, with smaller chunks of behavior and more frequent reinforcers, for a more developmentally disabled client.

3. According to Bandura's self-efficacy theory (1986), those who lack confidence in their own ability may have greater difficulty in successfully imitating models. Research by Salomon (1984) has shown that a client's perceived self-efficacy partly determines the mastery of new skills, which then, reciprocally, boosts self-judgment.

4. The client's capacity to process and retain information can be enhanced by minimizing outside distractions, simplifying the procedures, and commenting on pertinent modeling activities.

5. If the observer is too anxious, this will interfere with assimilation, processing, and retention of modeling skills. Such clients might need prior training in relaxation techniques or, if indicated, small temporary doses of tranquilizers prescribed by a psychopharmacologist.

6. For children, being imitated by the model is highly reinforcing and provides greater incentive for learning. Children also respond more favorably to peer models only if they perceive that the model's imitation of them is spontaneously genuine rather than falsely deliberate. Helpers must try to invoke the child's natural curiosity.

7. Goldstein, Sprafkin, and Gershaw (1976) summarized some principles that have been effective in their structured learning training programs: provide training in situations most similar to the client's everyday encounters; appropriate reinforcement of desirable behaviors is usually more effective if given by significant others; present and modify behaviors within a multitude of situations to help clients practice and gain competence in a variety of conditions.

CLINICAL APPLICATIONS OF MODELING AND ROLE-PLAYING

The beneficial effects of modeling have been well-documented both in laboratory research and clinical trials (Perry & Furukawa, 1986;

Rachman, 1976; Rosenthal & Bandura, 1978). Their straightforwardness and multiple, facile applicability make them useful in a wide variety of clinical applications.

Modeling and role-playing can be used with developmentally delayed psychotic or institutionalized clients by building new skills or by retrieving previously acquired, but no longer utilized, social skills. Working with these clients requires patience and persistence. Complex behaviors must be broken down into elementary subskills, which then must be frequently rehearsed and reinforced to provide incentives in carrying out the tasks.

The goal-specific and active, solution-oriented nature of these approaches helps counterbalance the fears and powerlessness people experience when anxious or depressed. Hence, they are useful in treating many behavior disorders, from primarily cognitive (e.g., test anxiety or phobias) to interpersonal difficulties, by augmenting insufficient social repertoires. The fostering of effective interpersonal skills has been advocated by clinicians working with alcoholics, delinquents, and addicts. Peer models are also enrolled to help decrease the defensive resistance in these populations.

These strategies can be applied in individual, group, or family counseling in various settings. Given their emphasis on learning rather than on psychopathology, modeling and role-playing can be applied to many systems: educational, work, medical, family, and community. Their psychoeducational nature makes them useful for a wide range of developmental concerns, hence, their promulgation in self-help publications. They are pragmatic, time-limited, and directive and are applied to well-delineated targets. According to Okun (1990), by minimizing the importance of individual deficits and emphasizing here-and-now interactions, modeling and role-playing provide a more optimistic view of the human capacity for change. It is this innate human potential to become aware of and alter the impact of their thoughts and behaviors that empowers clients to take charge of their lives. That potential is inherent in their humanity. Therapists cannot give it to them.

Modeling can also be used to teach child behavior management skills to teachers, parents, and other nonprofessionals. It has been useful in eradicating fears of animals and reducing dental anxiety and fears about medical procedures.

The current trend is toward incorporating modeling and role-playing as one element of a treatment package, thus, enhancing skills acquisition and broadening the applicability of treatment effects. In preventing or treating symptoms prior to the onset of medical disability, the developing fields of preventive sports and behavioral medicine promise a greater outlet for their dissemination.

Clinical research done in specific areas are listed below:

modeling for assertiveness training (Kazdin, 1975; Nietzel, Martorana, & Melnick, 1977),

independence training modeling (Goldstein et al., 1973),

use in explosive rages (Foy, Elser, & Pinkston, 1975),

treatment of aggression (Goodwin & Mahoney, 1975),

language training in autistic children (Coleman & Stedman, 1974),

treating enuresis (Johnson & Thompson, 1974),

treating anxiety in children and adults (Bandura, 1969, 1977),

uses in establishing social skills (Quinsley & Varney, 1977),

strategies for obsessive-compulsive (Roper, Rachman, & Marks, 1975),

interventions in social withdrawal (Ross, Ross, & Evans, 1971).

CRITIQUE POTENTIAL MISAPPLICATION — WHAT NEEDS ADDRESSING

The linear, cause and effect "old science" tried to uncover basic, nonchanging universal laws. The "new science" investigates cybernetic, circular, interactive, and constantly changing effects. It questions whether or not there exists some "one and only truth," and it posits that there may, indeed, be several "truths" and several ways of knowing it. It is useful to examine such notions when addressing psychological interventions. Glerck's theory of "chaos" (1988) implies that no single scientific discipline can totally understand behavior and its causes. Psychology must be flexible enough to be precisely focused when necessary but also open to novel ways of conceptualizing and problem solving. Bandura (1977), in his explication of reciprocal determinism and self-efficacy theory, further clarified that the interdependent personal and environmental factors that affect human functioning do not necessarily exert an equal amount of reciprocal influences. Evaluation of strategies of modeling and role-playing can be analyzed logically by seeing how well they address the needs of individuals, the environmental milieu, and the interactions between these two.

Observational and rehearsal learning are versatile, broadly applicable, helping strategies. However, some clients lack the mental flexibility to envision taking on another person's position; they cannot or will not release their internal controls so as to imagine themselves into their future, or, objectively, they cannot or will not address their situation. It is their right. Therapists must exert caution in using imaginal techniques when there has been some impairment in reality testing, troublesome perceptual distortions, dissociative states, poor judgment, and loss of the ability to remain in control of impulses.

If discrepancies exist between the model's and the observer's thinking and behaving, very few skills will be effectively learned or maintained. Inconsistency in standards most likely will generate conflict. Furthermore, adopting new practices initially creates stress barriers to change, which can disrupt routine patterns of functioning. In the literature, how such possible side effects and risks of treatment affect clients and their significant others is rarely addressed and needs to be done more frequently.

Modeling and role-playing are not, in and of themselves, coercive, but the emphasis on technique-driven formats may foster manipulation of vulnerable clients. Potentially, there could be careless mismatches between interventions and participants, and the therapeutic relationship might decline into coercion and control by a powerful other (the therapist). Clients could be overtly or covertly prescribed thoughts and behaviors that come merely from the therapist, not from therapist and client. Preventing this requires professionals to frequently evaluate themselves, their work, and their ethics.

Do helpers ask themselves: Who defines what is healthy and socially adaptive? What serve as criteria for social norms? The civil rights movement and feminist and constructive theories have made explicit that dominant or privileged groups benefit from the existing social arrangements and maintain the status quo by rigorously advocating for their standards of what is right and wrong. If we are defining such nebulous sociobehavioral concepts as adaptive and maladaptive, does it not behoove us to question whose criteria we are trying to emulate? According to Kantrowitz and Ballou (1992), proponents of cognitive behaviorism (including modeling and role-playing) have neglected to make visible who defines what is normative behavior and have failed to name their underlying assumptions and epistemologies.

The use of statistical norms in science and research can be linguistically confounding for many clients. Research paradigms attempt to establish the patterns of the normative or average population. Hence, they emphasize sameness and may devalue differences, but the use of the statistical words "normal" and "abnormal" does not connote the moral value of rightness and wrongness, and, yet, that might be exactly what those words mean for the general public. The United States, however, is multicultural, not a homogeneous society, and what is normal for one person may not be normal for another. Modern clinicians must always take into account the fit between interventions and a client's strengths, limitations, and needs and whether a particular strategy can be utilized by that person within a certain sociocultural context. Several authors have discussed that psychological theories based on dominant cultural norms may not be relevant to those whose racial, gender, cultural, and socioeconomic status vary from such norms.

Like most psychological interventions, modeling and role-playing are subject to the limitation of how their parent theory (cognitive behaviorism) views humankind, the nature of health and disease, the preferred empirical research methodologies, and the emphasis on rationality and control over one's perceptions and behaviors. This narrowed view of human functioning makes it easier to target and change specific behaviors. However, its drawback is that it implies that other methods of knowing, such as those utilized by women and non-European peoples (e.g., intuition, creativity, and subjectivity), are not as valid and that autonomy and self-sufficiency are seen as more mature ways of living, rather than relational and nonindividualistic modes. Proponents of modeling and role-playing could learn from the feminist counselors who explain to clients their professional worldview and their particular intervention styles. This gives a client more information on which to base decision making, to give informed consent, and to develop a truly corroborative working relationship. True, it takes more time, but the therapist is realistically seen as knowledgeable, rather than expert or omnipotent.

Modeling and role-playing are grounded in a belief that people are responsible for and can increase their well-being. This is hopeful, because it underscores that past learning can be unlearned and new learning mastered. On the other hand, it is overly simplistic and might contribute to a "blame the victim" mentality. The victim might take on too much responsibility for externally caused situations and might internalize self-blame. Counselors need to be aware of such ramifications. There has not been enough attention paid in modeling and role-playing literatures to the necessity of addressing specific individual and societal circumstances that spawn unfavorable situations. The nitty gritty of who, what, when, where, how, and why must be addressed so that in utilizing these strategies, therapists can remember and inform clients that these interventions are addressing only one part of a complex system.

Bandura (1961), in his self-efficacy formulation, stated that behavioral success not only was dependent on individual skills, change efforts, resiliency after setbacks, or the maintenance of gains but also is based on belief in one's capacity to master problems. However, how do you assess a person's self-efficacy? What serve as guideposts? If there are deficits, how do helpers facilitate remediation? Schwarzen's work (1992) deals at length with this topic; yet, much modeling and role-playing literature does not even raise this thorny issue. This is a glaring neglect and deserves more research. To facilitate persons' believing in themselves is essential and usually fairly difficult. If self-efficacy is so crucial to success in modeling and role-playing, then ways of helping those handicapped with insufficient self-belief must be addressed. Also, the broader, preventive means for nurturing this vital capacity in the general public must be addressed.

Schwarzen's review (1992) of this matter of self-efficacy is a reminder that in a specialized, compartmentalized world like ours, perplexing questions often have been answered, but the information gleaned then is not always integrated with previous knowledge or with other disciplines nor, often, disseminated in practical ways that could help our entire social structure. This plight is not unique to psychology, but as Staats (1991) underscores, "Psychology has developed the prolific character of modern science, without the ability to articulate its knowledge. . . . Sheer production must be counterbalanced by an equally strong investment in weaving the unrelated knowledge elements together into the fabric of organized science" (p. 899). This tendency to focus on parts, as in individual problems, without including the relationship of parts to the entire gestalt, can be seen in the application of modeling and role-playing. Paradoxically, the targeting of individuals by removing the spotlight from the greater social contexts also needs modifying. There must be a way to address both individuals and their environment, rather than merely either/or, as is proposed in the pluralistic psychotherapeutic methods reviewed by Okun (1990).

Worth considering: If we are able to be instructed by an external, expert other, in a piecemeal fashion, what does that communicate about who we are inside? That we are not quite competent? That knowledge comes from the outside? That our own thoughts should be scrutinized? Does this not lead to more self-doubt, rather than empowerment?

There has been a distressing rise in crime, violence, and penal recidivism in this country. This is ironic, when so many people understand so much more about the societal conditions that foster violence, and if we believe that, while watching television, we can learn to become more violent, surely we would not want to be continually inundated by violent images. Logically, we should not want such toxic stimuli in our homes, and, yet, it is there. Some of us find them entertaining, exciting, thrilling. They might even make us feel more powerful or more alive. How can we hope for a more peaceful, cooperative society if, at the same time, we are learning to be more violent? Yet, the actual practical significance of this seems to have bypassed us. Or has it? Is there something more to be discovered about what motivates us to learn?

It appears that we do not totally understand behavior or its causes. Hence, one should practice psychotherapy with a grain of humility while continually asking, How do we instruct without being pedagogic? How do we help without violating human integrity? It is hoped that the answers will evolve soon.

REFERENCES

Allport, G. W. (1937). *Personality: A psychological interpretation*. New York: Holt, Rinehart & Winston.

Anderson, M., & Borkovec, T. (1980). Imagery processing and fear reduction during repeated exposure to two types of phobic imagery. *Behavior Research and Therapy, 18*, 537–540.

Arnkoff, D., & Stewart, J. (1973). The effectiveness of modeling and videotape feedback on personal problem solving. *Behavior Research and Therapy, 13*, 127–133.

Bailey, K., & Sowder, W. (1970). Audiotape and videotape confrontation in psychotherapy. *Psychological Bulletin, 74*, 127–137.

Bandura, A. (1986). *Social foundations of thought and action: A social cognitive theory*. Englewood Cliffs, NJ: Prentice-Hall.

Bandura, A. (1977). *Social learning theory*. Englewood Cliffs, NJ: Prentice-Hall.

Bandura, A. (1969). *Principles of behavior modification*. New York: Holt, Rinehart & Winston.

Bandura, A. (1961). Psychotherapy as a learning process. *Psychological Bulletin, 58*, 143–159.

Bandura, A., & Walters, R. H. (1963). *Social learning and personality development*. New York: Holt, Rinehart & Winston.

Cautela, J. R. (1971). Covert conditioning. In A. Jacobs & L. Sacks (Eds.), *The psychology of private events: Perspectives on covert response systems*. New York: Academic Press.

Coleman, S., & Stedman, J. (1974). Use of a peer model in language training in an echolalic child. *Journal of Behavior Therapy and Experimental Psychiatry, 5*, 275–279.

Danet, N. (1968). Self confrontation in psychotherapy reviewed. *American Journal of Psychotherapy, 22*, 245–258.

Ellis, A., & Grieger, R. (Eds.). (1977). *Handbook of rational emotive therapy*. New York: Springer.

Ellis, A., & Harper, R. (1975). *A new guide to rational living*. Englewood Cliffs, NJ: Prentice-Hall.

Foy, E., Elser, R., & Pinkston, S. (1975). Modified assertion in a case of explosive rage. *Journal of Behavior Therapy and Experimental Psychology, 5*, 275–279.

Glerck, J. (1988). *Chaos: Making a new science.* New York: Viking-Penguin.

Goldstein, A., Martens, J., Hubben, J., von Belle, H., Schaaf, W., Wiersma, H., & Goedhart, A. (1973). The use of modeling to increase independent behavior. *Behavior Research and Therapy, 11*, 31–42.

Goldstein, A., Sprafkin, R., & Gershaw, J. (1976). *Skills training for community living: Applying structured learning therapy.* Elmsford, NY: Pergamon Press.

Goodwin, S., & Mahoney, M. (1975). Modification of aggression through modeling: An experimental probe. *Journal of Behavioral Therapy and Experimental Psychology, 6*, 200–202.

Griffith, R. (1974). Videotape feedback as a therapeutic technique: Retrospect and prospect. *Behavior Research and Therapy, 12*, 1–8.

Hay, W., Hay, L., & Nelson, R. (1977). The adaption of covert modeling procedures to the treatment of chronic alcoholism and obsessive-compulsive behavior: Two case reports. *Behavior Therapy, 8*, 70–76.

Hergenhahn, B., & Olson, M. (1993). *An introduction to theories of learning* (4th ed.). Englewood Cliffs, NJ: Prentice-Hall.

Johnson, J., & Thompson, D. (1974). Modeling in the treatment of enuresis: A case study. *Journal of Behavior Therapy and Experimental Psychiatry, 5*, 93–94.

Kanfer, F., & Goldstein, A. (Eds.). (1986). *Helping people change: A textbook of methods.* New York: Pergamon.

Kantrowitz, R., & Ballou, M. (1992). A feminist critique of cognitive-behavior behavioral therapy. In L. Brown & M. Ballou (Eds.), *Personality and psychopathology: Feminist reappraisals.* New York: Guilford.

Kazdin, A. (1984). Instructional format: Covert modeling. In P. Kendall (Ed.), *Advances in cognitive-behavioral research and therapy* (Vol. 3). New York: Academic.

Kazdin, A. (1975). Covert modeling, imagery assessment and assertive behavior. *Journal of Counseling and Clinical Psychology, 43*, 716–724.

Meichenbaum, D. (1977). *Cognitive-behavior modification.* New York: Plenum.

Miller, N., & Dollard, J. (Eds.). (1941). *Social learning and imitation.* New York: Holt, Rinehart & Winston.

Moreno, J. (1946). *Psychodrama,* (Vol. 1). New York: Beacon House.

Nietzel, M., Martorana, R., & Melnick, J. (1977). Effects of covert modeling with and without reply training on the development and generation of assertive responses. *Behavior Therapy, 8*, 183–192.

Okun, B. (1990). *Seeking connections in psychotherapy.* San Francisco, CA: Jossey-Bass.

Peris, F. (1969). *Gestalt therapy verbatim.* Lafayette, CA: Real People.

Perry, M., & Furukawa, M. (1986). Modeling methods. In F. Kanfer & A. Goldstein (Eds.), *Helping people change: A textbook of methods* (3rd ed.). New York: Pergamon.

Quinsley, V., & Varney, G. (1977). Social skills game: A general method for the modeling and practice of adaptive behavior. *Behavior Therapy, 8*, 279–281.

Rachman, R. (1976). Observational learning and therapeutic modeling. In M. Feldman & A. Broadhurst (Eds.), *Theoretical and empirical bases of the behavior therapies.* New York: Wiley.

Ritter, B. (1968). The group treatment of children's snakes phobias using vicarious and contact desensitization procedures. *Behavior Research and Therapy*, *6*, 1–6.

Roper, G., Rachman, S., & Marks, I. (1975). Passive and participant modeling in exposure treatment of obsessive-compulsive neurotics. *Behavior Research and Therapy*, *13*, 271–279.

Rosenthal, T., & Bandura, A. (1978). Psychological modeling: Theory and practice. In S. Garfield & A. Bergin (Eds.), *Handbook of psychotherapy and behavior change* (2d ed.). New York: Wiley.

Ross, D., Ross, S., & Evans, J. (1971). The modification of extreme social withdrawal by modeling and guided participation. *Journal of Behavior Therapy and Experimental Psychology*, *2*, 273–279.

Salomon, G. (1984). Television is "easy" and print is "tough": The differential investment of mental effort in learning as a function of perceptions and attributions. *Journal of Educational Psychology*, *76*, 647–658.

Schwarzen, R. (Ed.). (1992). *Self-efficacy: Thought control of action*. Washington, DC: Hemisphere.

Staats, A. (1991). Unified positivism and unification psychology: Fad or new field. *American Psychologist*, *46*(9), 899–912.

3

Cognitive Restructuring

Lucia Matthews and Lawrence Litwack

Cognitive therapy is based on the premise that cognition, or the process of acquiring knowledge and forming beliefs, is a primary determinant of mood and behavior. The overall aim of any cognitive intervention is to reduce emotional distress and corresponding maladaptive behavior patterns through correcting errors in thoughts, perceptions, and beliefs. Cognitive restructuring involves collaboration on the part of the therapist and the client to assist the client in identifying and altering perceptions and/or faulty beliefs about one's self, others, or the world.

THEORETICAL BACKGROUND

Cognitive orientations hold that a person's perceptions, attributions, and schematic organization and beliefs influence behavior and play a prominent role in emotion and meaning making. These internal processes are referred to as "cognitions" (Beck, 1976). The major philosophical assumption of cognitive psychotherapeutic interventions is that, by changing people's thinking, one can change their belief system, which, in turn, alters emotions and behavior. Vital to this assumption is the premise that clients must notice how they think, feel, and behave before behavior can change. Emotional disturbance stems from faulty cognitions. Once identified, effective strategies can be employed to modify the faulty cognitions that are causing a problem.

A change strategy, cognitive restructuring, traces its roots back to cognitive psychology and from some of the early work of Albert Ellis

(1973, 1989). Donald Meichenbaum (1985) and Aaron Beck (1988) are two current practitioners who have been instrumental in further developing the concept and strategy.

The ideas underlying cognitive restructuring are that cognitions (i.e., thoughts, beliefs, attitudes, personal attributions) affect both feelings and behavior. Changing such cognitions to Ellis's more rational term, to Beck's more concretely data based and reality tested conclusions, to Meichenbaum's more externally caused term (feminist), to more adaptive and coping oriented (Meichenbaum), to more "real world" thoughts (Glasser) is the key. The therapist identifies and defines the existing thoughts and attributions of a particular client and targets these for change or restructuring, so that the client can move toward more appropriate and adaptive attitudes and actions. Beck and Meichenbaum focus specifically upon the individual and the logic or coping of his or her thoughts. Feminists call for a view of external reality and awareness of sociocultural conditions in changing clients' attributions. Glasser concentrates on the individual's perceptual system as it determines how she or he experiences the real world. Finally, Ellis ascribes to challenging irrational beliefs commonly held.

Cognitive restructuring focuses on replacing maladaptive thinking with new, rational thinking. Although it originally emerged from Albert Ellis' rational-emotive therapy model, it has been incorporated into most cognitive strategies and feminist consciousness-raising. It is based on the premise that cognitive structure is the organizing aspect of thinking, which appears to monitor and direct the choice of thoughts (Meichenbaum, 1977).

Ellis (1973) posits that people are born with a tendency to be both rational and irrational. Through social conditioning stemming from parents, people and culture become more and more irrational by incorporating the world's irrationality into their belief system. He claims that irrationality causes emotional disturbances but that we can learn to give ourselves different messages. Aaron Beck expands upon Ellis' concepts. He formulates the psychoanalytic view of depression to incorporate the negative attitudes apparent in his depressed patients. This inclusion of depression (Beck, 1976) is a key element of his theory. It consists of negative thoughts about oneself, the world, and the future. Other aspects of Beck's cognitive model include schemas and cognitive errors.

THE PROCESS OF COGNITIVE RESTRUCTURING

Cognitive restructuring is one of the change strategies used to alter thinking. Cormier and Cormier (1979) describe a six step sequence to be used in cognitive restructuring with a client. The first two steps deal with the clear identification of the client's verbal set and thoughts during problem or stressful situations. The therapist clearly identifies how the process of cognitive restructuring works and then identifies the existing maladaptive perceptions and beliefs of the client as well as the possible positive ones.

The next two steps are designed to enhance the coping thoughts of the client, that is, to increase the client's ability to cope more successfully with the problem or stressor. These steps include introduction and practice of coping thoughts and shifting from maladaptive to coping thoughts. These are built on the premise that, as the client improves in coping thoughts, coping skills and behaviors will improve and enable the client to become more oriented toward the change goal in attitude and action.

The fifth step involves the introduction and practice of positive or reinforcing self-statements. Here, the therapist works with the client to help the client move beyond merely coping to active, positive, self-statements designed to enhance self-concept. In the final step, the therapist continues to work collaboratively with the client through homework assignments to practice the positive statements and behaviors and follow-up to support the client's continued growth. As Gilliland, James, Roberts, and Bowman (1984) state: "The counselor role is that of consultant, facilitator, mentor, and coach. It is quite important that a client understanding of the process, desire to change, and commitment to a plan of action be obtained (p. 174).

Through the process of cognitive restructuring, the client learns initially to identify self-defeating thoughts and then to gradually replace them with more objective, self-promoting, problem-solving thoughts and behaviors. This process incorporates a number of specific strategies that are used in the various phases or steps. Identifying these strategies helps a therapist learn to effectively apply the concepts described.

At the beginning of the strategy, the therapist and the client explore together the client's typical thoughts in troublesome situations. At this time, similar to the first step described by Cormier and Cormier (1979), the therapist questions the client about specific thoughts before, during, and after the problematic situations (Cormier & Hackney, 1987). If the client has difficulty recalling specific thoughts, the therapist may suggest using a daily log to record upsetting thoughts and the feelings and events that triggered them.

Imagery can also be helpful to gaining specificity in clients' thoughts. In imagery, a client is asked to imagine himself or herself in the stressful situation and then to identify the internal dialogue at the time: what thoughts are occurring. Through the use of imagery, the client is better able to move from the abstract to the concrete, from the words to the thoughts and feelings that have given him or her difficulty. This sometimes is referred to as "cognitive rehearsal."

Role-playing also can be helpful in expanding client awareness by showing possible alternative thoughts and behaviors in a given situation. It is usually more effective for the therapist to assume the role of the client and for the client to assume the role of a significant person in the client's life, because in each case, the role player is more knowledgeable about the role being assumed. The use of role play is limited only by the client's willingness to participate in the role-playing process. It provides an opportunity for a client to test out different thoughts and behaviors in a safe environment. Videotaping the role-playing for viewing and discussion by the participants increases the power of this strategy.

In cognitive modeling, the therapist demonstrates, in a series of modeling episodes, both desired behavior and the step-by-step description of the process. Developed by Beck (1976), the approach is somewhat similar to role-playing except that it emphasizes less the therapist-client interaction and more the therapist modeling and the client imitating, practicing, and integrating into personal change in thought and behavior.

Cognitive restructuring concentrates much more on thoughts and behaviors than on feelings. The client's feelings are neither ignored nor denied; rather, they are accepted. For example, if a client states that he or she is depressed, the therapist accepts the stated feeling and concentrates on what the client is thinking that produced that feeling and what will help the client feel better.

Feminist analysis of gender beliefs as well as multicultural perspectives and recognition of the individual influence of sociopolitical and economic factors have added importantly to cognitive restructuring. It has become an important strategy in consciousness-raising and reinterpreting individual thoughts to their external-social-gendered origins. Gender or cultural ascripted norms can be seen as particular messages with a purpose, rather than as universal standards. For example, believing that women are supreme to men in child care and relationships can be restructured to cultural norms and social structures assigning women emotional-interpersonal responsibility and men money-generating responsibility.

Cognitive restructuring requires an investment in time outside the therapy sessions as well, and homework is necessary. The client may maintain a log of stressful situations with descriptors of thoughts and feelings before, during, and after the event. Possibly of more importance is the maintenance of a log of positive statements to diffuse the negative thoughts. It may be helpful to tape the introductory sessions so the client may refer to them as needed. Follow-up in subsequent meetings reinforces success and helps to remind the client that work on the strategy and time are necessary to combat general cultural messages and negative self-evaluations. As with any other strategy, if concern does not diminish in a timely fashion, the counselor needs to reassess the situation and consider an alternative approach. Implementing cognitive restructuring is an active, directive, and structured approach. It is a time-limited, collaborative effort between therapist and client. Rationality and responsibility are key concepts. The therapist and client are partners in the process of problem solving. The therapist acts as investigator, teacher, and guide in helping the client discover new, more adaptive ways of thinking. Through practice, these skills become more automatic responses, and the client is no longer dependent upon the therapist. The status of the therapist as a teacher is transformed into that of a consultant. Ultimately, the client becomes empowered to take management of his or her own attributions, attitudes, and actions.

The therapist must take care in the use of cognitive restructuring not to impose ideology. Unexamined beliefs, whether of the client, culture, or therapist, are not appropriate in cognitive restructuring. Thoughts (perceptions, attitudes, and attributions) are not value free, nor is the judgment maladaptive or irrational independent from particular normative criteria. Cognitive restructuring can be a powerful strategy that must be used with awareness and care.

APPROPRIATE USES AND RESEARCH

The success of cognitive restructuring is dependent upon the client's identification of the problem and discrimination between negative and positive self-statements. The strategy utilizes the client's own intellect and motivations. It requires the intellectual capacity to understand cognitive restructuring principles and rationale. It is more effective with clients who possess the level of cognitive development required to apply logical reasoning to problem situations. As such, cognitive restructuring is more appropriate with clients who are grounded in reality, are verbal, possess an adequate memory, and are intellectually competent.

Cognitive restructuring relies on the client's motivation for change. It is most effective with clients who are not dogmatic and are open to experimentation. Cognitive restructuring utilizes in vivo exposure, in that the therapist models alternative rationales and behaviors. Clients must possess the concentration skills required to focus on their thoughts and to practice alternative self-statements. Clients are expected to complete homework assignments. Such an expectation requires a certain level of commitment and self-discipline on the part of the client.

The success of cognitive restructuring is also dependent upon the client's level of awareness and insight. Although it is considered a pragmatic intervention that relies on conceptual understanding and rational analysis, cognitive restructuring also encourages the client to experience both the self and others in new ways. Clients must be insightful and aware of how they form their thoughts, feelings, and behaviors. They must possess the ability to perceive their impact on others. There must be a willingness and ability to listen to one's self-statements. These abilities are necessary so that clients may interpret the scripted nature of their behavior long enough to evaluate it.

Cognitive restructuring endorses personal responsibility and may not be appropriate for clients demonstrating strong defenses or those who disavow responsibility. This also implies that the client must be in contact with reality. It is inappropriate for clients exhibiting flat affect, loose associations, hallucinations, or delusions. It is also inappropriate for clients with pathologies such as autism, mental deficiencies, and severe characterological flaws. Although applicable with affective disorders, cognitive restructuring may not be appropriate for clients in highly manic or extremely emotional states. If too caught up in emotion, clients may not have the capacity to attend to the rationalism espoused by this strategy.

The efficacy of cognitive restructuring has been extensively studied. It has been examined within a wide variety of settings: classrooms (Cramer, Post, & Behr, 1989), correctional facilities (Nickell, Witherspoon, & Long, 1989), industry (Chesney, Black, Swan, & Ward, 1987), pastoral care (Parsons & Wicks, 1986), in-patient hospital units (Cockett, 1992), and college campuses (Brewer & Shillinglaw, 1992).

Beck and Weishaar (1989, p. 316) claim that cognitive therapy (with emphasis on cognitive restructuring) has proven to be successful in treating such diverse disorders as drug abuse, alcoholism, major depression disorders, generalized anxiety disorder, dysthymic disorder, panic disorder, anorexia, bulimia, hypochondriosis, personality disorders, and obsessive-compulsive behavior. Used in conjunction with psychotropic medication and other cognitive therapeutic techniques, cognitive restructuring has contributed to the effective treatment of both delusional and manic-depressive disorders.

Despite the extensiveness of this research, the efficacy of cognitive restructuring as a viable therapeutic strategy has not been conclusively determined. Many of the studies involve the use of cognitive restructuring in conjunction with other cognitive or behavioral strategies. They do not distinguish cognitive restructuring as a discrete variable outside of the cognitive therapy model or independent of other therapeutic interventions. It remains unclear whether change can be attributed solely to cognitive restructuring.

This does not imply that cognitive restructuring is not an integral part of the therapeutic process. It seems that there is an ubiquitousness in cognitive restructuring that makes it a significant component of most therapeutic interventions. Okun (1990, p. 173) comments that it is difficult to imagine that any type of psychotherapy can occur without some form of cognitive restructuring. Although Walker (1984, p. 158) cites success rates of 70 to 80 percent using behavioral strategies, such as flooding in the treatment of obsessions, it is also noted that "it might be useful to modify the person's definition of unacceptable thoughts and impulses." Yalom (1985) concedes that catharsis is not, in itself, enough to foster a corrective experience. He states that cognitive restructuring "seems necessary for the patient to be able to generalize group experiences to outside life" (p. 226). Nichols and Schwartz (1991, p. 474) observe that structural family therapists, such as Minuchin, use words and concepts to alter the way family members perceive reality. In a study conducted by Valentich and Gripton (1985), a cognitive restructuring intervention was combined with a psychodynamic orientation to produce favorable results in the treatment of sexual dysfunction.

Cognitive restructuring is included regularly in skills training and self-help interventions. It has been used to foster coping skills in parents of disabled children (Gammon & Rose, 1991), encourage more competent use of decision criteria by sexual offenders in high-risk situations (Neidigh, 1991), and manage stress (Tolman & Rose, 1989). Cognitive restructuring has been used to help herpes patients curb the recurrence of lesions (McLaron & Kaloupek, 1988). It is regularly used when assisting clients during life transitions. Bogolub (1991) maintains that overall treatment for supporting women during midlife divorce should include cognitive restructuring of maladaptive beliefs. Dellmann-Jenkins, Hofer, and Chebra (1992) suggest that cognitive restructuring of the care-giving experience is a viable way to educate families to care for elderly relatives in the home environment.

Cognitive restructuring attempts to alter the client's perceptual field. This, combined with its educative qualities, enables the coping skills learned in one area of a client's life to be generalized to another. Numerous studies have investigated the enduring qualities of cognitive restructuring. In a five year follow-up study on patients disabled by spinal cord injuries, Hanson, Buckelew, Hewett, and O'Neal (1993) observed that cognitive restructuring was positively associated with acceptance of the disability. Although Murphy, Simons, Wetzel, and Lustman (1984) found that combining cognitive therapy with drug treatment was no more effective in the treatment of unipolar depression than pharmacological intervention alone, a one year follow-up study (Simons, Murphy, Levine, & Wetzel, 1986) indicates that the patients exposed to the cognitive restructuring strategy were significantly less likely to relapse than the patients who had been given only pharmacotherapy.

Mitchell and Krumboltz (1987) demonstrated cognitive restructuring to be significantly more effective than decision-making training in the reduction of anxiety concerning career decision making and increased vocational exploratory behavior. The clients in the cognitive restructuring group reported that the skills they learned were considerably more useful to them than did the clients in the decision-making training group. Not only was the anxiety surrounding career decision making reduced for the cognitive restructuring clients but also their vocation exploratory behavior was increased, and they learned valuable skills that they reported continuing to use after treatment was discontinued (p. 173).

Fortunately, not all research has investigated cognitive restructuring in combination with other strategies. When studied as a discrete variable, cognitive restructuring appears to be most effective when utilized as a short-term strategy that deals with a specific, well-defined problem. Ellis (1989, p. 222) believes it is best used with clients who show a single major symptom and with those who exhibit less severe forms of a disorder.

As a discrete variable, cognitive restructuring has been employed to help athletes and musicians overcome performance anxiety (Fremouw & Hamilton, 1985; Sweeney & Horan, 1982), curb eating disorders (Fremouw & Pecsok, 1988), regulate self-control (Goldfried, Decenteceo, & Weinberg, 1974), quell social phobia (Mattick &

Delongis, 1988), and manage pain (Fremouw, Heyneman, & Nicholas, 1990).

Although most outcome research involving cognitive restructuring has been conducted on individual adults in outpatient settings, other studies have explored its efficacy in different genre. Jabichuk and Smerigilio (1976) conducted a study with socially isolated preschoolers who evidenced low levels of social responsiveness. The children were shown two modeling films depicting a child playing alone, then approaching other children, and, ultimately, interacting with peers in a variety of situations. The soundtrack described feelings of isolation, suggested coping responses, and modeled self-reinforcement. Those exposed to the film demonstrated significantly greater improvement in behavioral responses than did children in a control group.

Other research supports the use of cognitive restructuring with children and adolescents (Cormier & Hackney, 1993). Bornstein and Quevillion (1976) used cognitive restructuring in the treatment of three hyperactive preschool boys. The children were given specific tasks and were then trained to verbalize the nature of the task and their problem-solving strategies. Treatment resulted in significant and stable changes in classroom behavior. Improvement was still evident after a 72 week follow-up study.

Williamson, Prather, Bennett, Davis, Watkins, and Grenier (1989) have evaluated the merits of cognitive restructuring when used as an inpatient versus outpatient intervention in the treatment of bulimia nervosa. Results indicate that the inpatient program led to very rapid progress, whereas those in the outpatient program showed more gradual improvements. However, there was a trend toward relapse for inpatients. Interestingly, other psychological disturbances (e.g., depression) appear more improved among the inpatients than the outpatients.

Traditionally, cognitive restructuring has been thought to be an inappropriate strategy in crisis situations, with clients exhibiting extreme pathology, or with victims of abuse. Recent studies have attempted to explore the efficacy of this premise. Davis (1991) investigated the utility of extending cognitive restructuring to victims of robbery, nonsexual assault, and burglary. Although deemed inappropriate with subjects who have been severely traumatized, cognitive restructuring does appear to be effective when victims recognize that they are experiencing debilitating emotions and are motivated to change. Cognitive restructuring has been used to treat paranoid personality disorder (Williams, 1988) and multiple personality disorder (Fine, 1991). Although care must be taken to ensure that victims of abuse do not feel blamed, cognitive restructuring can be a particularly empowering strategy (Dutton-Douglas, 1992). In cases of sexual abuse, cognitive restructuring has been employed effectively to combat feelings of low self-esteem, guilt, and depression (Jehu, 1989).

Recent studies have explored the applicability of cognitive restructuring with regard to gender, race, ethnicity, and cross-cultural perspectives. It appears to be equally effective among males and females (Barak, Shiloh, & Haushner, 1992), although there has been discussion that its use may need to be altered to compensate for the differing perspectives between males and females (Okun, 1990). In issues regarding race and ethnicity, the focus of cognitive restructuring has been on helping clients to become aware that their own subcultures' values are not inferior to, but merely different from, those of the dominant culture. The client is encouraged to develop behavior patterns that allow him or her to achieve self-acceptance and to function appropriately within both environments (Sophie, 1987; Giannini, Quinones-Delvalle, & Blackshear, 1990; Piotrowski & Franklin, 1990; LaFromboise & Bigfoot, 1988).

Corey (1990) maintains that a central part of the work done in group psychotherapy consists of challenging and exploring beliefs about situations. He argues that the process of cognitive restructuring forms a central role in several therapeutic group approaches, including Adlerian groups (p. 123). In a comparison of strategies exploring the efficacy of group therapy on cancer patients, Telch and Telch (1986) found that groups exposed to cognitive restructuring evidenced a consistent superiority over both supportive group therapy and a no-treatment control group. Similar results have been obtained by Gallagher (1981). Subjects having an elevated MMPI Depression Scale score were randomly assigned to four groups: two structured and two supportive. Groups met for ten sessions over a five week period. Although both interventions yielded lower post-treatment scores, subjects exposed to cognitive restructuring in the highly structured group yielded significantly better results when compared with the relatively unstructured group.

Unfortunately, these results are not conclusive and have been disrupted by more recent studies. Deberry, Davis, and Reinhard (1989) compared cognitive techniques (inclusive of cognitive restructuring) with a meditation-relaxation approach in the group treatment of geriatric depression. They hypothesized that geriatric depression is a function of stress and that cognitive restructuring could help alleviate this stress and, thereby, reduce depression. The cognitive modality failed to reach significance. These results confirm those found by Chaisson, Beutler, and Yost (1984) and shed doubt upon the efficacy of cognitive restructuring within this milieu.

Although questionable within a geriatric group setting, there is evidence to support the use of cognitive restructuring as an intervention with older people (Bates, Johnson, & Blaker, 1982; Weiner & Weinstock, 1979). In particular, Lazarus and Delongis (1983) maintained that it is an effective strategy in the treatment of geriatric depression, because old age is typically characterized by sudden change and loss. Cognitive restructuring deals with these potentially depressive aspects of life.

Depression is one of the most extensively studied applications of cognitive restructuring. Beck (1988) contends that depression stems from a lack of structure in one's life and that cognitive restructuring's emphasis on active, problem-solving techniques helps correct this deficit. Results have been mixed. Craighead (1983) found that its use (in conjunction with other cognitive-behavioral methods) is more effective in reducing unipolar depression than behavioral therapy or pharmacotherapy. Other research (Simons et al., 1986) suggests that depressed clients who endorse ideas about self-control respond to cognitive restructuring, while those who do not subscribe to cognitive beliefs respond better to drugs. Still other research (Chan, 1992) purports that depression actually may undermine a cognitive restructuring strategy because of a client's tendency to brood over problems and the inherent passivity that typically accompanies depression.

Despite the abundance of research, the efficacy of cognitive restructuring remains debatable. As noted, there have been studies that dispute its effectiveness when compared with other therapeutic interventions. Baucom and Lester (1986) evaluated cognitive restructuring when used in conjunction with behavioral marital therapy. They found no significant difference between this application and the use of behavioral marital therapy alone. They concluded that further research into factors such as sequencing of techniques, the length of treatment, the manner of presenting concepts, and the cognitive factors involved in marital distress must be completed before cognitive restructuring can be ruled out as a viable strategy in treating marital partners (p. 401).

This example clearly illustrates the need for ongoing research into the efficacy of cognitive restructuring. Although many studies provide compelling support for its effectiveness, its capabilities as a discrete therapeutic intervention must be explored further. Additionally, the limitations of this strategy remain unclear. More research, with emphasis placed on variables, such as those mentioned above, is required before the efficacy of cognitive restructuring can be established fully.

EVALUATION

If one accepts that cognitions cannot be divorced from human functioning, then cognitive restructuring may be viewed as a powerful promoter of behavioral change. The strategy is based on the premise that there is synergy between one's thoughts and behaviors. Rather than focus on psychopathology, cognitive restructuring encourages clients to broaden their perceptual field and to reconstruct faulty schema. The strategy operates from the assumption that all behavior is learned. As the perceptual field broadens, the homeostasis of the client's intraactional and interactional system is altered. Once altered, the stage is set for change. Old behaviors are replaced with new, more adaptive skills.

The goal of cognitive restructuring is to normalize a client's prevailing thoughts. The strategy does not seek to change one's entire being. Rather, it strives to alter a part of the perceptual field so that a client can feel more comfortable within the world. As perceptions change, the client begins to experience life in different ways. The effects are cumulative in that each new experience in turn influences other thoughts and behaviors.

An effective therapeutic strategy, cognitive restructuring promotes optimism. It examines ways in which life can become more fulfilling. It is a skills-building strategy designed to improve one's interpersonal functioning. Rather than encourage a client to cope, cognitive restructuring motivates a client to change. It enables clients to navigate the interplay between the environmental, psychological, and physiological variables of life. Cognitive restructuring rejects biased assumptions, advocates autonomy, and cultivates personal responsibility. It urges clients to take control of their lives.

A specific strength of cognitive restructuring is that it does not promote a long-term dependency on a therapist. The mechanism for change lies more in the client's ability to assume responsibility than in the therapeutic relationship. Its benefits can be acquired in a short time and can be generalized to future situations. It is an active, problem-solving strategy that helps the client focus on and fix the presenting problem. An added benefit of cognitive restructuring might be derived in that, as results occur, the client may become motivated to work on less obvious problems.

Cognitive restructuring operates within the tenets of cognitive therapy. It espouses pragmatism and rationality but does so within the context of a warm, respectful therapeutic relationship. This supportive environment is the essential ingredient for the establishment of a collaborative relationship between client and therapist. Collaboration and flexibility are critical when challenging a client's thought processes. They enable confrontation to occur while maintaining respect for the client's dignity.

Cognitive restructuring can become coercive if incorrectly applied. The therapist must take care not to become manipulative or controlling or impose his or her values on the process. Evaluation of a client's cognitions must be made independent of the therapist's opinion of what is appropriate or rational. It is imperative that a therapist continually strive to broaden his or her own perceptual field and not fall victim to myopic thinking. Cognitive restructuring becomes detrimental when therapists believe theirs is the only rational perspective. The strategy is most effective when both client and therapist adopt an exploratory, experimental attitude.

Cognitive restructuring may seem reductionistic and simplistic because it emphasizes cognitions and tends to minimize the affective components of a client's persona. Although this may appear as a shortcoming to some, it can be a benefit to clients who are hesitant to delve too deeply into their psyche. Additionally, opportunities exist to use cognitive restructuring as a tactic for deeper exploration. As a trusting relationship develops, a therapist might probe the motivation behind a specific negative thought. Although remaining in a here-and-now orientation, such a strategy enables past situations and feelings to be incorporated into the therapeutic process. It can provide valuable insight into how the past influences current perspectives.

Cognitive restructuring is an educative process that is easy to learn and self-manage. Its language is noncolloquial, and its methodology is logical. This simplicity can be beguiling. There is the perception that the strategy provides a "quick fix" for all problems. Cognitive restructuring requires commitment, motivation, and practice. It is not effective with all clients, especially one who is unfocused, nor can the process be implemented in a generic manner. It must be customized to suit the problems being treated and the uniqueness of each client's perceptual field.

Despite a plethora of studies, the efficacy of cognitive restructuring has not been clearly determined. However, this does not detract from the contribution it makes to the therapeutic process. It is a useful strategy, especially when a specific cognitive-behavioral problem has been targeted for change. It appears to be most effective when used in conjunction with other psychotherapeutic interventions and is typically coupled with behavior modification. It is being applied to an ever-widening field of disorders and populations. Recent studies demonstrate cognitive restructuring to be effective on gender issues and ethnic concerns, perhaps because cognitive restructuring does not solicit clients to abandon respect for their individuality. It encourages an examination of the influence of sociopolitical and economic factors on the thought process and then challenges the client to evaluate the consequences of these cognitions.

Cognitive restructuring has fallen prey to the same criticisms levied against most cognitive interventions. There is a concern that, despite claims to be value free, its empiricism and rationality are characteristic of a dominant white male culture (Okun, 1990). Correctly applied, cognitive restructuring supersedes gender, ethnicity, and other social issues. It attends to the concerns raised by the individual client. It attempts to normalize perceptions. It seeks alternatives that will enable a client's unique internal variables to coexist with external factors. Granted, if it is used in a coercive manner, complex issues of gender, race, and ethnicity can be oversimplified — for example, consideration must be given to the notion that men and women perceive phenomena differently and are conditioned to behave based on these perceptions. However, used within an ecological context, cognitive restructuring becomes a powerful catalyst for change.

REFERENCES

Barak, A., Shiloh, S., & Haushner, O. (1992). Modification of interests through cognitive restructuring: Test of a theoretical model in preschool children. *Journal of Counseling Psychology, 37*(4), 490–497.

Bates, M., Johnson, C., & Blaker, K. E. (1982). *Group leadership: A manual for group counseling leaders.* Denver, CO: Love.

Baucom, D. H., & Lester, G. W. (1986). The usefulness of cognitive restructuring as an adjunct to behavioral marital therapy. *Behavioral Therapy, 17*, 358–403.

Beck, A. T. (1988). Interview with S. G. Weinrach: Cognitive therapist: A dialogue with Aaron Beck. *Journal of Counseling and Development, 67*(3), 159–164.

Beck, A. T. (1976). *Cognitive therapy and the emotional disorders.* New York: New American Library.

Beck, A. T., & Weishaar, M. E. (1989). Cognitive Therapy. In R. J. Corsini & D. Wedding (Eds.), *Current psychotherapies* (4th ed.). Itasca, IL: F. E. Peacock.

Bogolub, E. B. (1991). Women and mid-life divorce: Some practice issues. *Social Work, 36*(5), 4289–4433.

Bornstein, P., & Quevillion, R. (1976). The effects of a self-instructional program on overactive preschool boys. *Journal of Applied Behavior Analysis, 9*, 179–188.

Brewer, B. W., & Shillinglaw, R. (1992). Evaluation of a psychological skills training workshop for male intercollegiate lacrosse players. *Sport Psychologist, 6*(2), 139–147.

Chaisson, M., Beutler, L., & Yost, E. (1984). Treating the depressed elderly. *Journal of Psychosocial Nursing, 22*(5), 25–30.

Chan, D. W. (1992). Coping with depressed moods among Chinese medical students in Hong Kong. *Journal of Affective Disorders, 24*(2), 109–116.

Chesney, M. A., Black, G. W., Swan, G. E., & Ward, M. M. (1987). Relaxation training for essential hypertension at the worksite. *Psychosomatic Medicine, 49*(3), 250–263.

Cockett, A. D. (1992). Logical refeeding: An adolescent specific approach to the in-patient treatment of severe anorexia nervosa. *British Review of Bulimia and Anorexia Nervosa, 6*(1), 9–22.

Corey, G. (1990). *Theory and practice of group counseling* (3rd ed.). Belmont, CA: Wadsworth.

Cormier, W. H., & Cormier, L. S. (1979). *Interviewing strategies for helpers: A guide to assessment, treatment, and evaluation.* Monterey, CA: Brooks-Cole.

Cormier, L. S., & Hackney, H. (1993). *The professional counselor: A process guide to helping,* 4th ed. Englewood Cliffs, NJ: Prentice-Hall.

Cormier, L. S., & Hackney, H. (1987). *The professional counselor: A process guide to helping,* 3rd ed. Englewood Cliffs, NJ: Prentice-Hall.

Craighead, E. (1983). Psychological therapy for depressive disorders. *Terapia Psicologica, 2,* 7–11.

Cramer, K. A., Post, T. R., & Behr, M. J. (1989). Cognitive restructuring ability, teacher guidance, and perceptual distracter tasks: An adaptive-treatment interaction study. *Journal for Research in Mathematics Education, 20*(1), 103–110.

Davis, R. C. (1991). A crisis intervention program for crime victims. *Response to the Victimization of Women and Children, 14*(2), 7–11.

Deberry, S., Davis, S., & Reinhard, K. E. (1989). A comparison of meditation and cognitive/behavioral techniques for reducing anxiety and depression in a geriatric population. *Journal of Geriatric Psychiatry, 22*(2), 231–247.

Dellmann-Jenkins, M., Hofer, K. V., & Chebra, J. (1992). Eldercare in the 1990's: Challenges and supports for educating families. *Educational Gerontology, 18*(8), 775–784.

Dutton-Douglas, M. A. (1992). Treating battered women in the aftermath stage. *Psychotherapy in Private Practice, 10*(1–2), 93–98.

Ellis, A., (1989). Rational-emotive therapy. In R. J. Corsini & D. Wedding (Eds.), *Current psychotherapies* (4th ed.). Itasca, IL: F. E. Peacock.

Ellis, A. (1973). Rational-emotive therapy. In A. Burton (Ed.), *Operational theories of personality.* New York: Brunner/Mazel.

Fine, C. G. (1991). Treatment stabilization and crisis prevention: Pacing the therapy of the multiple personality disorder patient. *Psychiatric Clinics of North America, 14* (3), 661–675.

Fremouw, W. J., & Hamilton, S. A. (1985). Cognitive-behavioral training for college basketball free-throw performance. *Journal of Cognitive Therapy and Research, 14,* 63–77.

Fremouw, W. J., Heyneman, N. E., & Nicholas, G. (1990). Individual differences and the effectiveness of different coping strategies for pain. *Journal of Cognitive Therapy and Research, 9,* 479–483.

Fremouw, W. J., & Pecsok, E. H. (1988). Controlling laboratory binging among restrained eaters through self-monitoring and cognitive restructuring procedures. *Journal of Addictive Behaviors, 13*, 37–44.

Gallagher, D. (1981). Behavioral group therapy with elderly depressives: An experimental study. In D. Upper & S. M. Ross (Eds.), *Behavioral group therapy.* Chicago, IL: Research Press.

Gammon, E. A., & Rose, S. D. (1991). The coping skills training program for parents of children with developmental disabilities: An experimental evaluation. *Research on Social Work Practice, 1*(3), 244–256.

Giannini, A. J., Quinones-Delvalle, R. M., & Blackshear, G. (1990). The use of cognitive restructuring in cross-cultural therapy. *Psychiatric Forum, 15*(2), 30–32.

Gilliland, B. E., James, R. K., Roberts, G. T., & Bowman, J. T. (1984). *Theories and strategies in counseling and psychotherapy.* Englewood Cliffs, NJ: Prentice-Hall.

Goldfried, M., Decenteceo, E. T., & Weinberg, L. (1974). Systematic rational restructuring as a self-control technique. *Behavior Therapy, 5*, 247–254.

Hanson, S., Buckelew, G. P., Hewett, J., & O'Neal, G. (1993). The relationship between coping and adjustment after spinal cord injury: A 5-year follow up study. *Rehabilitation Psychology, 38*(1), 41–52.

Jabichuk, Z., & Smerigilio, U. (1976). The influence of social behavior of preschool children with low levels of social responsiveness. *Child Development, 47*, 838–841.

Jehu, D. (1989). Mood disturbances among women clients sexually abused in childhood: Prevalence, etiology, treatment. *Journal of Interpersonal Violence, 4*(2), 164–184.

LaFromboise, T. D., & Bigfoot, D. S. (1988). Cultural and cognitive considerations in the prevention of American Indian adolescent suicide. *Journal of Adolescence, 11*(2), 139–153.

Lazarus, R. S., & Delongis, A. (1983). Psychological stress and coping in aging. *American Psychologist, 38*(3), 245–254.

Mattick, R. P., & Delongis, A. (1988). Treatment of severe social phobia: Effects of guided exposure with and without cognitive restructuring. *Journal of Consulting and Clinical Psychology, 56*(2), 251–260.

McLaron, L. D., & Kaloupek, D. G. (1988). Psychological investigation of genital herpes recurrence: Prospective assessment of cognitive-behavioral intervention for a chronic physical disorder. *Health Psychology, 7*(3), 231–249.

Meichenbaum, D. H. (1985). *Stress inoculation training.* New York: Pergamon Press.

Meichenbaum, D. H. (1977). *Cognitive-behavior modification.* New York: Plenum.

Mitchell, L. K., & Krumboltz, J. D. (1987). The effects of cognitive restructuring and decision-making training on career indecision. *Journal of Counseling and Development, 66*, 171–174.

Murphy, G. F., Simons, A. D., Wetzel, R. D., & Lustman, P. J. (1984). Cognitive therapy and pharmacotherapy: Singly and together in the treatment of depression. *Archives of General Psychiatry, 41*, 33–41.

Neidigh, L. (1991). Implications of a relapse prevention model for the treatment of sexual offenders. *Journal of Addictions and Offender Counseling, 11*(2), 42–50.

Nichols, M. P., & Schwartz, R. C. (1991). *Family therapy: Concepts and methods.* Boston, MA: Allyn & Bacon.

Nickell, E. B., Witherspoon, A. D., & Long, C. K. (1989). Decreasing speech anxiety of female prisoners. *Psychological Reports, 65*(3), 1351–1357.

Okun, B. F. (1990). *Seeking connections in psychotherapy.* San Francisco, CA: Jossey-Bass.

Parsons, R. D., & Wicks, R. J. (1986). Cognitive pastoral psychotherapy with religious persons experiencing loneliness. *Psychotherapy Patient, 2*(3), 47–59.

Piotrowski, C., & Franklin, G. (1990). A rational-emotive approach to problems of Black adolescents. *Journal of Training and Practice in Professional Psychology, 4*(2), 44–51.

Simons, A. D., Murphy, G. E., Levine, J. L., & Wetzel, R. D. (1986). Cognitive therapy and pharmacotherapy for depression: Sustained improvement over one year. *Archives of General Psychiatry, 46*, 43–48.

Sophie, J. (1987). Internalized homophobia and lesbian identity. *Journal of Homosexuality, 14*(1–2), 53–65.

Sweeney, G., & Horan, J. (1982). Separate and combined effects of cue-controlled relaxation and cognitive restructuring in the treatment of musical performance anxiety. *Journal of Counseling Psychology, 29*(5), 486–497.

Telch, C. F., & Telch, M. J. (1986). Group coping skills instruction and supportive group therapy for cancer patients: A comparison of strategies. *Journal of Consulting and Clinical Psychology, 54*(6), 802–808.

Tolman, R. M., & Rose, S. D. (1989). Teaching clients to cope with stress: The effectiveness of structured group stress management training. *Journal of Social Service Research, 13*(2), 45–66.

Valentich, M., & Gripton, J. (1985). A periodic case strategy for helping people with sexual problems. *Journal of Sex Education and Therapy, 11*(2), 24–29.

Walker, S. (1984). *Learning theory and behavior modification.* New York: Methuen.

Weiner, M. B., & Weinstock, C. S. (1979). Group progress of community elderly as measured by tape recordings, group tempo, and group evaluation. *International Journal of Aging and Human Development, 10*(2), 177–185.

Williams, J. G. (1988). Cognitive intervention for a paranoid personality disorder. *Psychotherapy, 25*(4), 570–575.

Williamson, D. A., Prather, R. C., Bennett, S. M., Davis, C. J., Watkins, P. C., & Grenier, C. E. (1989). An uncontrolled evaluation of inpatient and outpatient cognitive-behavior therapy for bulimia nervosa. *Behavior Modification, 13*(3), 340–360.

Yalom, I. D. (1985). *The theory and practice of group psychotherapy* (3rd ed.). New York: Basic Books.

4

Bibliotherapy

Mary Ballou

Reading about the thoughts and life situations of others has long been one of the human forms of healing, education, and prevention. In fact, according to Pardeck (1993), the inscription over the door in a library in ancient Thebes was "Healing Place of the Soul." In more contemporary times, bibliotherapy has become an adjunct to a variety of psychotherapeutic interventions. It is seen as offering guidance in problem solution; facilitating developmental progress; offering information about situational, environmental, and topical issues; and providing for dynamic interaction between the client and the material read. Bibliotherapy can be useful in several stages of therapy with a variety of clients and in addressing numerous concerns.

The basic principles of bibliotherapy were first practiced by two physicians, Benjamin Rush in 1815 and John Minson Galt II in 1853, who recommended reading to their patients. Bibliotherapy was recognized as an aspect of librarianship in 1904, when a partnership between psychiatry and librarianship was formed at McLean Hospital in Waverly, Massachusetts.

One of the first formalized studies that recorded the use of books in a therapeutic setting was conducted in the United States by William C. Menninger during the late 1930s. He utilized the book *The Human Mind*, written by his brother Karl A. Menninger, to study how mental health professionals and laypersons used books as a tool for dealing with mental health problems. As a result of positive responses to the use of the book, the Menningers became vocal advocates of bibliotherapy as a treatment strategy. They advised that bibliotherapy was most appropriate for individuals with mild neuroses and alcoholism and least appropriate for psychotic individuals with anxiety states or obsessional neuroses.

Since the Menningers' introduction of bibliotherapy as a treatment strategy, many mental health professionals have incorporated this technique into their treatment plans. During the 1970s and 1980s, bibliotherapy experienced a second surge of popularity, partly because of the human potential movement and the increased publication of self-help books. Self-help books have a wide range of topics that address such issues as incest, weight loss, personal growth, assertiveness, and anger management. Currently, millions of Americans are using some form of bibliotherapy to deal with personal mental health issues. A recent survey of psychologists revealed that 11.4 percent used some form of bibliotherapy quite often, 37.1 percent used it often, 47.6 percent used it sometimes, 3.8 percent used it rarely, and 0 percent never used bibliotherapy (Starker, 1988). Self-help materials vary dramatically in quality when considering vital attributes such as thoroughness, knowledge of psychology, and responsibility to the reader.

THE USE OF BIBLIOTHERAPY

General Procedures

Bibliotherapy may be used with both adults and children, individually or in groups. The therapist recommends books that she or he perceives as meeting the needs of the client. Typically, the client reads the material alone, outside of session, though in some cases, it is read aloud in groups. The formats are diverse and include self-help books, novels, poetry, plays, and newspaper and magazine articles. The form and content chosen depend upon the client's situation and the most appropriate materials available that will address these issues. After reading the material, the client discusses it with the therapist, who clarifies the client's interpretations and explores new insights gained.

Bibliotherapy is a general therapeutic strategy with many possible variations. Craighead, McNamara, and Horan (1984) described four separate levels of therapist/client contact in utilizing written material in a treatment plan. These four levels are self-administered, minimal-contact, therapist-administered, and therapist-directed (Pardeck, 1993). In the case of the self-administered strategy (often called the no-contact approach), the client receives written material from the therapist and has no further contact with the therapist. The minimal-contact strategy refers to a situation where the client has minimal contact with the therapist and relies primarily on the written material. When contact is made with the therapist, it can take the form of a meeting, a phone call, or written correspondence. The therapist-administered strategy consists of the client receiving written material while also meeting regularly with the therapist. The material and possible change interventions are discussed with the therapist in either an individual or a group setting. The highest level, therapist-directed bibliotherapy, provides for weekly contact between client and therapist, with the therapist highly involved in the client's use of the materials as part of treatment. Clients are often asked to use self-monitoring or complete homework assignments between therapy sessions.

Before a therapist decides to introduce the use of written materials as a treatment modality, there are several factors that must be considered. The most important is the client's readiness. If a strategy is introduced at an inappropriate time, it can damage the existing client/therapist relationship. Ideally, the client and the therapist should be working in the context of an established relationship based on mutual trust and respect. In addition, the client and the therapist should have done some preliminary exploration of the presenting problem.

The next factor that needs to be considered is the selection of appropriate materials. Not only must the content address the client's issues in a believable and realistic way, but also the material must be compatible with the client's reading level and interests. The form of publication is also a consideration if a handicapping condition exists. Many books are available in Braille, on cassette, and in large type.

Once the therapist selects the material, it is imperative that she or he have a thorough understanding of the contents and be familiar with the specific details. The therapist also needs to consider how to present the reading to the client. Most therapists agree that it is better to suggest, rather than prescribe, it (Pardeck & Pardeck, 1984).

Once reading has been initiated, the client typically experiences three stages in processing the material. In the first stage, identification and projection, the client begins to see similarities between her or his life and the characters in the story. The therapist and client explore the motives of the characters and assess the relationships in the story. How the meaning of the story relates to the presenting problem is also discussed. The next phase, abreaction and catharsis, is characterized by emotional release followed by catharsis. Once catharsis has occurred, clients move into the insight and integration stage. During this stage, clients gain insight and recognition of the self and significant others in the characters. This helps the client discover new ways of solving the presenting problem (Pardeck & Pardeck, 1984). Although most therapists would agree that a process exists, proponents of other theoretical orientations would explain this process differently, each according to his or her own constructs.

The client's reaction to the reading material can be expressed in several ways. The reaction can occur in individual or group discussion (Yauman, 1991), through role-playing (Moody & Moody, 1991), or through the use of nonverbal materials, such as drawing (Pardeck, 1990; Moody & Moody, 1991). The client's response can reflect his or her own mood as a result of what has been read, or the reaction can be the portrayal of a character's mood. Ultimately, the end result of the bibliotherapeutic process is expected to be the client's implementation of a resolution to his or her own problem.

In a broad sense, bibliotherapy is meant to yield "affective change and promote personal growth and development" (Lenkowsky, 1987, p. 123). There does not appear to be one specific aspect of a client that biblio-therapy is intended to change. The literature on this approach implies that bibliotherapy is successful in altering a client's conceptualization of his or her problem (attitude change) and can, thus, produce behavioral change. Schrank and Engels (cited in Pardeck, 1990) say that biblio-therapy is effective in changing attitudes. Lenkowsky (1987) says that bibliotherapy has a positive effect on children's personal and social development.

When clients feel utterly alone, as if no one understands them, it is often difficult to convince them otherwise. However, if she or he reads an account of someone else who is faced with and overcomes a comparable obstacle, the client will probably feel less alone in her or his plight. For example, a child whose parent has died has many difficult issues to work through. If the child's peers cannot fully appreciate the pain, the child will feel isolated. By reading about a character who goes through the loss of a parent and then deals with it in an adaptive manner, the child is able to identify with the character. The child then can vicariously experience the stages "with" the character in the book and thereby gain some resolution of his or her own feelings.

Identification with one another (or characters in a story) is a powerful force that can help people cope with the difficulties of life. Just to know that one is not alone in facing adversity can be a comforting thought, even if those with whom the common problem is shared are characters in a book. This identification helps the individual form new attitudes and gain a different perspective. Thus, the client might think, "If they could do it, so can I." The realization that others have the same problems helps create self-acceptance and gives the client permission to open up and reveal feelings that he or she was previously reluctant to show. It is at this point that the real work of emotional healing can begin. When a client develops a more "healthy" attitude toward his or her problem (e.g., that it can be dealt with), he or she is ready to embark on the journey of resolution.

Bibliotherapy with Children

According to McInnis (1982), bibliotherapy with children usually involves the use of fiction that portrays a situation that is similar to the child's own. He maintains that stories should present a realistic resolution of conflict that allows children to develop good problem-solving skills. However, Brown (1975) says that although young children (ages 2–6) enjoy stories concerning familiar events, older children tend to develop an interest in fantasy and tales of imagination and adventure. These genres typically do not involve a realistic resolution of conflict; yet, Brown believes that this type of literature still can be beneficial to children. It appears that general prescriptions cannot be made; the type of book recommended depends upon the child's particular situation.

Bibliotherapy with children is best used as a preventive strategy and focuses on problem-solving skills, self-understanding, and self-efficacy. Books reinforcing a positive self-image are especially important for adolescents, who tend to be low in self-acceptance (Wilkin, 1978). Use of bibliotherapy for children with developmental transitions or situational crises (e.g., menstruation, death of a sibling) can be very helpful and important. Suggestions for reading should be made carefully. Children should be allowed choice in whether to read the books and not feel that they are obliged to do so. A good strategy is to leave books lying around for them to pick up and start reading on their own or giving them a few books from which to make choices. In the discussion phase, children need guidance to be sure that they come to sound conclusions and grow through their reading (Hanna, 1970), but advice giving should be avoided. In a permissive atmosphere, with no answers given, children must explore potential solutions. This allows them to integrate their insights into their lives, improves problem-solving skills, and increases self-efficacy (Brown, 1975).

Sargent (1985) discusses the use of bibliotherapy with children of mentally ill parents. Because they may not receive adequate nurturing and are often stigmatized by the parent's illness, such children are quite vulnerable. Useful materials for these children present information that helps them attain some cognitive understanding of mental illness, some coping skills, and the assurance that they are not to blame for the parent's illness. The material also should provide models of environments in which the child can develop and individuate from the family in spite of the potentially engulfing nature of a parent's mental illness. An important part of this modeled environment is the portrayal of healthy peer relationships and the development of relationships with surrogate parents as a necessary aspect of these children's lives.

Another special case is that of children living in the United States whose native language is not English. These children may feel alienated from both cultures. Bibliotherapy using books written in their native language can help children to achieve a sense of dignity and value for their native culture as well as knowledge and skills for living in their new culture.

Bibliotherapy with Groups

Group bibliotherapy usually involves material being read aloud by individual group members or the therapist, or in the case of a play, individuals each take on a role. The reading is then followed by reaction and discussion. With mental patients, Brown (1975) recommends reading poetry or prose that is descriptive, colorful, and evocative of memories. The sessions should provide an atmosphere of friendship to foster feelings of belonging and acceptance and promote interpersonal relationships. The therapist may wish to have art supplies available for the clients to work with while they listen to the readings. This artwork may have diagnostic value when evaluating the client's state of mind. The discussion should be nondirected — members should be allowed to talk about their reactions to the material without being led in a particular direction by the therapist. Individual contact with the therapist for further discussion is sometimes useful and should be used to correct any mistaken interpretations made by the client (Brown, 1975).

There are some clear advantages to using group bibliotherapy with more acutely troubled clients. Their illnesses and medications may leave patients unable to read; therefore, group reading may be the only opportunity for the use of bibliotherapy. Because the material is not known to the patients before the session and its impact is fresh, clients are more easily able to share their experiences. Group bibliotherapy often leads to improvement in the socialization skills of the members (Brown, 1975).

APPROPRIATE USES

Virtually all of the literature cautions against using bibliotherapy as a lone therapeutic strategy and recommends that it always be used in conjunction with other therapies (Lenkowsky, 1987; Pardeck, 1990; Yauman, 1991). Attempts to use bibliotherapy alone would deprive the client of the additional benefits that a broader therapeutic context offers. The literature also suggests that bibliotherapy can be effective with children, adolescents, young adults, adults, and elderly clients (Phinney, 1977; Bernstein, 1983).

Because bibliotherapy is a relatively recent therapeutic strategy, it is still unclear for whom and under what conditions it is most appropriate. Nevertheless, the therapist should be aware of some important issues before choosing a bibliotherapeutic strategy. It is important to know how reading fits into a client's lifestyle. If the client does not enjoy reading and views it as a chore rather than a pleasure, using bibliotherapy may not be the best strategy. In contrast, for the client who reads for pleasure, bibliotherapy may be a very natural adjunct to therapy. Another consideration is the client's level of commitment to the therapeutic process. Reading and thinking about the material (and, often, completing homework assignments) outside of session is a time and energy intense undertaking and requires a great deal of motivation. Also, it is important to realize that accomplishing reading assignments is sometimes a matter of opportunity, not of motivation. For example, if the client is a single working mother without the benefit of household and child care assistance, bibliotherapy may not be a realistic strategy.

The healthier a person is, mentally and emotionally, the more benefit she or he will derive from reading (Brown, 1975). McInnis (1982) claimed bibliotherapy is most effective when the client is of above-average intelligence and is not severely disturbed, thus, raising questions about its use with some clients. Mildly neurotic patients are more likely to benefit than are severely neurotic or psychotic patients, and people who ask for psychotherapeutic help also are more likely to benefit.

From the research that has been conducted, it appears that bibliotherapy is useful for problems that are typically approached with cognitive-behavioral strategies. A good example is assertiveness, a behavior that often is effectively learned by altering irrational thinking, utilizing behavioral techniques, and prescribing bibliotherapy. Hackney and Cormier (1994) link bibliotherapy with cognitive strategies and see the most benefit for those clients who engage in logical and systematic behavior involving analysis and synthesis. Strategies closely associated with cognitive change assume that people will need to change their beliefs, attitudes, and perceptions if change is to be sustainable. If distortions in these areas can be replaced with more constructive thoughts, then clients are more likely to satisfy their goals within the counseling process. Bibliotherapy can be an important tool in providing accurate information and enhancing analysis and rational conclusions.

Bibliotherapy often is useful when a client is unable to personalize and verbalize certain thoughts and feelings. This approach allows the client to look at problems in terms of the characters rather than in terms of themselves. Although this may be necessary only during the initial stage of therapy, it is important, because it allows the client to depersonalize the problem and feel more comfortable with the therapeutic process. For example, Pardeck (1990) reported particular success using bibliotherapy with physically abused children.

Although there are specific client profile characteristics that increase the potential success of bibliotherapy, they are sufficiently general that almost any client, at some point in therapy, will probably benefit from this intervention strategy. Thus, it often is not an issue of whether to use bibliotherapy but of when to use it. Brown (1975) believed that the timing was critical and suggested that bibliotherapy was most appropriate in the final stages of therapy, when emotional and cognitive growth need to be reinforced.

There are a few important cautions that must be noted. The client must be willing to participate, and the therapist must use professional judgment to determine if the client is sufficiently prepared for bibliotherapeutic intervention. The selected materials must be carefully previewed for theme and reading level. If the client is fragile, reactions to the material must be carefully monitored. Misinterpretation can exacerbate depressive symptoms, especially with socially withdrawn and depressive personalities. It also is possible for the reading to engender false expectations in the client and reinforce client problems (Brown, 1975). If inappropriate material is selected, the client may fail to see the positive and increase their negative thoughts and feelings. Issues such as reading disabilities, moral or religious beliefs, and countereffective role models can all result in client resistance to the intervention.

It generally is wise to avoid bibliotherapy with clients who are out of touch with reality and have difficulty separating fantasy from reality. If bibliotherapy is considered for neurotic or psychotic patients, the severity of their condition must be carefully considered and modifications made to accommodate individual situations.

Bibliotherapy recently has been subdivided into two fields. Hynes and Hynes-Berry (1986) note that bibliotherapy reference lists and therapeutic use now are divided between "clinical" and "developmental" bibliotherapy. "Clinical bibliotherapy" refers to the treatment of residential patients in mental hospitals, chemical dependency treatment centers, and correctional institutions. "Developmental bibliotherapy" refers to use by clients who are seeking increased self-understanding. A further distinction is made between "situational" and "contextual" areas within the bibliotherapy literature. For example, Worell and Remer (1992) present bibliotherapy as important to feminist therapy clients learning about sex roles, gender ascriptions, and systemic discrimination. They hold that education about sexism, resocialization about sex roles, and learning about coping skills are facilitated by reading.

EFFECTIVENESS

The research conducted on the effectiveness of bibliotherapy can be categorized into roughly eight areas: academic achievement, assertiveness, attitude change, behavioral change, marital relations, fear reduction, self-concept, and self-development. Bibliotherapy has been relatively effective with assertiveness, attitude change, behavioral change, and self-development. In contrast, bibliotherapy failed to show significant effectiveness in academic achievement, reducing fear, changing self-concept, and marital dysfunction. The Borenstein and others (1984) study of marital therapy did not support the utility of bibliotherapy for couples with marital dysfunction. One hypothesis for this failure is that marital difficulties are more resistant to change because they require the efforts of more than one person. A related idea is that gaining information is not the same as the willingness and effort required to change power relationships and other dynamics.

Bibliotherapy has several strengths and weaknesses. Cost-effectiveness is an important strength. In many situations, a therapist can loan a book to a client or the client can purchase it for a relatively low cost. Another strength is the ease with which it can be administered, without need of specialized training in the specific technique, by a trained and experienced therapist. Bibliotherapy also allows the client to be very involved in the direction of therapy. The client participates in selecting the book, initiating discussion, and discerning its meaning.

One of the weaknesses of bibliotherapy is the dependence upon the client's ability to follow through with the readings. The less structured the relationship with the therapist, the less likely is the client to follow through with the readings (Glasgow & Rosen, 1978). Another issue is bibliotherapy's inability to affect a client's environmental system (Glasgow & Rosen, 1978). This inability to affect surrounding systems is a problem shared by many psychotherapeutic approaches. The attention to the surrounding systems as well as their impact on the individual is precisely the focus of feminist psychology (Brown & Ballou, 1992). This perspective has been brought to bear on bibliotherapy by Worell and Remer (1992).

Bibliotherapy is a process that has existed in one form or another since the time of ancient Greece. Using literature to deal with mental health issues has evolved into a widely practiced therapeutic strategy. The clinical opinions regarding appropriate use are fairly broad and consistent, though differing theoretical positions apply their own constructs in explanation. As with many other strategies, however, the research investigating effectiveness is vague, inconsistent, nonrigorous, and unconvincing. Careful research, through a variety of methods by those using bibliotherapy, needs to be done if effectiveness claims are to be made beyond clinical impression.

REFERENCES

Bernstein, J. E. (1983). *Books to help children cope with separation and loss* (2d ed.). New York: R. R. Bowker.

Borenstein, P. H., Wilson, G. L., Balleweg, B. J., Weisser, C. E., Bornstein, M. T., Andre, J. C., Woody, D. J., Smith, M. M., Laughna, S. M., McLellarn, R. W., Kirby, K. L., & Hocker, J. (1984). Behavioral marital bibliotherapy: An initial investigation of therapeutic efficacy. *The American Journal of Family Therapy*, *12*(4), 21–28.

Brown, E. F. (1975). *Bibliotherapy and its widening applications*. Metuchen, NJ: Scarecrow.

Brown, L., & Ballou, M. (1992). *Personality and psychopathology: Feminist reappraisals*. New York: Guilford.

Craighead, J., McNamara, N., & Horan P. (1984). In J. T. Pardeck (Ed.), *Using bibliotherapy in clinical practice* (pp. 54–72). Westport, CT: Greenwood.

Glasgow, R. E., & Rosen, G. M. (1978). Behavioral bibliotherapy: A review of self-help behavior therapy manuals. *Psychological Bulletin*, *85*(1), 1–18.

Hackney, H., & Cormier, S. (1994). *Counseling strategies and interventions*. Boston, MA: Allyn and Bacon.

Hanna, G. R. (1970). Promoting adolescent growth through reading. In D. Thomison (Ed.), *Readings about adolescent literature*. Metuchen, NJ: Scarecrow.

Hynes, A., & Hynes-Berry, M. (1986). *Bibliotherapy — the interactive process: A handbook*. Boulder, CO: Westview.

Lenkowsky, R. S. (1987). Bibliotherapy: A review and analysis of the literature. *Journal of Special Education*, *21*, 123–132.

McInnis, K. M. (1982). Bibliotherapy: Adjunct to traditional counseling with children of stepfamilies. *Child Welfare, 61,* 152–160.

Moody, R. A., & Moody, C. P. (1991). A family perspective: Helping children acknowledge and express grief following the death of a parent. *Death Studies, 15,* 587–602.

Pardeck, J. A., & Pardeck, J. T. (1984). An overview of the bibliotherapeutic treatment approach: Implications for clinical social work practice. *Family Therapy, 3,* 241–252.

Pardeck, J. T. (1993). *Using bibliotherapy in clinical practice.* Westport, CT: Greenwood.

Pardeck, J. T. (1990). Using bibliotherapy in clinical practice with children. *Psychological Reports, 67,* 1043–1049.

Phinney, E. (Ed.). (1977). *The librarian and the patient.* Chicago, IL: American Library Association.

Sargent, K. L. (1985). Helping children cope with parental mental illness through use of children's literature. *Child Welfare, 64,* 617–628.

Starker, S. (1988). Psychologists and self-help books: Attitudes and prescriptive practices of clinicians. *American Journal of Psychotherapy, 42*(3), 448–455.

Wilkin, B. T. (1978). *Survival themes in fiction for children and young people.* Metuchen, NJ: Scarecrow.

Worell, J., & Remer, P. (1992). *Feminist perspectives in therapy.* New York: Wiley.

Yauman, Beth E. (1991). School-based group counseling for children of divorce: A review of the literature. *Elementary School Guidance and Counseling, 26,* 130–138.

5

Expressive Therapies

Mary Ballou

The expressive therapies are primarily nonverbal and rely on the modalities of dance, movement, art, and music as the means of expression in various therapeutic environments. These nonverbal interventions are sometimes referred to as "creative therapy" or "activity therapy." Although not entirely nonverbal, each modality facilitates communication through body movements, drawings, or music. Through participation in these therapeutic activities, the individual has the opportunity to discover and overcome the harmful and maladaptive habits and behaviors that create intrapersonal and interpersonal conflicts.

Expressive therapies may be used in groups or when individual clients have difficulty verbally expressing themselves. Emotions may be expressed in a drawing, by playing an instrument, or by simply moving about the room in a manner reflective of their mood. These are examples of the many ways a therapist may use expressive therapy to give nonverbal clients the freedom to speak in a nontraditional manner. Expressive therapy gives the individual the opportunity to interpret their emotions in a highly individualized manner at a self-chosen level of complexity.

The expressive therapies involve individuals in an activity that elicits creativity and participation. The goals are to develop body awareness, to focus on body image, and to link body movement and emotional responses. It is made clear to the client that aptitude or ability in the chosen format is not a factor. The goal is the freedom to communicate, rather than artistic accomplishment. However, tailoring the therapy to the client's interests does facilitate the client's participation.

Each of these therapies has unique methods and mediums, but all share common ground. All have historical roots in accepted and well-documented theory, and the events that occur during a session are interpreted within a therapeutic frame of reference. The common goal of intervention in each modality is effective healing. Each modality has produced specialists, but the otherwise trained and experienced therapist can effectively employ these intervention strategies. During the past 50 years, committed practitioners of all the expressive therapies have significantly advanced the conceptual base and refined the intervention techniques.

Although the expressive therapies share commonalities with each other and with other interventions, each has unique applications and techniques. Two of these interventions, art therapy and movement-dance therapy, will, therefore, be discussed separately.

ART THERAPY

Theoretical Background

Art as a therapeutic modality did not come into its own until the 1940s. Initially, it relied on psychoanalytic theory and practice and encouraged individuals to draw spontaneously and to free-associate with their creations. Today, many techniques have been developed for using art as a communication vehicle with all types of clients.

Art Therapy offers an opportunity to explore personal problems and potential through verbal and non-verbal expression, and to develop physical, emotional, and/or learning skills through therapeutic art experiences. . . . Therapy through art recognizes art processes, forms, content, and associations as reflections of an individual's development, abilities, personality, interests and concerns. The use of art as therapy implies that the creative process can be a means both of reconciling emotional conflicts and of fostering self awareness and personal growth. (Feder & Feder, 1981, p. 10)

Art can be the primary therapeutic intervention, or it can be an adjunct to other strategies. In addition to being a means of alternative client communication, art has proven to be an effective diagnostic tool and a means of identifying client issues.

Margaret Naumburg and Edith Kramer are recognized as the fore-mothers and primary developers of art therapy. Both began their work with children — Naumburg in an education setting and Kramer in a hospital setting. They left education and medicine, respectively, to study psychoanalysis. Although both women had a psychoanalytic orientation, each used different aspects of psychoanalytic theory in the development and justification of the use of art as therapy. According to Rubin (1984), Naumburg believed that art was a symbolic form of speech evoked from the subconscious, much like dreams, and could be understood through spontaneous free associations. Kramer, on the other hand, believed that art was the "royal road to sublimation." She viewed art therapy as a way of integrating conflicting feelings and impulses in an aesthetically satisfying form, helping the ego to control, manage, and synthesize via the creative process.

Currently, there is debate within art therapy concerning the critical mechanism of this intervention's effectiveness. Feder and Feder (1981) raise the question of whether the art is itself a complete form of therapy or a strategy for conducting therapy. They then place Edith Kramer and Irene Jakab as asserting that the creation of art is itself therapeutic, allowing the individual to channel sexual and aggressive drives into socially acceptable activities. Through this process, there is a release of tension. Generally, however, most psychoanalysts, in Feder and Feder's view, see art therapy as a means by which a therapist creates "the meeting ground of the world inside and the world outside" and not, in and of itself, a means of catharsis.

Many therapists consider artistic communication superior to verbal communication because it facilitates a more direct and intense expression of the client's emotions, dreams, and fantasies. When presented with the opportunity to communicate in this manner, suppression and intellectualization are much less likely. The artwork that results is concrete evidence of a client's internal experience that can be examined for overt and covert messages. If collected and saved over time, artwork can be a means of following an individual's progress.

Implementation

Oster and Gould (1986, p. 7) state that, "Freud hypothesized that symbols represent forgotten memories and are likely to emerge through dreams or art expression due to intrapsychic stress." In art therapy, clients are supplied with a variety of materials with which they may express thoughts and feelings. Once the work is completed, the therapist looks at form, color, relationships, and symbols and facilitates the client's self-awareness. To avoid trauma, the therapist always must use a degree of caution in making latent messages apparent to the client. Further, the therapist assists the clients in the integration of their discovered inner selves with their external world. "The use of art for healing and for mastery is at least as old as the drawings on the walls of caves; yet the profession is itself an infant in the family of mental health disciplines. In a similar paradox, while art therapy itself is highly sophisticated, the art process itself is simple and natural (Rubin, 1984, p. 11).

The materials utilized in art therapy are those with which to draw, paint, model, and construct. An adequate work surface must be available, and the materials should be arranged in such a way that they can be used spontaneously and without unnecessary delay in the actualization of a creative impulse. The procedure generally involves three broad stages. First, the client focuses upon an event or feeling. Second, the client creates an image that represents the event or feeling. Third, the therapist considers the significance of the client's creation.

Sourkes (1991) provides an excellent illustration of this process in the creation and use of a mandala. "Mandala" is a Sanskrit term for a circle. Jungian analysts see the circle as a symbol of unity, and, thus, the ultimate dialogue between the conscious and the unconscious is the literal creation and use of a mandala.

A mandala is typically developed in six steps. First, the therapist defines a topic, for example, "How you felt when. . . ." The client is then lead through a guided visualization of the topic, for example, "Close your eyes and think about it. Remember where, who, what was there. Remem-ber how you felt." The process of visualization is the critical link be-tween the emotions and the concrete task that follows. The third step in the process is the client's inventory of his or her feelings. With children, a therapist facilitates this process by presenting a set of feelings commonly attributed to their experience. Each of the feelings is written on a separate file card, and the cards are shuffled to avoid biasing the child. The child then selects the feelings that apply to him or her.

After focusing on the feelings, the fourth step is for the client to choose a color to represent each of those feelings. Fifth, the client then colors in the mandala using the chosen colors in proportion to the extent of each of the identified feelings. Each of the colors is then labeled with its corresponding emotion.

The last step in the process is a consideration of the completed mandala. The therapist generally focuses upon the client's choice of feelings, colors, proportions, order, overall design, and verbal associations. The client and therapist process the experience and, thus, bring into play a verbal component to this primarily nonverbal process.

The unstructured nature of the mandala is advantageous because it permits use with any topic and can be as general or specific as the therapist chooses. The mandala technique also can be employed at different points in time and, thus, can provide a record of patient progress.

In contrast to the relatively unstructured approaches, such as the creation of a mandala, there are several highly structured techniques that can be used in art therapy (Feder & Feder, 1981). For example, Elizabeth Koppitz's "Human Figure Drawing Test" is designed to measure a child's emotional and mental development. Meaning is assigned to particular features of the drawing. For example, small figures are interpreted as timidity, while large figures suggest aggression. Hanna Kwiatkowska pioneered the use of family art therapy. Her psychoanalytic interpretations of the art work focused on the revealed roles and status of each individual and the relationships between family members. Robert Burns and Harvard Kaufman developed the Kinetic Family Drawing from which the therapist notes the style, symbols, actions, juxtaposition, and physical characteristics of each individual portrayed. Other dimensions examined include shading and scribbling, the degree of emphasis on details, and the enlargement, exaggeration, or omission of body parts.

Form and shape are generally considered to reveal thought, while color is the revealer of emotion. Often, those pleasantly disposed toward the outside world like color for color's sake, and those who are inwardly oriented do not. One study with a group of young children demonstrated the constancy of the relationship between emotions and their color representation. Blue and black suggest repression; red, aggression; yellow, infantile regression; and green, simplicity (Feder & Feder, 1981).

Color is used diagnostically in the "House, Tree, Person" exercise. The client first draws a house, a tree, and a person in pencil and then draws them again using color. Normally, a person will use three to five colors, but an inhibited individual will use a single crayon, and, in contrast, psychotics often make a wild use of many colors within their drawings.

The rigid interpretation of colors and shapes is often criticized. Helene Burt (1993) makes a strong case for interpreting a client's creative expression within the context of other known data. The client's socioeconomic status, class, culture, and individuality all contribute to his or her art. Thus, interpretation is best made within the context of these other known variables.

Art therapy appears to be appropriate with almost any population. It can be especially helpful with nonverbal or withdrawn individuals, children, and families with children. With art therapy, defenses often weaken, and more information becomes available than would have emerged from a strictly verbal interaction. Art therapy may be of cathartic benefit to psychotic individuals, although their artistic creations will mirror their garbled thinking. This makes interpretation difficult, if not impossible (Feder & Feder, 1981).

Case Studies

Comparative group research on the effectiveness of art therapy is difficult to find, but there are numerous case studies that describe its effectiveness in providing a mode of expression, catharsis, and the opportunity for the therapist to observe accompanying behaviors (Landgarten, 1987).

In one case study, during the process of art therapy, a child named Donnie began to remember more details about an attack he had experienced. He was able to draw a picture of his attacker, the print on his T-shirt, and his car. Thus, Donnie was able to identify the perpetrator. In addition, he also drew pictures of his attacker being physically punished and castrated, which served a cathartic purpose and a means by which he could communicate his emotions to the therapist.

The "here and now" of family interactions also can be explored through art therapy. By guiding a family through an assignment, the therapist is provided with an opportunity to observe the family in action as well as analyzing their artwork. In one case study, a young mother brought her six-year-old son in for counseling. The therapist suggested that the mother and son do a team art task nonverbally. The mother prompted her son to go first. The boy made a sculpture of a naked boy in a bathtub. The mother then sculpted a snake around the boy. When the boy became distraught, the mother responded with an amused indifference. The therapist then suggested that they work together in a verbal team art task, making a sculpture together with one color. The mother told her son to pick a color, then picked a second color for herself. She laughed at her son's protests that she had broken the rules. The boy molded the face of a little boy, which the mother then crushed. The boy began to cry, and the mother again responded with amused indifference. In focusing upon the artistic tasks, the mother and son behaved more characteristically than they would have if they had focused on speaking directly with the therapist. The mother's actions with the art materials mirrored her treatment of her son. This art therapy session helped to confirm the therapist's suspicions of the mother's neglect and abuse of the child (Landgarten, 1987).

Victims of trauma, such as abused children and war veterans, may also benefit from art therapy. Case and Dalley (1992) report Read's 1991 work which discusses a Vietnam veteran who would not talk about his war experiences. An intelligent and verbal person in most situations, he could express his feelings about Vietnam only through his artwork. The safety and sense of control provided through the art medium allowed the veteran to see and understand his trauma.

DANCE AND MOVEMENT THERAPY

History and Theoretical Background

Dance and movement have been forms of treatment for centuries. "The dance of the medicine man or shaman belongs to the oldest form of medicine and psychotherapy, in which the common exaltation and release of tensions was able to change man's physical and mental suffering into a new option on health" (Bernstein, 1975, p. 3). In 1873, Darwin's *The Expression of Emotions in Man and Animals* described the relationship between emotion and physical activity. A resurgence of awareness of the whole person, including bodily movements, occurred in the theories of Adler, Reich, and Jung.

Reich's theory emphasized the physical tensions that accompany mental tensions. He believed that muscular tension and emotional repression were parallel symptoms of the same problem (Feder & Feder, 1981).

Reich's focus on the relationship between movement and psychic tension had a strong influence on Marian Chace. In June 1942, Chace, the founder of modern dance therapy, created a pioneer program called "Dance as Communication" at St. Elizabeth's Hospital in Washington, D.C. In 1966, 73 therapists, under her leadership, founded the American Dance Therapy Association (Feder & Feder, 1981). Together with Chace, Liljan Espanek, Trudy Schoop, and Mary Whitehouse are the recognized originators of the field of dance therapy.

Interestingly, the association was formed in the absence of an official theory. However, the members did agree on the following official definition of dance therapy: "Dance therapy is the psychotherapeutic use of movement as a process which furthers the emotional and physical integration of the individual. Dance therapy works with individuals who require special services because of behavioral, learning, perceptual and/ or physical disorders. Dance therapy is used in treatment, rehabilitation, and education of the emotionally disturbed, physically handicapped, neurologically impaired, and socially deprived" (Feder & Feder, 1981, p. 159).

Although a psychoanalytic orientation dominates the field, dance-movement therapists practice from Sullivanian, Adlerian, Jungian, behavioral, and humanistic orientations. Common to all orientations, a set of assumptions provides the rational for the techniques of dance-movement therapy. "The basic view underlying the concept of dance therapy is that the expressive aspects of personality, in its gestures, movements, and postures, are a function of the individual totality: the intellectual, emotional, unconscious, and somatic totality. In posture, in pose, in mannerism, in attitude, in gesture, in movement, and in breathing, the individual communicates with an eloquence that transcends his verbalizations and that surpasses his own inner state" (Emilio, Hurwitz, & Carranza, 1983, p. 3).

Movement and dance are rooted in the physical expression of our relationship with our world. Our experience of the world and life events and our expressions of that experience are ultimately connected to physical movement. Our mental and emotional activities are inseparable from our physical freedom. An individual's characteristic movement patterns are believed to reflect the totality of his or her life and are viewed as a part of personality, rather than as a manifestation of personality. Movement therapy implies the use of a broad range of body movement styles that are rhythmic extensions of an individual's everyday movement.

Dance-movement therapists approach movement at physical, psychological, and social levels. Physically, the techniques aim to develop a repertoire of behavior that promotes meeting one's needs, adjustment to the environment, a definition of the physical self, and the expression of moods, attitudes, and ideas (Fleshman & Fryear, 1981).

Psychologically, the goals include bringing the unconscious to the conscious, encouraging free expression in movement, developing a means of emotional release, and facilitating adjustment to reality. Further, the therapist "works to develop new skills and interests so that the patient's attention is removed from his own symptoms" (Fleshman & Fryear, 1981, p. 92).

Finally, dance-movement therapy promotes participation in social activities. Individuals have the opportunity to develop interpersonal relationships, and this interaction serves to reestablish contact with the external world.

Implementation

To accomplish the goals of dance therapy, the therapist focuses on the movement of the individual. The therapist looks for undue muscle tension, uncontrolled or overcontrolled movement, and constricted movement. In observing and classifying movement, the therapist generally analyzes the function of movement (movement to perform a task), the symbolic use of posture and direction, and the existence of tension (Feder & Feder, 1981).

Labanotation and Effort/Shape are two descriptive and analytical systems utilized by therapists to systematically observe movement. Labanotation is used to record movement patterns, weight distribution, and quantitative aspects of movement. Effort/Shape expands the Laban system and adds the analysis of tensions, efforts, and shapes and the qualitative elements of movement. The systems are used diagnostically and to determine the specific areas of intervention.

A one-to-one approach may be used to facilitate the expression of spontaneous movement, or a group format may be used to promote socialization. In either case, the dance therapist will attempt to individualize treatment. The duration of the session will depend on the physical, intellectual, and tolerance levels of the individual(s). Group therapy sessions are usually held weekly, while individual sessions are typically scheduled for 50-minute sessions, two to three times per week. For mentally retarded individuals and for children, a short session of 30 minutes is generally mostly effective (Espanek, 1981).

Dance therapists use a variety of techniques within an organized sequence of activities. In the beginning, the group is allowed to choose the music selections, and typically, the music chosen is an accurate reflection of the group mood. Not surprisingly, a group dominated by a depressive tone will usually begin with music that has a slow tempo. In contrast to a depressed group, an escalated group may choose loud, lively music (Rosen, 1974).

Once the music has been selected, the therapist often will have the group form a circle. The circle, in addition to symbolic connotations, serves to establish communication and reduce anxiety. Further, the therapist can more easily observe and assess the emotional tone of the group.

Within the circle, warm-up exercises are executed. The exercises release tension, prevent pulled muscles, and stimulate body and mind. They also enable the therapist to establish initial and direct contact with the clients by moving in rhythm with them. The exercises include stretching, stamping the floor, clapping, swinging limbs or the trunk, and beating a drum.

Upon completion of the warm-up, the therapist begins to introduce simple steps. These steps are performed by all group members (including the therapist) in unison. The act of dancing with patients is extremely valuable. According to Chace, "The therapist by dancing with the patient says: I feel every emotion — I know hate, sadness, and loneliness; I know all these moods that separate you from people. I can feel all these things too. I accept you and we know one another for a moment" (in Rosen, 1974, p. 60).

Depending on the group's needs, the therapist can introduce a variety of steps. The steps may involve exploring different parts of the body, changes in locomotion, establishing one's space, cooperation in working with a partner, or working on movement to rhythm, impulses, and irregular beats (Wethered, 1973). All of these techniques promote an awareness of the body.

Because dance-movement therapists consider the walk the most fundamental expression of an individual, several techniques focus on the forward progression of the patient. Exercises that recapitulate the development of walking from quadruped to biped are repeated until the patient can smoothly and harmoniously move from all fours to an upright position. Variations of the forward progression include the leap, the run, and the tumble. Through these procedures, the patient is able to observe and experience his or her body language and understand the way in which his or her body expresses attitudes, feelings, and emotional release (Espanek, 1981). In addition to these whole-body techniques, intervention sometimes focuses on specific areas of function, such as breathing, posture, and balance. "Through a restructuring program in motor movement, sacrum development (Forward Progression), wings, posture, balance, and breathing, the patient begins to experience his [sic] body fully as a vehicle of movement in time and space" (Espanek, 1981, p. 76).

Eventually, the patients will claim the role of leader and introduce steps for others to follow. The therapist encourages this client-initiated activity, because it is the precursor to improvisation. Improvisation is spontaneous free movement that "has the function of embodying the feelings and of bringing them to the surface where their force can be experienced as the dynamic underlying body-ego disturbance" (Espanek, 1981, p. 81). Improvisation is a powerful technique, because emotional content is expressed regardless of conscious intent.

To facilitate improvisation, the therapist often will select a particular type of music, rhythm, or percussion to meet the clients' needs. The four types of stimulation used in improvisation are melody, rhythm, symbolism, and the images and emotional dynamics of everyday life. For example, a depressed patient might be exposed to a melody that arouses feelings of joy and happiness. Most importantly, the patient must develop an awareness of the feelings that accompany the physical experience.

As the emotional and physical intensity begins to diminish, the group listens to music in closing. The procedure for ending the session varies by therapist preference. Some advocate processing the members' experiences, because they believe that complete awareness comes through verbalization and insight into the experience. Other therapists strongly believe that the experience is all that is necessary for growth to occur.

Appropriate and Inappropriate Uses

The techniques of dance-movement therapy have been used with diverse populations. Dance-movement therapy had its genesis with psychotic patients who were unable to verbally communicate their feelings and thoughts or form interpersonal relationships. According to Chace (in Espanek, 1972, p. 112), "The first goal of a therapist in this situation is to break through the isolation of the patient." For many psychotic individuals, words are a means of further concealing their feelings. Movement enables the patient to reveal hidden emotions in a socially acceptable manner.

Further, Heber (1993) suggests the psychotic patient often needs to be resocialized. Dance-movement techniques facilitate the patient's participation in treatment. Once involved, the patient can share her or his feelings through expressive movement. As success in performing movements occurs, the patient can first learn to accept herself or himself and then come to accept others. Participation fosters identification with the group and relationships with group members.

Psychotic and autistic children can benefit from dance-movement techniques. The techniques are useful in developing a basic repertoire of behaviors necessary for the activities of daily living. The techniques are especially valuable for improving basic movements such as walking, bending, running, and jumping. Most importantly, the techniques provide severely disturbed children with an opportunity to communicate and express a variety of feelings.

Mildly mentally retarded individuals and individuals with mild brain damage respond positively to dance-movement techniques. The techniques often enable the individual to interact by using capacities that are not impaired. For example, the visually impaired, whose movement is usually restricted, learn to move freely and express their emotions through movement (Fleshman & Fryear, 1981).

There are several specific client populations for whom dance therapy has been proposed as a therapeutic intervention. Kreuger and Schofield (1986) proposed a model for working with patients suffering from eating disorders. Because these patients generally have restricted emotional expression and have difficulty connecting to their bodily experiences, dance-movement therapy would appear to be a logical intervention.

Alcoholic women who display a field dependent cognitive style, typically a global type of thinking, have been considered good candidates for dance-movement therapy (Reiland, 1990). Global thinking is believed to hinder recovery. Reiland's study determined that field dependent alcoholic women were able to achieve a "state of greater articulation," at least temporarily (Reiland, 1990, p. 353). Additionally, the characteristic denial, isolation, and low self-esteem were decreased with the group support in dance-movement sessions. This change was hypothesized to be beneficial to the substance abuser in terms of altering a potentially dysfunctional style.

Goodill (1987) proposed that dance-movement therapy is a beneficial treatment intervention with abused children. This intervention is believed to facilitate the development of a healthy sense of personal space. Additionally, through symbolic movement, children can communicate their experiences in less threatening and frightening ways. Finally, the dance-movement intervention can equip children with assertive traits that may aid in the prevention of further abuse.

Dance-movement techniques also can be beneficial for relatively healthy individuals. For example, the techniques can be used to raise self-esteem, and shy or extremely self-conscious individuals can learn to be more free with their bodily expressions.

There are individuals for whom dance-movement therapy is clearly inappropriate. The severely physically handicapped cannot effectively participate in the required activities. Similarly, the custodial retarded are not good candidates for this intervention, because participation would be likely to frustrate and disappoint such individuals.

Hyperactive children and adults with patterns of acting out violence are not recommended for dance-movement techniques. Unless the focus is specifically limited to relaxation, these individuals can gain greater benefit from other therapeutic interventions.

Exhibitionists and voyeurs are not appropriate candidates for dance-movement techniques. Because the techniques involve physical activities, such individuals may use the therapy as an opportunity to reinforce their neurosis (Espanek, 1981).

Research

According to Fleshman and Fryear (1981, p. 184), "the glaring weakness in dance-movement therapy is in the area of research. Few carefully designed outcome studies have been conducted and fewer yet reported." Although studies do exist, they are typically case studies, and the literature is obviously lacking in research using rigorous experimental design.

Emilio, Hurwitz, and Carranza (1983) reported success in treating paranoid and withdrawn patients. The patients were claimed to have actively participated in dance-movement groups. Children in a residential treatment center were less detached, had fewer instances of acting-out behavior, and were more receptive to adult contact following a dance-movement program (Shennum, 1987). Fersh (1981) elaborated on the positive effects of dance-movement techniques with the elderly. The therapy was reportedly successful in revealing unresolved conflicts over feelings of abandonment by family members, encouraging independent functioning, and preparing for death.

Dance-movement techniques appear to be a useful tool for the clinician. With an emphasis on the body and movement, the therapist gains an appreciation of many levels of communication. It is recommended that intensive training be completed before the techniques are utilized in clinical practice. Further, the practitioner needs to attend to future research findings on the efficacy of dance-movement techniques.

SUMMARY

The expressive therapies are primarily nonverbal therapeutic interventions. Art and dance are therapeutic approaches that explore human capacities outside the cognitive dimension. They are experiential and not within the domain traditionally addressed by psychology. In addition, the implementation of these strategies is organic and is dependent upon the individual client, the issue, and the "right moment." There are no set rules, and the experienced therapist often must be willing to take risks in initiating a spontaneous, but fitting, intervention strategy. Because of these inherent characteristics, it is sometimes difficult to adequately describe the process of the expressive therapies. It is equally difficult to research them using the Western scientific paradigm. Nevertheless, case studies, patient reports, and the clinical experience of therapists suggest that these methods are powerful tools both as therapy in their own right and as adjuncts to other, more traditional therapies.

REFERENCES

Bernstein, P. (1975). *Theory and methods in dance-movement therapy.* Dubuque, IA: Kendall/Hunt.

Burt, H. (1993). Issues in art therapy with culturally displaced American Indian youth. *Arts in Psychotherapy, 20*(2), 143–151.

Case, C., & Dalley, T. (1992). *The handbook of art therapy.* New York: Tavistock/Routledge.

Emilio, R. F., Hurwitz, A. J., & Carranza, V. (1983). Dance therapy in a therapeutic community for schizophrenic patients. *Arts in Psychotherapy, 10*, 85–92.

Espanek, L. (1972). Body-dynamics and dance in individual psychotherapy. *American Dance Therapy Association, 2*, 111–123.

Espanek, L. (1981). *Dance therapy.* Springfield, IL: Charles C. Thomas.

Feder, E., & Feder, B. (1981). *The expressive arts therapies.* Englewood Cliffs, NJ: Prentice-Hall.

Fleshman, B., & Fryear, J. L. (1981). *The arts in therapy.* Chicago, IL: Nelson-Hall.

Fersh, I. E. (1981). Dance/movement therapy: A holistic approach to working with the elderly. *Activities, Adaptation, and Aging, 2*(1), 21–30.

Goodill, S. W. (1987). Dance/movement therapy with abused children. *The Arts in Psychotherapy, 14*, 59–68.

Heber, L. (1993). Dance movement: A therapeutic program for psychiatric clients. *Perspectives in Psychiatric Care, 29*(3), 22–29.

Kreuger, D. W., & Schofield, E. (1986). Dance/movement therapy of eating disordered patients: A model. *The Arts in Psychotherapy, 13*, 323–331.

Landgarten, H. B. (1987). *Family art psychotherapy.* New York: Brunner/Mazel.

Oster, G. D., & Gould, P. (1986). *Using drawings in assessment and therapy.* New York: Brunner/Mazel.

Reiland, J. D. (1990). A preliminary study of dance/movement therapy with field dependent alcoholic women. *The Arts in Psychotherapy, 17*, 349–353.

Rosen, Elizabeth. (1974). *Dance in psychotherapy.* New York: Dance Horizons Republications.

Rubin, J. A. (1984). *Child art therapy* (2d ed.). New York: Van Nostrand

Shennum, W. A. (1987). Expressive activity therapy in residential treatment: Effects on children's behavior in the treatment milieu. *Child and Youth Care Quarterly,*

16(2), 81–90.

Sourkes, B. M. (1991). Mandala (color-feeling wheel). *Journal of Psychosocial Oncology, 9*(2), 81–96.

Wethered, A. (1973). *Movement and drama in therapy*. Boston, MA: Plays.

6

Imagery

Mary Ballou

HISTORY

According to Sheehan (1972), imagery is the way we learn to organize objects and experiences from our past and relate them to our present. He describes it further as a perception of forms, colors, and sounds in the absence of the stimuli themselves. Although Sheehan indicates that the human capacity for producing images is probably universal, he acknowledges that this capacity was not widely used in psychotherapy until the 1960s.

Although psychoanalysts, some dating back to the 1800s, were interested in the concept of imagery, their methodology prevented them from fully exploring it. Singer (1974) explains, "Psychoanalysis became so formed with restrictions on intervention and emphasis on the blank screen that it blocked experimentation with fantasy approaches" (p. 3). It is the behaviorists, according to Singer, who studied brain models and derived important findings around sleep cycles, dreams, and long-term memory who eventually brought great advances to the study and use of imagery.

During the 1950s, advances in the ability to methodically measure imagery and ongoing thought processes in the laboratory prompted breakthrough studies in the field. These procedures met high scientific standards and, so, were viewed as sufficiently objective to be replicated in other laboratories, thus, allowing widespread validation. Although the amount of ongoing experimental research is lacking when compared with other, more technically adaptable models of intervention, it is important to note that the verbal report of the client is often all a therapist should need to determine if progress is being made. According to Jerome Singer (1975), by the mid-1970s, many methods of psychotherapy were relying more heavily than ever upon the client's capacity to use imagery during the counseling process. Currently, the use of visualization as a therapeutic strategy is widespread, and evidence, indeed, does suggest that it can not only generate insight and help to bring about desired change in attitude but also be used to evoke spontaneous mental images that may hold significance (Goldberg, 1983).

Psychotherapists from many theoretical orientations use imagery in therapeutic communication and intervention. Following are brief descriptions of the development and use of imagery within four major orientations.

Psychoanalysis

Imagery used in psychotherapy can be traced back to Freud's use of hypnosis, verbal images, and associations (Singer, 1974). Carl Jung, a neo-Freudian, was aware of the symbolic nature of mental imagery and used it to enhance his dream work. Jung would ask his clients to visually recreate, in as much detail as possible, a previous dream. Jung called the process "active imagination." By reviewing and analyzing the symbolic content of these dream images, Jung attempted to increase client self-awareness (Singer, 1974).

Behaviorism

Although imagery techniques initially received criticism from staunch behaviorists (Watson, 1913), they were later integrated into many conditioning therapies. Images were found to be powerful stimuli, capable of eliciting emotional responses (Lazarus & Abramovitz, 1962; Stamfl, 1961; Wolpe, 1969). Imagery currently is used in a wide variety of behavior therapies (e.g., systematic desensitization and implosion).

Cognitive and Neurological

In his experiments on the human brain, Penfield (1963) discovered that images could be stored and recalled in a similar but more basic way than information presented verbally. Influenced largely by Penfield, Kubie (1965) suggested that sensory memories never may have been processed verbally, thus, proposing a previously unexplored aspect of human memory.

Transpersonal

The current, and most prolific phase, of imagery's development could be described as the transpersonal phase. It is characterized by its rediscovery of such neo-Freudians as Carl Jung and Roberto Assagioli, its integration of Eastern meditation techniques, and its eclecticism. Authors, such as Ahsen (1965, 1968), Assagioli (1965), Bandler and Grinder (1979), Borysenko (1987, 1993), Crampton (1969), Epstein (1989), Ferrier (1992), Gawain (1982), Ornstein (1987), and Pelletier (1977) have explored imagery and visualization techniques as adjuncts to psychotherapy. Some of these authors focus primarily on mind-body and psychosomatic illness issues, others on integrating subpersonalities, and others on achieving greater levels of spiritual insight, self-confidence, and peace of mind.

THEORY AND IMPLEMENTATION

The use of imagery techniques in therapy begins with a discussion with the client in order to assess his or her comfort with using imagery techniques. Schaub and Schaub (1990) discuss beginning with dream work (in a fashion similar to Jung's active imagination) as an effective means of introducing anxious clients to the imagery process.

Before initiating the imagery process itself, the therapist guides the client into a state of deep relaxation. This is sometimes referred to as grounding and centering (Schaub, Anselmo, & Luck, 1991). Grounding serves to relax the client, and centering enhances awareness and the ability to focus by directing attention inward to the body. Music sometimes is used to facilitate this relaxation stage. In the initial stage of relaxation, the clients must be taught to breathe diaphragmatically. Once this is accomplished, the client is directed toward awareness of the breathing rhythm and the rise and fall of the abdomen. Once proper breathing is established (usually 10 minutes), the client is asked to become aware of his or her subtle bodily sensations (e.g., feet on the floor, back on the chair). The client then systematically focuses on each body part and attempts to relieve tightness and tension by breathing into it.

By now, the client's breathing should be slow and deep, and his or her posture should be relaxed and quiet. Imagery sometimes starts (and ends) with an anchor image (a vivid image associated with a relaxed state, often a natural setting, such as a meadow). From this general state of relaxation and self-awareness, the client can then proceed to images more specific to the issue(s) being explored.

Case studies illustrate three major variations of imagery: guided, facilitative, and spontaneous. In guided imagery, the therapist is directive and describes predetermined images to the client. In facilitative imagery, the therapist provides some basic imagery structure but then allows the client to develop the specific images that unfold. Spontaneous imagery allows the client the greatest degree of freedom to imagine whatever she or he chooses.

To maximize effectiveness, care must be taken in the placement of descriptors (adjectives and adverbs) when initiating a scenario. Most therapists find it effective to place descriptors before the noun or verb that they describe (Brown & Brooks, 1991). For example, if a truck were to be described, it is more effective for the therapist to say, "It is a shiny, green truck," rather than, "The truck is shiny and green." In the latter example, after hearing "truck," the client could already have begun to imagine a truck quite different from the shiny, green one.

Common to all case studies reviewed is the care taken to reorient clients before ending the imagery process. Although not always used, the anchor appears to be useful in this reorientation. Further, prior to opening their eyes, clients are usually asked to visually return to the room in which they are sitting or lying.

At the conclusion of the imagery session, the experience is usually processed, although this is not always necessary. The counselor and client attempt to understand symbolic meaning and explore thoughts and feelings experienced by the client during the procedure. Both the therapist and client can keep a journal of the client's images to help delineate emerging themes. Sometimes it is helpful to have the client draw facsimiles of those images she or he has visualized.

The primary concept underlying imagery is that images (primarily visual, but also including other senses) are nonverbal, affect-laden stimuli that can be neurologically imprinted by direct experience and associative learning. Akhter Ahsen (1965, 1968) describes "eidetic" images, emphasizing the vividness and depth of mental images:

Eidetic images relate to fantasies, being akin to images which appear in a variety of neurotic phenomena. . . . In traumatic memories, eidetics reproduce actual historical data with detailed exactness. They are spontaneous, interior, demonstrable, repeatable, affect-laden images which appear over the developmental line and influence the mind of the adult in a powerful way. Capable of releasing a real somatic response, following certain lines of symbolic and mechanical operation, a simple eidetic image automatically sets off a complex mental reaction and elaborates the mind's dynamics through its own experiential exposition. (pp. 273–274)

Images stored within a client's memory (e.g., from some traumatic event) are more powerful than verbal recollections and provide more direct access to internal psychodynamics. Images can be a powerful tool to unlocking a client's resistances, negative self-concepts, dysfunctional behaviors, erroneous beliefs, fears, and anxieties. Further, in most imagery techniques, the client herself or himself is in charge of the breadth, intensity, duration, and interpretation of the imagery. The therapist is primarily a facilitator. "The [therapist's] role is one of facilitator or guide who brings structure to the interaction. The client's non-verbal behavior is cued to facilitate internal dialogue. Interpretation is always left up to the client who is responsible for deriving his or her own meaning from the experience" (Rancour, 1991, p. 33).

From a behavior modification perspective, images elicited in a therapeutic setting can and should be controlled. For example, in using the techniques of systematic desensitization and implosion, it is important that the clinician be able to adjust the level of intensity of the stimuli. Additionally, the client himself or herself can control the content and intensity of the stimuli (images) when they are imagined. Stimuli based in fantasy can effectively approximate real experience. Thus, learning and reconditioning can occur at the level of fantasy.

APPROPRIATE AND INAPPROPRIATE USES

Frequently, individuals experience physical problems that are not treatable by modern medicine. Some of these ailments may be the result of psychological disturbances that are manifested somatically. Individuals experiencing such psychosomatic disorders can benefit from addressing the relationship that exists between mind and body. Numerous psychologists and physicians have written about the mind-body connection (Epstein, 1989; Ornstein, 1987; Borysenko, 1987, 1993; Pelletier, 1977). In this approach, often called "holistic medicine," imagery is but one tool used by the practitioner and appears to be a particularly good way to address these mind-body issues.

In the state of disease, the direct connection between the mind and the body is sometimes severed, and the two are at odds. Used in holistic therapy, imagery techniques tap the inner strength and wisdom of the client's organism to integrate mind and body. The following case study is an example of imagery's application to the holistic treatment of a client experiencing chronic lower back pain.

After deep relaxation and focusing were obtained, the client (Lauren) was asked to allow the pain to form an image. The client was then asked to describe the image (a coiled rope) and any feelings associated with it. Following the description, the therapist provided questions for the client to ask the image. The dialogue that ensued (similar to a Gestalt dialogue) effectively targeted the cause of her pain. The client was then encouraged to identify with her image and ask questions from the perspective of the coiled rope. Lauren's identification with her back pain offered her insight into the "needs" of her back (the cause of the pain) and decreased her mind-body separation. By eidetically working with her back pain, Lauren was able to develop a more appropriate method of dealing with her pain (Rancour, 1991).

Imagery also has been used to circumvent verbal defenses (Singer, 1974). In the following case, imagery was used as an aid in dream work to help a client who was experiencing anxiety and also was resistant to expressing emotions in therapy (Schaub & Schaub, 1990). This client typically would intellectualize about his dreams and emotions, referring to them as "interesting" or "strange." In an attempt to have the client attach emotion to his dreams, the therapist asked him to eidetically relive them. As the client relived his dream, the therapist had the client focus on certain parts of his dream as well as his immediate affect. By reexperiencing his dream, the client was able to express his emotions in a less defended manner and achieve a greater awareness of the etiology of his anxiety.

Psychosynthesis is probably the therapeutic approach most often associated with the use of imagery techniques. Psychosynthesis posits that the human being exists on many levels, including the inner self, various subpersonalities (roles) one has taken on, and the social, global, and universal (transpersonal) being. Psychosynthesis uses imagery techniques at all of these levels and can be either directed or spontaneous.

When using spontaneous mental imagery, the therapist first guides the client into a state of deep relaxation, then simply asks the client to close his or her eyes and report what he or she is seeing and experiencing. In this type of free association using imagery, the therapist intervenes or offers occasional support or guidance. Martha Crampton (1969) has written that an imagery session often can lead to abreaction and the reexperiencing of repressed memories and fixations. She believes that the client's full catharsis, within safe limits, is to be encouraged. "It seems clear that the value of such methods does not depend on interpretation. The working through of conflicts on a symbolic level can definitely bring about growth regardless of whether the person is able to verbalize about or understand intellectually what has happened. On the other hand, once a person has lived something on the symbolic level, sound interpretation emerging from the person's own experience rather than imposed on him from the outside can add to the value of the experience" (p. 145).

Assagioli (1965) describes a directed technique (often referred to as "guided fantasy") that he calls the "Exercise of the Blossoming of the Rose." After a client has entered into deep relaxation, the therapist guides the client to imagine a rosebud, first closed, then slowly opening, then with its full perfume escaping. The client imagines the whole rosebush radiating its life force and is directed toward identification with the rose. "Symbolically we are this rose. The same life that animates the universe and has created the miracle of the rose is producing in us a like, even greater miracle — the awakening and development of our spiritual being and that which radiated from it" (pp. 214–215).

Assagioli states that this exercise elicits many psychoanalytic elements (resistance, doubt, oscillation, and so on). The therapist should encourage a discussion of these issues. He says, however, that many clients spontaneously have "a real self-realization, and awakening of hitherto latent inner qualities that certainly speeded up the healing process" (1965, p. 215).

Imagery techniques are likely to be especially effective with willing, insightful, self-aware individuals who will quickly internalize the association. It appears that imagery is appropriate and effective for the treatment of mild phobias and anxiety problems and for building confidence in situational settings (e.g., public speaking). The techniques also seem to have significant promise when used with children, via symbolic modeling, to develop social skills and appropriate behaviors.

Reexperiencing events through imagery can be appropriate for individuals who have not dealt with issues in the past that are affecting them now, who are in conflict with their emotions, and who are not in touch with their feelings. There also appears to be potential for imagery to enhance learning and performance in a variety of situations.

There are many situations where great caution must be taken before using imagery techniques and some instances where they should not be used at all. Issues of suicidal thoughts, rape, violent abuse, and death of loved ones are obviously in this category. The therapist must be cautious and sensitive in these, and all, abreactive cases.

Directed imagery can be used with the images of dreams, interpersonal relations (role-playing), self-image, and subpersonalities integration. Crampton (1969) says that such techniques should be used only after developing rapport with the client. She also cautions against using imagery techniques too early with clients not yet ready for them. "Spontaneous imagery procedures can produce experiences that may be too disturbing for some people to handle by themselves. Moreover, in assigning some of the techniques discussed, a therapist must observe caution and know his patient well" (p. 144).

Schaub and Schaub (1990) further emphasize that the timing of an imagery intervention is critically important. "Clients with strong issues related to trust may find the process initially too threatening. Those with a poor sense of self or with weak ego boundaries may experience a sense of depersonalization just from closing their eyes. It is important to assure the client that he or she has ultimate control in this situation and simply has to open his or her eyes to stop the experience" (p. 409). The client's understanding of his or her own control over the process is especially true in abreactive work involving past trauma. It is also important to debrief the client after the exercise to discuss and assess his or her emotional state.

Imagery techniques also may be inappropriate for individuals who are intellectually impaired or have neurological damage. It is likely that these individuals will have difficulty maintaining intense, vivid images and be unable to connect those images to the intended thoughts. Imagery techniques also may be less effective with individuals who are untrusting, skeptical, or pessimistic. The common thread is their failure to generate a sufficient quantity of imagery for work to begin. Other client characteristics that may preclude the use of imagery techniques are an incompatible learning style, difficulty in producing vivid images, and excessive daydreaming.

If used appropriately, imagery techniques can be powerful tools in helping individuals redirect energy, previously invested in denial and resistance, toward self-acceptance and increased self-esteem. By focusing attention on more positive images, individuals can discard and transcend old and dysfunctional patterns.

RESEARCH

Singer (1974) points out that there have been several studies that document the effectiveness of imagery techniques and at the same time raise issues about their use. For instance, he reports that some studies support the claim that systematic desensitization has a significant effect on a client's approach response, but it rarely eliminates the fear itself. Most likely, the basis for the fear itself has not been explored and dealt with and, so, it will remain. In this event, one wonders about the likelihood of the transfer of both the old avoidance and the new approach responses to other situations. Another question is the contribution of the relaxation technique itself to the overall effectiveness of this strategy. Perhaps further study should be focused on these issues.

Singer also reviews research on positive imagery, guided daydreams, and noxious imagery techniques. Although positive imagery and guided daydreams have shown results such as reduced therapy time and reduction of symptoms, the research lacks adequate controls and is relatively limited in scale. More reliable and valid measures are needed on such issues as the influence of client characteristics (e.g., confidence), the ability to produce detailed images, the vividness and controllability of images produced by an individual, and the ability to internalize the imagery association. Generally, the studies have not controlled for relevant variables in the individual's life. Noxious imagery techniques, employed in the traditional behavioristic approach, raise concerns. They do not permit the client to deal with the underlying reasons for the behavior. As a result, they most likely suppress them. Further, it appears that this approach implies that the client himself or herself, as well as his or her behavior, is bad.

Several studies highlighting the effectiveness of symbolic modeling techniques are examined by Singer (1974). His analysis shows these techniques to be valuable, although more so in some circumstances than in others. For example, it seems that adults with highly formed values and attitudes are less susceptible to identifying with and integrating modeled behaviors and attitudes than are children and students. In addition, differences in perception and value of the modeled situation indicate that cultural and socioeconomic values will impact the effectiveness of this approach.

Cox (1985) cites research indicating that internal and external imagery techniques are almost as effective as physical practice. He also points out that it is most effective with physical activities that depend heavily upon cognitive processes. As with the research on other therapeutic techniques, the question remains about the extent to which the subject is using the techniques and the certainty that the control subjects are not using them.

Allender (1991) reviews studies on the application of imagery techniques in teaching and learning. He states, "Self-indulged images together with active student involvement greatly facilitate associative learning" (p. 30). He also suggests that imaginative thinking and being "verbally interactive" (p. 30) are significant variables in learning through imagery. Although this use of imagery may be useful, there are some obvious concerns, for example, the individual student's ability to learn this way (some studies show that information processing is predominantly visual, auditory, or tactile for any given individual) and the teacher's ability to teach this way. It would be damaging if the teaching profession came to assume that learning with imagery was appropriate for all students and did not recognize the variety of learning styles. Therefore, it is important to conduct research comparing groups taught with imagery techniques with groups taught with visual, auditory, and tactile techniques.

In summary, there is supportive evidence for the effectiveness of imagery techniques with anxiety, phobias, learning, and sports performance. There are, however, individual differences in degree of control, accuracy, vividness, and awareness of images. Differences also exist in the ability to learn and associate by way of an image. Another factor affecting the success of imagery techniques is the individual's willingness or ability to fully invest in a procedure that sometimes requires a great deal of creativity and energy. These differences remain largely unmeasured.

The medical field has explored the efficacy of imagery in the treatment of various illnesses. Research with cancer patients has been the focus of much of this research. Achterberg (1984) conducted a study wherein he compared the mental images held by two groups of cancer patients. He found that subjects who held images of cancer cells as weak (e.g., slugs) and white blood cells as strong (e.g., white knights) tended to outlive those whose images of cancer cells were strong and those of white blood cells as weak. There is some evidence that one's created images do have effects on bodily functions that have been considered to be outside the domain of personal control. For example, patients have been able to lower blood pressure and control body temperature as a result of imagined scenarios. Achterberg contends that one's images affect the immune system and can, to some degree, influence it. Research is being continued in the hope that further exploration will validate his hypothesis.

One issue that must be considered when using imagery techniques with seriously ill patients is the degree of responsibility taken on by the patient as both the causative and the curative agent. The therapist must be aware that the patient may conclude that she or he is to blame for causing the disease because of "faulty" images or feel that they have failed if they are not able to influence the course of the disease.

Documented case studies supporting the use of imagery are plentiful. Although imagery is used in a wide variety of therapeutic approaches, there is a lack of strong empirical evidence to support its effectiveness. Until such time as more definitive research evidence is presented, the thoughtful clinician will want to review the documented case studies that pertain specifically to his or her clients' issues in order to assess the benefits and dangers associated with imagery techniques.

REFERENCES

Achterberg, J. (1984). Imagery and medicine: Psychophysiological speculations. *Journal of Mental Imagery, 8*(4), 1–14.

Ahsen, A. (1968). *Basic concepts in eidetic psychotherapy.* New York: Brandon House.

Ahsen, A. (1965). *Eidetic psychotherapy: A short introduction.* Lahore: Nai Matbooat.

Allender, J. S. (1991). *Imagery in teaching and learning.* Westport, CT: Praeger.

Assagioli, R. (1965). *Psychosynthesis.* New York: Hobbs, Dorman.

Bandler, R., & Grinder, J. (1979). *Frogs into princes.* Moab, UT: Real People Press.

Borysenko, J. (1993). *Fire in the soul: A new psychology of optimism.* New York: Warner Books.

Borysenko, J. (1987). *Minding the body, mending the mind.* Reading, MA: Addison-Wesley.

Brown, D., & Brooks, L. (1991). *Career counseling techniques.* Needham Heights, MA: Allyn & Bacon.

Cox, R. H. (1985). *Sports psychology.* Dubuque, IA: William C. Brown.

Crampton, M. (1969). The use of mental imagery in psychosynthesis. *Journal of Humanistic Psychology, 9*, 139–153.

Epstein, A. (1989). *Mind, fantasy and healing.* New York: Delacorte.

Ferrier, L. (1992). *Dance of the selves.* New York: Fireside Books.

Gawain, S. (1982). *Creative visualization.* New York: Bantam Books.

Goldberg, P. (1983). *The intuitive edge: Understanding and developing intuition.* Los Angeles, CA: Jeremy P. Tarcher.

Kubie, L. S. (1965). The struggle between preconscious insights and psychonoxious rewards in psychotherapy. *American Journal of Psychotherapy, 19*, 365–371.

Lazarus, A., & Abramovitz, A. (1962). The use of "emotive imagery" in the treatment of children's phobias. *Journal of Mental Science, 108*, 191–195.

Ornstein, R. (1987). *The healing brain.* New York: Touchstone Books.

Pelletier, K. (1977). *Mind as healer, mind as slayer.* New York: Delacorte.

Penfield, W. (1963). The brain's record of auditory and visual experience — a final summary and discussion. *Brain, 86*, 595–696.

Rancour, P. (1991). Guided imagery: Healing when curing is out of the question. *Perspectives in Psychiatric Care, 27*, 30–33.

Schaub, B., Anselmo, J., & Luck, S. (1991). Clinical imagery: Holistic nursing perspectives. In R. Kunzendorf (Ed.), *Mental imagery*. New York: Plenum.

Schaub, B., & Schaub, R. (1990). The use of mental imagery techniques in psychodynamic psychotherapy. *Journal of Mental Health Counseling, 4*, 405–415.

Sheehan, P. W. (1972). *The function and nature of imagery*. Corpus Christie, TX: Academic.

Singer, J. (1975). *The inner world of daydreaming*. New York: Harper & Row.

Singer, J. L. (1974). *Imagery and daydream methods in psychotherapy and behavior modification*. Orlando, FL: Academic.

Stamfl, T. G. (1961). *Implosive therapy: A learning theory*. Paper presented at the University of Illinois, Urbana.

Watson, J. B. (1913). Psychology as the behaviorist views it. *Psychological Review, 20*, 158–177.

Wolpe, J. (1969). *The practice of behavior therapy*. New York: Pergamon.

7

Systematic Desensitization

Suzanne St Onge

THEORY

"Systematic desensitization" is the term the South African psychiatrist Joseph Wolpe (1958, 1981, 1990) applied to the sequential pairing of incompatible states. In particular, he paired relaxation and imaging of anxiety-provoking situations, in order to alleviate patterns of maladaptive anxiety. Metaphorically speaking, a person has become "allergic" to a certain situation and has developed troublesome anxiety or avoidance mechanisms (symptoms). Desensitization is the slow imaginal recalling (inoculation) by the client of the past allergy-producing situation while in a relaxed physical state in order to develop a tolerance or immunity to the original allergy. This chapter examines the systematic desensitization paradigm, its theoretical substrates, its effectiveness, its limitations, and the areas for future research.

In 1924, Mary Cover Jones was the first to publish a report on counterconditioning-type procedures used to treat anxiety. In the 1940s, Wolpe developed systematic desensitization treatment while experimenting with cats. He wanted to see if eating satisfactorily would inhibit the anxiety of entering a room in which the cats had previously been electroshocked. By 1958, he had clarified what the fear-reduction factors were and had produced systematic desensitization, the first major practical application of behavioral principles in outpatient mental health.

Borrowing from the physiologist Sherrington (1906), Wolpe (1958) termed his new procedures "reciprocal inhibition." Anxiety, he said, results from the neurophysiological arousal of the sympathetic nervous system, and through Pavlovian classic conditioning, people come to associate those sympathetic sensations with the presence of situational stimuli. Treatment based on teaching a response (following Hull's 1943 learning theory) physiologically competes with and effectively inhibits the sympathetic nervous pattern by enervating opposing, and more pleasing/relaxing, parasympathetic nervous responses. Wolpe believed that many activities were capable of doing this, such as sexual behavior, eating, and assertion. However, he chose Jacobson's (1938) more utilitarian progressive muscle relaxation exercise. Gradual, repeated exposure to anxiety-producing stimuli while in an anxiety-incompatible state of physical relaxation causes loss of the stimuli's anxiety-evoking capacity and extinguishes the phobic response.

Among behaviorists, controversy exists regarding the exact underlying mechanisms of systematic desensitization. Is it the counterconditioning and extinction of physiological processes or the learning of cognitive and expectation alternatives? Is it because of therapist suggestions and attention, thus, making a hierarchical stimulus presentation unnecessary? According to Wolpe, most psychotherapy reduces anxiety about 50 percent of the time by the soothing effects of the therapist's reputation, demeanor, and attention. This, he says, is no better than chance, and, to be recommended on empirical grounds, an effective therapeutic intervention must identify the exact anxiety-reducing mechanisms and exceed the 50 percent success rate. Wolpe (1990) has documented an 88 percent success rate.

No proof, yet, exists that any single mechanism accounts for the success of desensitization, but Schroeder and Rich (Wachtel, 1992) suggest that each client may combine particular therapeutic components differently, depending on his or her specific problem and learning modality. Some people may utilize cognitive and positive self-efficacy interventions better, a la Bandura, Beck, or Ellis. Others may find different physiological explanations useful, such as Rachman (1990), who designates the decrease of anxiety to a reduction in the particular activating system and the creation of a state of habituation or tolerance. Others (Marks, 1987) utilize behavioral measures, such as total exposure to fearful stimuli (flooding) or in vivo exposure, a gradual physical encounter with anxiety-provoking situations. Agras, Kazdin, and Wilson (1979) and Wachtel (1992) suggest that desensitization works because therapists create conditions that motivate the clients to expose themselves to past feared situations without reexperiencing past anxieties and negative consequences, thus, decreasing avoidance behaviors.

Other anxiety-incompatible responses are humor, laughter, and emotive imagery. Because they are easy and do not have to be learned, they may be advantageous, especially with children. Other strategies that facilitate relaxation are meditation (Mahesh Yogi, 1969), Benson's (1984) relaxation response, yoga and biofeedback, and metronome-conditioned relaxation exercises (Brady, 1971). Recent posttraumatic stress-disorder treatments have used relaxing effects of saccadic eye movements (Shapiro, 1989), for example, following a moving finger, side to side, for several minutes. Wachtel (1992) cites Silverman, Frank, and Dachinger as having successfully treated insect phobic individuals by exposing them to the tachistoscopically flashed message, "Mommy and I are one," hypothesizing that fantasies of merger with the therapist as a mother substitute underlie the effectiveness of systematic desensitization.

GROUP SYSTEMATIC DESENSITIZATION

Lazarus (1961), Anton (1976), and Renneberg, Goldsteing, Phillips, and Chambliss (1990) have adapted and studied the effectiveness of group systematic desensitization. Because clients share similar problems, similar or individual fear hierarchies can be presented, making this an expedient intervention. Some authors caution that this method may be more boring for "quick" learners, but reports indicate that this does not affect its overall usefulness.

COPING SYSTEMATIC DESENSITIZATION

Goldfried (1971; Goldfried & Davison, 1976) teaches a coping type of systematic desensitization. The therapist helps clients to become aware of sensations associated with tension and learning and to use these sensations as cues to relax, and, thus, the particular events that elicit anxiety become less critical. The more important focus becomes learning to relax whenever experiencing anxiety. These coping procedures then can be generalized to help in other anxiety-provoking situations.

SELF-ADMINISTERED DESENSITIZATION

A final version of this treatment technique is called self-administered desensitization. Rosen, Glasgow, and Barrera (1976) teach clients how to self-administer a desensitization protocol through the use of written instructions, audiotapes, or videotapes. Some authors cite more problems with client follow-through with this version, while others suggest it might enhance therapist-demonstrated techniques.

DESCRIPTION OF SYSTEMATIC PARADIGM AND STRATEGEMS

Generally, systematic desensitization is utilized in treating specific fears, usually caused by external inanimate sources that cannot be logically or verbally dealt with (e.g., all types of classical phobias). Because a variety of methods may be useful, the specific interventions chosen will reflect the counselor's preference and their applicability to a client's learning style and concern, that is, whether cognitive, emotional, physiological, or motoric (behavioral) symptoms predominate.

A typical format includes exploration of all these areas:

1. a thorough biopsychosocial assessment to help identify problems and achieve treatment goals,
2. instructions about the nature of desensitization,
3. development of reference points by measuring baseline levels of anxiety through the use of self-report inventories and subjective distress scales,
4. selection and training in the counterconditioning response (e.g., relaxation, meditation),
5. hierarchical ranking of increasingly fearful situations,
6. training in visualizing scenes and assessing of imagery effectiveness,
7. pairing of the relaxation response with imagery from the fear hierarchy, and
8. practicing the procedure, homework, follow-up.

BIOPSYCHOSOCIAL ASSESSMENT

In a therapeutic atmosphere of respect, sensitivity, and genuine concern, the clinician ascertains who the client is, what circumstances have and continue to influence him or her, and what past coping strategies were effective. The presenting problem is ordinarily a specific, delineated, nonrational fear of external situations, a physiologically determined fear, not merely a cognitively based fear. Desensitization should not be used when a client's anxiety is nonspecific or free-floating, or when the anxiety is caused by a client's skill deficits.

Shaffer (1984) has described the diagnostic criteria that correspond best to desensitization:

The client's defined problem entails something that needs changing, not a choice they are worried about making.

The client is psychologically intact and can comprehend and implement change strategies.

The identified problems result from the client's behavior, rather than from the system in which he or she functions.

No more than three behaviors need changing, and the client is neither too rigid nor too unsuccessful in previous change attempts.

The counselor has expertise, resource, and interest in working with the client.

EXPLAINING SYSTEMATIC DESENSITIZATION

Clients are told that they will be learning anxiety-incompatible responses that will help eliminate the fearfulness previously associated with particular situations, thus, enabling them to cope more effectively.

BASELINE MEASUREMENT

Clients are encouraged to fill out the Willoughby Neuroticism and Fear Survey Questionnaires (Wolpe, 1990). These are used to assess the nature, frequency, duration, intensity, and context of disturbing symptoms. Wolpe (1990) also teaches clients to rate varying levels of distress and corresponding circumstances by using the subjective distress scale (suds). Anxiety ordinarily is rated from 1–100 (or 1–10), with the highest number representing greater discomfort. This facilitates the differentiating and naming of varying degrees of tension, or relaxation, by assigning numerical or categorical ranks (low, medium, high) to the sensations experienced. All items in the fear hierarchy usually are separated by a distance of five to ten suds in order to ensure uniformity and achievable levels of relaxation. Training in the chosen relaxation response is to continue until the client can discriminate differing levels of anxiety and can achieve a state of relaxation after a training session equivalent to 10 on a suds scale of 100 (Marquis, Morgan, & Piaget, 1979). Usually, the client is asked to rate the experienced level of anxiety on the suds scale before and after each fear hierarchy and relaxation prevention.

SELECTION AND TRAINING IN THE COUNTERCONDITIONING RESPONSE — RELAXATION TRAINING

Before and after each training session, the therapist has the client rate his or her anxiety on the suds. A usual starting point is a baseline level of suds.

The client should sit in a comfortable chair in a room with a minimum of distractions. Suggesting that he or she close his or her eyes may facilitate relaxation. In a soft, gentle tone, the therapist explains that the client is going to tense and relax opposing muscles while paying attention to the physical sensations in the muscles. The client is instructed to become completely absorbed by and focus on the physical sensations he or she will be experiencing. The client is reminded that the entire goal of relaxing is not to force relaxation but, instead, to simply notice and become immersed in bodily sensations. Because each relaxation step lasts about 10 seconds, with a 10–15-second pause between successive steps, the entire procedure spans about 25 minutes.

During the first session, the therapist can practice the relaxation procedure with the client to give him or her encouraging physical cues. Because it is easier, most therapists begin relaxing the hands and arms first, then proceed to the head region, where the greatest anxiety-relieving effects are obtained, and then move onward through the body.

RELAXATION SCRIPT

The following is adapted from Morris (1991) and Wolpe (1990). Additional rationales for clinicians are bracketed. Repeat only if helpful. Caution the clients not to strain themselves while tightening muscles.

1. Take a deep breath, hold it (about 10 seconds). Hold it. Now, let go, feeling the release.

2. Stick your arms out and make a tight fist. Really tight. Feel the tension in your hands; notice the discomfort. I am going to count to three, and when I say "three," drop your arms and hands. One. . . . Two. . . . Three. . . . Relax. . . . Just let go. . . . Notice the difference (perhaps there's even some heaviness).

3. Raise your arms again, and bend your fingers back toward your body. Hold it. Now drop your arms and hands; just let go. Notice the sensations; feel the difference; feel the comfort.

4. Tense your forearms and upper arms by pressing your elbows down

against the chair. Feel the tightness. . . . Hold it. Now, relax. The muscles are letting go; your arms may even be getting warmer. Let your forearms really rest on a chair (or lap). Let go even more. [It is the act of relaxing these additional fibers that will bring about the greatest emotional effect.] Let the whole arm go limp, soft. Good.

5. [If one arm is done at a time, sensations in one can be compared with those in the other. Clients can also be asked to verbalize what relaxation feels like for them, to notice finer and finer degrees of letting go. Softly encourage clients that there is nothing to accomplish here, other than to be aware of and report sensations. All attention should go on the muscle sensations. Sensations of relaxation may consist of tingling, numbness, warmth, or heaviness.]

6. Hunch your shoulders forward. Hold it. Breathe normally. Let go. Notice the release. Now push the shoulders backward. . . . Hold. . . . Breathe. . . . And let go. That's right, let it all go.

7. Now roll your head slowly, feeling all the muscles strain, and then relax, as your head makes a slow, steady circle. Slowly now — let it stop wherever it wishes. Feel it like a heavy ball, just resting on your shoulders. . . . Now roll it slowly again three or four times, in the opposite direction. [The client should not be encouraged to bend his or her neck either all the way back or forward.]

8. [From an emotional point of view, the head muscles are most important.] Now, relax the muscles of your face. First, contract your forehead. . . . Wrinkle it as much as possible. Hold it. . . . Okay. . . . Now relax, let go. . . . Feel the smoothness, even when you think you're completely relaxed. . . . Let go some more. [According to Wolpe, it is this relaxation beneath the surface that produces the most emotional relaxation.]

9. Now close your eyes. Squeeze them tight; raise your eyebrows. Notice tension. Breathe naturally. Now, relax. . . . The pain slips away so easily when you relax.

10. Open your mouth as much as possible. Pull your lips tight. Feel the tension. Now, let it go, feel the drooping. . . . Feel the relaxation.

11. Now bite your teeth, push your tongue to the roof of your mouth. Press hard. Harder. . . . Relax. . . . Let your tongue rest comfortably.

12. You are becoming more and more relaxed. . . . While you're sitting there, with your eyes softly closed, imagine looking at something far away, something pleasant, like mountains and lazy, drifting clouds. See those clouds. Nice, puffy, lazy clouds. Breathe naturally . . . easily. . . . Sense your head resting on your shoulders . . . like a heavy ball. . . . Just sitting there . . . easily . . . relaxed.

13. Breathe slowly and deeply. . . . Breathing with your belly, expanding it fully. Hold it . . . and let go. Let all the air out . . . feel the air move out

. . . enjoy the relaxing peace. . . . Good.

14. Now, pull your stomach muscles in tightly. Tighter. Your entire back is becoming firm and straight. Hold it. Okay, let it go. [Make sure client does not strain back, especially if there have been previous injuries. Do not tighten beyond the point of comfort.]

15. Now extend your chest muscles as if you were a prize fighter. Make your stomach hard. Relax. . . . It is easier and easier to relax.

16. Tighten your buttocks . . . tighter. Hold it. Now, let go. It feels so good to let go.

17. Search the upper part of your body and relax any part that is tense. First, let the facial muscles go . . . your throat . . . feel your neck, your shoulders soften . . . and droop. . . . Relax any part that is tense. Your arms and fingers can curl up . . . just relaxing. . . . Fine. You are becoming very relaxed.

18. While maintaining this upper body relaxation, raise both of your legs to a 45 degree angle. Hold it . . . feel the tension. Lower your legs. Now let everything go. . . . See how much more relaxed you're becoming.

19. Now, bend your feet back so that your toes point toward your face. Bend them hard. Dig your heels into the floor. Hold it. . . . Now relax. . . . Let go.

20. Bend your feet the other way, away from your body. Not too far . . . good. Notice the tension. Okay . . . relax, let go.

21. Now curl your toes together . . . as hard as you can. Tighter. Okay. [If there's cramping, shake the muscles loose.] Okay . . . relax, feel the relaxation spread all over.

22. Explore your entire body. Every part is becoming more and more relaxed. Your toes . . . your feet . . . your legs. . . buttocks. . . stomach. . . shoulders . . . neck. . . eyes. . . and, last, your forehead. . . . All of you is more relaxed. . . more comfortable. Lie there, feeling very relaxed, noticing the warmth. . . the comfort. Listen to your breathing; feel it gently move in and out. Each time you begin to exhale, say a soothing word, like "calm" or "peace". . . or "relax". . . or "let go." Whatever word you like. You're feeling very comfortable, very relaxed. . . . Breathe slowly. . . imagining yourself completely at peace. Whatever word you use, it will cue you into a deeper and deeper relaxation. Breathe your word into yourself. . . breathe in the relaxation. . . breathe out the tension. Easily. . . naturally.

   [Pause for a few moments.] Stay this way for about another minute, and then I am going to count to five. When I reach five, you can open your eyes. . . feeling very calm and refreshed. . . . One. . . feeling very calm; two. . . very calm, very refreshed; three. . . very relaxed; four. . . better and better in every way; five. . . . Whenever you want, open your eyes, feeling calm, relaxed, comfortable.

23. [The most common error for the beginning therapist is to rush through the relaxation exercise. Do not race through it. It is not calisthenics. Practice it on yourself; become more aware of the sensations of relaxation in your own body; sink into them, and speak slowly from that comfortable place.]

24. [Ask the client to make a mental picture of what he or she feels like, so that he or she will be able to return to it whenever he or she wants. At this point, he or she also can indicate whether or not he or she has reached at least a level of 10 on a 100-point suds scale. The signs of being relaxed are smooth breathing; heaviness of limbs; smoothness about the face, mouth, forehead; a softness in the body, like a rag doll.]

Some clients, for many reasons, have difficulty relaxing, no matter how motivated they are. They have learned over the years not to relax, to be tense and be strong, and it might take them time to change. As they practice, their uncomfortableness will lessen. Asking them to describe their bodily sensations, as they occur, might help them realize that there is no right or wrong way to do this; there is no goal to accomplish — there is only letting their attention become fully absorbed, fascinated by their physical sensations, their breathing, the gentle letting go, the natural resting into themselves.

CONSTRUCTING THE ANXIETY HIERARCHY

At the end of the first relaxation session, clients are asked to describe in detail the fearful situations they wish to master. They are asked to assign increasing suds values, separated by ten suds, to aspects of the situation that become progressively stressful. One hundred suds represents the most dreaded situation. Hierarchies typically have 10 to 20 items and represent situations the clients themselves can initiate. The hierarchy is useful only if it represents small enough variations of a painful situation that the clients are capable of mastering.

The scenes are to reflect, clearly, vividly, and concretely, actual or future situations the clients have to face. Hierarchy items usually differ according to levels of anxiety, the number of people present, the perceived attitudes of others, and/or differing time and space dimensions. Control items are neutral or relaxing scenes, for example, nature scenes, placed at the bottom of the hierarchy. They are totally satisfying and comforting and are unrelated to the client's fears. They can be used as safe "rest areas" for destressing and relaxing.

TRAINING IN VISUALIZATION AND ASSESSMENT OF IMAGERY

Clients are asked to imagine a hierarchy item as if they were actually participating in the scene and not merely observing. If scenes contain several sensory modalities, for example, sight, touch, and smell, clients have an easier time visualizing. When clients are relaxed and can picture the control scene, the therapist ascertains whether or not the images are anxiety free and which inhibiting factors might be present. Clients can experiment with scene control by switching a scene on and off at will and by maintaining the scene for as long as possible before the images fade away.

PAIRING OF RELAXATION AND HIERARCHY IMAGERY — DESENSITIZATION PROPER

In the initial session, clients relax to a suds level of ten or less. Therapist and clients corroborate on a nondistracting signaling system, for example, raising a finger, to indicate when a scene is visualized. When anxiety increases and clients need to relax, they can signal by raising the whole arm. Some people prefer to verbalize "anxious" rather than raising limbs. To make the transition smoothly from session to session and to check on learning and prevent relapse, the therapist begins subsequent sessions with the last item successfully completed.

After describing the first hierarchy item, the counselor asks the client to visualize it and to signal when the image is clear. After 20 to 40 seconds, the client is instructed to stop visualizing, take a deep breath, and relax for about a minute. Some clients may need additional time.

If anxiety is experienced during visualization, the counselor can (in traditional desensitization) instruct the client to stop visualizing and relax or to go to a neutral relaxing image. (In coping desensitization, the client starts relaxing away the tension while staying with the scene.)

After relaxing to a suds level of ten, the client can begin to revisualize the situation. The counselor uses standardized instruction whether or not the client signals high or low anxiety. Because neither being anxious nor being calm is judged as "better," the client learns that performance is not being judged, that simply experiencing images and sensations is what matters, and that they need not fear revealing anxieties.

In a climate of understanding and concern, the counselor presents the scenes in a conversational manner and utilizes a notation system to track progress. When two scene presentations produce no anxiety, scenes are considered mastered (Marquis, Morgan, & Piaget, 1979). However, Foa, Steketee, and Milby (1980) suggest three or four no-anxiety repetitions with distressing scenes. If discomfort continues or the clients cannot visualize the scene, they should stop the sequence and relax. Difficulties then can be explored, or the therapist and client can modify the relaxation procedure or insert easier fear situations into the hierarchy.

The particular phobia and severity of anxiety determine the amount of scene presentations and the therapeutic pace. The tempo tends to be slower as scenes become more complicated. Those involving increasing numbers of people or objects should be expanded on with the scene at a fixed distance. Once all the persons or objects are in place, the client imagines the scene slowly approaching.

Because desensitization requires considerable effort and concentration, the client should be observed for signs of fatigue or frustration. The pace of learning is determined by the client's tolerance. Ordinarily, desensitization proper stops after 15 to 30 minutes or on completion of three to four hierarchy items. To avoid ending on an anxious note, no new hierarchy items should be explored toward the session's end. Sufficient time needs to be set aside to discuss any issues or concerns.

HOMEWORK AND FOLLOW-UP

Daily practice of the relaxation procedure is essential to effective desensitization. Repeated visualization of completed items is encouraged. Sessions can even be recorded and replayed at home. According to Rimm and Masters (1979), it is risky for clients to try out hierarchy items that have not yet been covered, and this should be discouraged. Until hierarchy items evoke little anxiety, clients are advised against physically entering the real-life feared situations in order to preserve whatever desensitization has occurred.

EFFECTIVENESS

Considerable experimental and case-study literature endorses systematic desensitization for treating conditional phobias and other anxiety-related disorders (Marks & Gelder, 1969; Wolpe, 1990; Masters, Burish, Hollon, & Rimm, 1987). In a landmark 1978 study, Kazdin and Wilson reviewed over 100 controlled studies and found that desensitization was more effective than insight or placebo treatment in reducing cognitive and physiological anxiety symptoms. Some studies indicate that training in systematic desensitization helps to physiologically "toughen" the autonomic nervous system and facilitate greater self-confidence, thereby aiding management of stress-induced pressures. Characteristics of good treatment candidates are:

They have three or less phobias.

Their fears are not due to skill deficits.

Their level of arousability is not exceedingly high.

With prompting, they can imagine negative scenes and related emotional experiences.

With training in deep muscle relaxation, or another alternative, they become sufficiently relaxed. (Rimm & Masters, 1979)

Undoubtedly, the benefits of systematic desensitization are numerous. Ordinarily a small number of sessions (8 to 12) results in behavioral improvement without generating further symptom substitution. Because it is fairly painless and nonthreatening, desensitization facilitates the client's collaboration with treatment. As his or her anxiety threshold and discomfort level lessen, previously anxiety-blocked coping strategies may emerge (Deffenbacher & Suinn, 1988). Because target symptoms are so clearly defined, the client becomes encouraged by his or her progress and tends not to terminate therapy prematurely.

Many difficulties can be treated through systematic desensitization. These include alcoholism (Hedberg & Campbell, 1974), anger (Rimm, DeGroot, Boord, Herman, & Dillow, 1971; Schloss, Smith, Santora, & Bryant, 1989), racial prejudice (Cotharin & Mikulas, 1975), dating anxiety (Curran & Monti, 1982), insomnia (Steinmark & Borkovec, 1974); anticipatory nausea in cancer patients (Morrow, 1986), posttraumatic disorder (Brom, Kleber, & Defares, 1989), and children with animal phobias (King & Gillone, 1990).

LIMITATIONS

Generally, systematic desensitization is not used when the clients wish to undergo uncovering psychotherapy. Its therapeutic goal always has been limited to symptom reduction, not to personality reorganization or to achieving greater insight into one's emotional and psychological functioning.

Usually, desensitization applies only when a client can identify the antecedents of anxiety that trigger the maladaptive cognitive, behavioral, or psychological responses. Hecker and Thorpe (1992) suggest that systematic desensitization is effective for neither obsessive-compulsive disorders nor agoraphobia. When used alone, neither cognitive restructuring nor systematic desensitization effectively treats generalized or free-floating anxiety, but a combination of both may be helpful. If passivity or dependency is the prominent personality trait and there is much secondary gain and reinforcement of maladaptive behavior by social consequence, desensitization may not be effective (Brady, 1972). Secondary gains can be treated through other means, (e.g., extinction, or by substituting more appropriate rewards for adaptive behavior. By itself, systematic desensitization is not useful in treating difficulties caused by other problems. Primarily, problems must be addressed (Cormier & Cormier, 1991). Similarly, desensitization is not as effective with social phobias, because they normally involve interpersonal skill deficits and are better managed through role-playing, social skill training, and assertiveness. Generally speaking, desensitization is most appropriate when target behaviors need increasing or decreasing, but, by itself, it is not appropriate for introducing new adaptive behaviors.

One to three years post–systematic desensitization, Lazarus (1971, 1976) found fairly high (40 percent) relapse rates and subsequently developed his multimodal approach to behavior therapy. Cormier & Cormier (1991) agree that few clients present with unidimensional problems. Diverse variables influence most difficulties and necessitate implementing multidimensional change strategies. A well-integrated program, he claims, will employ interventions that address a client's performance and cognitive skills, emotional and body responses, and contributing environmental factors.

In 1977, a meta-analysis of Smith and Glass (1977) showed no significant difference between the effectiveness of behavioral treatments and psychoanalytic-oriented brief psychotherapies. In 1981, Andrews and Harvey reanalyzed the Smith and Glass data. When the meta-analysis was restricted to neurotic patients, they said behavior therapy was more effective than psychoanalytically-oriented therapy. Such contradictory data analyses only highlight that the efficacy of various stages may well be affected by the experimental lens through which they are being observed and that human difficulties are so complex that no single approach has all the answers.

The results are mixed as to whether or not desensitization can be used in treating psychotic disorders. Brady (1972) felt it useful for removing severe obsessional thoughts and interpersonal anxieties with hospitalized schizophrenics. Because the underlying patterns of psychotic thought are usually unpredictable and unaffected by logic, a clinician would have to be well-skilled in managing clients with major mental illness before undertaking such interventions.

TREATMENT OF COMMON DESENSITIZATION PROBLEMS

According to Wolpe (1990), systematic desensitization can be problematic when clients experience no reduction of anxiety with the successive scene presentations and anxiety still occurs in a real-life situation, despite its reduction during training sessions. The most common reasons for such failures are difficulties in relaxing or the presence of relaxation-induced anxiety, misleading or irrelevant fear hierarchies, difficulty in achieving imagery clarity, and insufficient emotional involvement.

If, after relaxing, clients cannot lower their anxiety to ten or less suds, Wolpe (1990) recommends the adjunct use of tranquilizers or carbon dioxide-oxygen inhalation minutes before treatment. Hypnosis, psycho-physiological monitoring, and biofeedback, as well as alternative counterconditioning responses, also have been successful.

Ineffective hierarchies usually result when the context of the patient's fear has been mistaken for the trigger of the anxiety, for example, low self-efficacy rather than external situations. Additional hierarchy items may be introduced to facilitate the mastery of disparate hierarchy items, or one can resort to "circumscribing the danger" by enclosing it in time (i.e., by beginning in the past and progressing toward the present) or by enclosing it spatially (i.e., placing it far away before bringing it closer).

According to Wolpe (1990), 85 percent of people can project themselves into imagined anxiety-evoking situations. After all, this is what "worrying" is all about. However, clients who have been trained to control feeling display may be less able to evoke emotion by use of imagery. If this occurs, the therapist can describe a scene in greater detail or have clients describe out loud whatever scene comes, rather than imagining one. Otherwise, concrete representations, that is, pictures, or real stimuli may have to be substituted.

UNANSWERED QUESTIONS

In 1990, Wolpe noted, while surveying behavioral clinical practices, that surprisingly few behaviorists (18–42 percent) had used questionnaires to investigate the antecedents of patients' maladaptive anxieties. Further, few had followed his original systematic desensitization format.

He compared this "failure to use these instruments [as] a serious deprivation of data, parallel to a physician's nonuse of the electrocardiogram in suspected heart disease" (Wolpe, 1990, p. xi). He considered the degeneration of behavioral standards of practice quite serious. It is a point well-taken.

Review of the literature yields few texts or articles that document what a thorough assessment entails and what training a therapist must undergo to qualify her or him to administer systematic desensitization. Procedures in desensitization look deceivingly simple on the surface. This might paradoxically seduce nonbehaviorally trained therapists to apply them without having understood the complexities involved in helping clients to relax and imagine anxiety-invoking situations. Professionals are ethically bound not to practice beyond their levels of expertise. It is unfortunate that this warning may be heeded in carrying out highly skilled practices, such as psychoanalysis, but may not be adhered to when it comes to behavioral methods, like systematic desensitization.

Helpful texts would contain such warnings and highlight the needed clinical skills. Therapists then would understand the subtler effects of relaxation and anxiety-evoking imagery, thus, enabling them to enlist client corroboration effectively. Much psychotherapy involves abstract discussions of problems, but systematic desensitization involves facilitating the client's reexperiencing of frightening activities and thoughts. Through such encounters, insight and mastery are concretely experienced, not merely discussed. However, in helping a client face their deepest fear, the therapist is entering "the lion's den" with the client and needs to be aware of how to manage the dangers that may lurk therein.

Wolpe (1990) acknowledged that the use of technical interventions did make behavior therapy mechanistic but that to label it "nonhumanistic" was unjustified. "Internal medicine is not dehumanized when penicillin replaced bloodletting as a treatment for infections," he said, "and no more is psychotherapy when conditioning replaces free association" (p. vi). His rebuttal has some merit, and, yet, it does not eradicate the tendency of technique-driven formats like systematic desensitization to be applied in ways that are more mechanical than humane, more piecemeal than integrative, and, perhaps, more coercive than empowering. As Wachtel (1992) has pointed out, behaviorists themselves may have contributed to their "bad press" because past publications tended to coldly discuss stimulus-response bonds, behavior control, and manipulation of variables.

What appears to be needed is more literature devoted to stopping the polarization between behavioral and psychodynamic methods by bridging their areas of overlap. A technology-based science does, indeed, carry the potential for becoming dehumanized and short-sighted. We need look only at the ecological costs of the past, of advocating progress as more beneficial, rather than taking a closer look at interdependent components of life. It is, perhaps, time that psychology examine the roots of its love of empirical scientific experimentation as the only mark of a true scientific method. Psychology need no longer be so terrified of being subsumed by its philosophical/religious/intuitive roots and can, perhaps, start to see that other mainstream sciences are accepting that "truth" and "certainty" and "objectivity" are not as true and certain and objective as they had been touted to be. Psychological phenomena, especially, are multiply determined and may, perhaps, be best treated, as Cormier and Cormier (1991) stated, through multiple channels.

Because of this reliance on empirical evidence and rational thought, behaviorism can be discriminatory to the many people who do not espouse an androcentric, European epistemology. The literature contains scarcely any descriptions of applying desensitization to non-European cultures, minority and oppressed populations, and all those who adopt a more relational, less individualistic life approach, such as women. By sidestepping such populations in outcome studies, behaviorists only reinforce how narrow their focus is and how tied their interventions are to animal experimentation studies, rather than to the multifaceted, multiracial natures of real-world people. The feminist behaviorist Fodor (1974) has cited the central role of interpersonal factors and the importance of context in treating clients. Developing clinicians must begin seeing their clients as living, dynamic, complexly interrelated multidimensional beings. Only when one glimpses the totality of factors affecting people can one implement interventions that best match the people at which they are aimed and the worlds in which these people live.

Our experience of reality consists of a unique intermingling of internal and external events. Quite often the internal events are not rational or verifiable by empirical, scientific means. Wachtel (1992) states that even when real-life exposure is used in desensitization, therapists must recognize that situations to which clients are exposed may not depend strictly on what is externally presented; they also may depend on how that is perceived. Reality consists of the internal and external, and the two may not always be closely related.

Much of the systematic desensitization literature obsessively focuses on which theorist correctly identifies underlying mechanisms, on whether exposure should be brief or all at once, on whether or not belief affects success, on questioning the importance of the therapeutic relationship, and on whether or not external events can physiologically affect us without first being processed cognitively. Could it be that behaviorists are too closely scrutinizing the trees rather than the forest? Have they overlooked (with the exception of, perhaps, Goldfried) what hidden treasure systematic desensitization can actually offer clients? Is this because behaviorists need to deny that, in systematic desensitization, they employ techniques that are quite difficult to verify in an external, measurable way? Certainly, imaginary scenes cannot be made to stay still and cannot be guaranteed to be reproducible at the same levels every time. In other words, behaviorists are using nonrational techniques, the very things they have so long denounced in other psychotherapies. It is a paradox for which they have not yet accounted.

Teaching relaxation through any method offers clients (as well as therapists) a means of coping, another way to manage life stress. However, more than that, it offers a new way of seeing, a way to shift perceptual frameworks, and, perhaps, that is what underlies the effectiveness of any psychotherapy.

When clients are taught relaxation, they are essentially taught to use non–goal-directed, focused attention. They are trained to passively observe the products of their own minds, the constant shifting of images, thoughts, and feelings. Behaviorists do not address that they are teaching a kind of mind control, a thought stopping, a stopping of the world, a means of exercising mental flexibility that is rarely discussed in the West. In relaxation training, clients are shown how their own minds work, the interplay between pictures and thought, emotions and physical reactions. They are shown how to focus attention or consciousness on what one chooses, rather than on the "programmed in the past" images our mental computers often automatically display. It is this ability to stop the flow of thinking, to practice mindfulness, to wonder about our mental products that is rarely explained in any school. We are taught how to study, what information to know, how to inquire, what others said, but we are rarely taught how to begin to use our magical mental computers in a planned fashion. In many ways, we do not quite know when to listen to our bodies, our minds, and our emotions or when to ignore them. We seem to pay too much attention either to not questioning or to always questioning. We need to combine both. This is the treasure systematic desensitization contains and what few behaviorists have addressed.

Relaxation helps us step out of our everyday way of seeing the world. It helps us step out of automatic assumptions and automatic modes of behaving and brings curiosity, openness, and freshness. It brings an alive presence, rather than the efficient and sometimes deadening effects of habitual patterns.

Feather and Rhoads (1972) outcome studies raise many questions. When traditional desensitization did not work, they successfully modified the desensitization procedures based on their dynamic conception of phobia. Their conception was that anxiety was provoked by the arousal of forbidden wishes. They asked patients to imagine the worst possible thing happening in the particular situations they feared and pursued this questioning until patients gave vivid, concrete descriptions. Most patients fantasized antisocial acts. Once they learned to distinguish how to gratify these wishes in fantasy but not act on them in reality, their anxiety significantly decreased. Interestingly, once one begins to entertain the hypothesis that anxiety is not just an automatic result of a particular stimulus but is a function of the patients' interpretation of that stimulus (and, perhaps, the need to repress hostile interpersonal reactions), the simple straightforward experimental model of stimulus-response comes under questioning. Feather and Rhoads applied systematic desensitization to the wish-related fantasies that may have caused avoidance behaviors, rather than to the environmental stimulus being avoided. In a similar vein, Davison and Neale (1974) noted that there is little solid evidence for the accidental conditioning view of human anxieties. Cues that evoke anxiety, they say, are largely a matter of accidental pairing. What actually provokes anxiety is whether or not clients can successfully relate to themselves and others.

Countertransference issues are ignored by behaviorists. They may state that such issues do not exist but may actually only be closing their eyes to the pitfalls clinicians face in becoming involved in someone else's emotional life, in appearing to be knowledgeable and wise, in being capable of rescuing and fixing. Understandably, given its theoretical underpinnings, there is not much discussion of how systematic desensitization can contribute to further self-understanding. Because part of the technique involves a component where clients and therapists can actually become better acquainted with themselves (relaxation exercise), it is an omission that the uses of mental imagery are not expanded on at greater length.

Finally, there are many questions that can and should be raised about the nature of therapeutic influence in desensitization. Is therapist influence being exerted in the patient's interest or in the therapist's interest?

This is quite difficult to explore unless one looks at things like counter-transference. Are some worthy goals, such as reduction of anxiety, being achieved at the expense of others, for example, an increased sense of self-directedness? Who decides which goals are better: the client, the thera-pist, society? Developing and seasoned clinicians need to remember that all psychotherapies are situations in which one human being (therapist) tries to enable another human being (client) to think, act, and feel differently. As such, these are situations that are vulnerable to power inequities. Behaviorists tend to dismiss these notions, but that does not mean they should be dismissed. In using systematic desensitization, a clinician must be quite clear on why, how, and when to use his or her influence on highly suggestible clients while using suggestibility-inducing interventions.

REFERENCES

Agras, W., Kazdin, A., & Wilson, G. (1979). *Behavior therapy: Toward an applied clinical science*. San Francisco, CA: W. H. Freeman.

Andrews, G., & Harvey, R. (1981). Does psychotherapy benefit neurotic patients? *Archives General Psychiatry, 38*, 1203.

Anton, W. (1976). An evaluation of outcome variables in the systematic desensitization of test anxiety. *Behavior Research and Therapy, 14*, 217–224.

Benson, H. (1984). *Beyond the relaxation response*. New York: Berkeley.

Brady, J. (1972). Systematic desensitization. In W. S. Agras, (Ed.), *Behavior modification: Principles and clinical applications*. Boston, MA: Little, Brown.

Brady, J. (1971). Metronome-conditioned speech retraining for stuttering. *Behavior Therapy, 2*, 129.

Brom, D., Kleber, R., & Defares, P. (1989). Brief psychotherapy for post-traumatic stress disorder. *Journal of Counseling and Clinical Psychology, 57*, 607–612.

Cormier, H., & Cormier, S. L. (Eds.). (1991). *Interviewing strategies for helpers: Fundamental skills and cognitive behavioral interventions* (3rd ed.). Pacific Grove, CA: Brooks/ Cole.

Cotharin, R., & Mikulas, W. (1975). Systematic desensitization of racial emotional responses. *Journal of Behavior Therapy and Experimental Psychiatry, 6*, 347–348.

Curran, P., & Monti, P. (Eds.). (1982). *Social skills training: A practical handbook for assessment and treatment*. New York: Guilford.

Davison, G., & Neale, J. (1974). *Abnormal psychology*. New York: Wiley.

Deffenbacher, J., & Suinn, R. (1988). Systematic desensitization and the reduction of anxiety. *The Counseling Psychologist, 16*, 9–30.

Feather, B., & Rhoads, J. (1972). Psychodynamic behavior therapy: 2. Clinical aspects. *Archives of General Psychiatry, 26*, 503–511.

Foa, E., Steketee, G., & Milby, J. (1980). Differential effects of exposure and response prevention in obsessive-compulsive washers. *Journal of Consulting and Clinical Psychology, 48*, 71.

Fodor, I. (1974). The phobic syndrome in women: Implications for treatment. In V. Franks & V. Burtle (Eds.), *Women in therapy: New psychotherapies for a changing society.* New York: Brunner/Mazel.

Goldfried, M. (1971). Systematic desensitization as training in self-control. *Journal of Consulting and Clinical Psychology, 37,* 228–234.

Goldfried, M., & Davison, G. (1976). *Clinical behavior therapy.* New York: Holt, Rinehart & Winston.

Hecker, J., & Thorpe, G. (1992). *Agoraphobia and panic: A guide to psychological treatment.* Boston, MA: Allyn and Bacon.

Hedberg, A., & Campbell, I. (1974). Comparison of four behavioral treatments of alcoholism. *Journal of Behavior Therapy and Experimental Psychiatry, 5,* 251–256.

Hull, C. L. (1943). *Principles of behavior.* New York: Appleton-Century-Crofts.

Jacobson, E. (1938). *Progressive relaxation.* Chicago, IL: University of Chicago Press.

Jones, M. C. (1924). A laboratory study of fear: The case of Peter. *Pedagogical Seminar, 31,* 308–315.

Kazdin, A., & Wilson, G. (1978). *Evaluation of behavior therapy: Issues, evidence, and research strategies.* Cambridge, MA: Ballinger.

King, N., & Gillone, E. (1990). Acceptability of fear reduction procedures with children. *Journal of Behavior Therapy, 21,* 1–8.

Lazarus, A. A. (1976). *Multimodel behavior therapy.* New York: Springer.

Lazarus, A. A. (1971). *Behavior therapy and beyond.* New York: McGraw Hill.

Lazarus, A. A. (1961). Group therapy of phobic disorders by systematic desensitization. *Journal of Abnormal and Social Psychology, 63,* 504.

Mahesh Yogi, M. (1969). *Maharishi Mahesh Yogi on the Bhagavad-Gita: A new translation and commentary.* New York: Penguin.

Marks, I. (1987). *Fears, phobias & rituals: Panic and anxiety and their disorders.* New York: Oxford University Press.

Marks, I., & Gelder, M. (1969). *Fears and phobias.* London: William Heinemann.

Marquis, J., Morgan, W., & Piaget, G. (1979). *A guidebook for systematic desensitization* (3rd ed.). Palo Alto, CA: Veterans Workshop.

Masters, J., Burish, T., Hollon, D., & Rimm, D. (1987). *Behavior therapy techniques and empirical findings* (3rd ed.). San Diego, CA: Harcourt, Brace, Jovanovich.

Morris, R. (1991). Fear reduction methods. In F. Kanfer & A. Goldsteing (Eds.), *Helping people change: A textbook of methods.* New York: Pergamon.

Morrow, G. (1986). Effect of the cognitive hierarchy in the systematic desensitization treatment of anticipatory nausea in cancer patients. *Cognitive Therapy and Research, 10,* 421–446.

Rachman, S. (1990). *Fear and courage* (2d ed.), San Francisco, CA: Freeman.

Renneberg, B., Goldsteing, A., Phillips, D., & Chambliss, D. (1990). Intensive behavioral group treatment of avoidant personality disorder. *Behavior Therapy, 21*(3), 363–377.

Rimm, D., DeGroot, J., Boord, P., Herman, J., & Dillow, P. (1971). Systematic desensitization of an anger response. *Behavior Research and Therapy, 9,* 273–280.

Rimm, D., & Masters, J. (1979). *Behavior therapy: Techniques and empirical findings* (2d ed.). New York: Academic Press.

Rosen, G., Glasgow, R., & Barrera, M. (1976). A controlled study to assess the clinical efficacy of totally self-administered systematic desensitization. *Journal of Consulting and Clinical Psychology, 44*, 208–217.

Schloss, P., Smith, M., Santora, C., & Bryant, R. (1989). A respondent conditioned approach to reducing anger responses of a dually-diagnosed man with mild retardation. *Behavior Therapy, 20*, 459–464.

Shaffer, W. (1984). *Heuristics for the initial diagnostic interview.* Reprinted in W. Cormier & S. Cormier (Eds.), *Interviewing strategies for helpers: Fundamental skills and cognitive behavioral interventions.* Pacific Grove, CA: Brooks/Cole.

Shapiro, F. (1989). Eye movement desensitization: A new treatment for post-traumatic stress disorder. *Journal of Behavior Therapy and Experimental Psychiatry, 20*, 211–217.

Smith, M. L., & Glass, C. V. (1977). Meta-analysis of psychotherapy outcome studies. *American Psychologist, 32*, 752–760.

Steinmark, S., & Borkovec, T. (1974). Active and placebo treatment effects on moderate insomnia under counterdemand and positive demand instructions. *Journal of Abnormal Psychology, 83*, 157–163.

Wachtel, P. (1992). *Psychoanalysis and behavior therapy: Toward an integration.* New York: Basic Books.

Wolpe, J. (1990). *The practice of behavior therapy* (3rd ed.). Elmsford, NY: Pergamon.

Wolpe, J. (1981). The dichotomy between directly conditioned and cognitively learned anxiety. *Journal of Behavior Therapy and Experimental Psychiatry, 12*, 35.

Wolpe, J. (1958). *Psychotherapy by reciprocal inhibition.* Stanford, CA: Stanford University Press.

8

Focusing

Mary Ballou

DESCRIPTION

Focusing, an affective intervention derived from phenomenological theory, places emphasis upon the internal reality of the individual. Focusing draws from the theoretical background of the client-centered and experiential approaches. It utilizes client-centered concepts, including the necessity of a sound therapeutic relationship and an emphasis on the exploration of the client's immediate experience. Focusing is also based on the client-centered premises of the need for positive regard and a nonjudgmental acceptance of the client's experience (Cormier & Hackney, 1993).

From the experiential theories, the technique of focusing draws on the practice of continually referring back to the client's felt sense. The reason for this is to check the accuracy of the counselor's and the client's verbal descriptions of the client's experience. This practice results in more accurate and more diverse insight into the client's experience. Basing "knowing" on body reactions avoids lengthy intellectual discussions of verbal content and may give access to an additional way of knowing. On either account, it offers experience-based awareness.

Reality resides in the individual's perception of experience, rather than in some domain outside of and independent of the person. Client-centered, Gestalt, experiential, and some aspects of existential personality theories rest on this philosophical position. In common, they hold that health lies in increased self-awareness and choice. Gestalt and experiential theories often find the body a source of awareness. Hence, bodily sensations, beyond a physical experience, are a source of increased awareness and knowledge. Some of the experiential therapies hold that the body stores experience that can be reclaimed through bodily attention and release.

Discussion of levels and states of consciousness are strange to ears filled with words of the 1990s. "Individual" and "movement conscious-ness" are words of earlier eras and of vocabularies out of the mainstream of psychological theory and practice. Consciousness is a powerful concept and one that calls for newer paradigms and pluralistic concep-tions. Consciousness and affect require worldviews, values, and reality constructs quite different from the usual themes of the 1980s and 1990s.

Focusing, although certainly another intervention strategy, requires a differing consideration of the many aspects of human capacity and functions. Consciousness, emotion, and body are all meaningful additions to cognitions, behavior, and social motivation.

Focusing developed as a result of psychotherapy research (Gendlin, 1969). The goal of the research was to examine successful therapy outcomes and the experiential level of discourse. The two were found to be significantly associated. There were additional unexpected results. In successful therapy, clients seemed to direct inward attention to a bodily sense of an unclear edge of awareness; this phenomenon did not occur in individuals who had unsuccessful outcomes. Further, this finding held true during the beginning, middle, and end of·therapy across a variety of therapeutic methods. Thus, it appeared that successful therapy was related to something these clients did inside themselves. A method for teaching this mode of inner attention or inner act was devised, and it is called "focusing."

Eugene Gendlin developed this strategy in the late 1960s and early 1970s after years of observing clients move successfully and unsuccess-fully through therapy. He discovered that successful clients were those who used what he later termed "focusing" as a technique in their therapy, that is, these clients were able to obtain information from their physical awareness, not just their psychological awareness, and were able to use this information to produce permanent change in their lives.

During the focusing process, the individual accesses an internal bodily awareness that Gendlin calls a "felt sense" (Gendlin, 1981). This is the bodily version of a problem. By attending inside one's body, a felt sense will form if the individual has an accepting attitude. At first, it is vague and undefined because it is a body-sense; however, it feels significant. This felt sense is a complex physical experience that represents a deep level of awareness that is unfamiliar. A felt sense in body knowledge lies below and is different from emotion. However, an awareness of one's feelings can be an important avenue and outcome of focusing.

When focusing is successful, the felt sense will acquire more definition, and a change will take place (Gendlin, 1981). This is a physical change, and it is called a "body shift." The felt sense of the problem will change with the body shift, and the individual also will change. A body shift is a physical feeling of a change or movement; something inside becomes unstuck. One is able to sense the difference, and it feels good. The body's way of having a problem does not necessarily follow the mind's logic. Any given body shift may clarify, elaborate, change direction, or contradict the previous body shift. Because focusing brings hidden knowledge into conscious awareness, one might expect to feel worse. However, a body shift has the sensation of freedom or of release. It feels pleasant and relaxing.

A familiar experience that Gendlin (1981) offers as analogous to focusing is the strange feeling of having forgotten something but not knowing what it is. For example, suppose you are going away for the weekend. While driving toward your destination, you have a felt sense of something forgotten nagging at you. You try going over mental checklists of possibilities, and you try to shake the feeling in order to enjoy the drive. Yet, nothing works. Suddenly, the answer hits you: you forgot to pack a jacket. Your vague felt sense changes and moves into a body shift; you feel physical release, unstuck, and relaxed. You may not be glad about forgetting the jacket, but the body shift feels good. You have experienced change.

IMPLEMENTATION

Focusing is appropriate only in the context of a sound therapeutic relationship. The exercise in and of itself should not be considered therapy but should be viewed as a part of the therapeutic process.

There are six movements to the inner act of focusing. Following are the basic instructions that the therapist would give to the client. Gendlin (1981) refers to this as the focusing manual.

1. Clearing a space
   What I will ask you to do will be silent, just to yourself. Take a moment just to relax. . . . All right — now, inside you, I would like you to pay attention inwardly, in your body, perhaps in your stomach or chest. Now see what comes there when you ask, "How is my life going? What is the main thing

for me right now?" Sense within your body. Let the answers come slowly from this sensing. When some concern comes, DO NOT GO INSIDE IT. Stand back, say "Yes, that's there. I can feel that, there." Let there be a little space between you and that. Then ask what else you feel. Wait again, and sense. Usually there are several things.

2. Felt sense
From among what came, select one personal problem on which to focus. DO NOT GO INSIDE IT. Stand back from it. Of course, there are many parts to that one thing you are thinking about — too many to think of each one alone. However, you can *feel* all of these things together. Pay attention there where you usually feel things, and in there, you can get a sense of what *all of the problem feels like*. Let yourself feel the unclear sense of *all of that*.

3. Handle
What is the quality of this unclear felt sense? Let a word, a phrase, or an image come up from the felt sense itself. It might be a quality word, like "tight," "sticky," "scary," "stuck," "heavy," or "jumpy," or a phrase or an image. Stay with the quality of the felt sense till something fits it just right.

4. Resonating
Go back and forth between the felt sense and the word (or phrase or image). Check how they resonate with each other. See if there is a little bodily signal that lets you know there is a fit. To do it, you have to have the felt sense there again, as well as the word. Let the felt sense change, if it does, and also the word or picture, until they feel just right in capturing the quality of the felt sense.

5. Asking
Now ask, "What is it, about this whole problem, that makes this quality" (that you have just named or pictured)? Make sure the quality is sensed again, freshly, vividly (not just remembered from before). When it is here again, tap it, touch it, be with it, asking "What makes the whole problem so _____?" or you ask, "What is in *this* sense?" If you get a quick answer without a shift in the felt sense, just let that kind of answer go by. Return your attention to your body and freshly find the felt sense again. Then ask it again. Be with the felt sense till something comes along with a shift, a slight "give" or release.

6. Receiving
Receive whatever comes with a shift in a friendly way. Stay with it awhile, even if it is only a slight release. Whatever comes, this is only one shift; there will be others. You probably will continue after a little while, but stay here for a few moments.

IF DURING THESE INSTRUCTIONS SOMEWHERE YOU HAVE SPENT A LITTLE WHILE SENSING AND TOUCHING AN UNCLEAR

HOLISTIC BODY SENSE OF THIS PROBLEM, THEN YOU HAVE FOCUSED. It doesn't matter whether the body shift came or not. It comes on its own. We don't control that. (pp. 43–45)

The counselor guides the client through this sequence, although the specific instructions can be modified by individual counselors. Despite individual differences in technique, the main goal remains for the counselor to help the client to "recognize, reflect, and clarify their internal experiences and withhold judgment of it and interference with it" (Bassoff, 1984, p. 268). Mcguire (1991) refers to the larger application of focusing as a flood of symbols and memories that accompany the bodily release in the felt shift. The felt shift is Gendlin's (1981) term for the body knowledge that occurs in focusing.

After the focusing exercise, the counselor and client may discuss new awarenesses that were reached during the process. If the client is still unclear about his or her feelings experience, he or she may refocus. If the client finds that he or she has difficulty focusing, this resistance then may be the subject of a new focusing exercise. This technique also may be accompanied by other techniques that work with the awareness affectively, cognitively, and behaviorally (Gendlin, 1969).

Gendlin (1981) thinks that focusing (whether a preexisting skill or acquired during therapy) is the critical determiner of successful or unsuccessful therapeutic outcome, because the attention inward helps clients become "unstuck." Western therapies traditionally have not allowed for the individual's body awareness of a problem to influence or be influenced by the therapeutic process. In order to subscribe to this interpretation of focusing, one must acknowledge (as Gendlin does) the holistic mind-body connection. From this, it follows that the body has an integral role in the process of change. "The problems inside you are only those parts of the process that have been stopped, and the aim of focusing is to unstop them and get the process moving again" (Gendlin, 1978, p. 67). However, as Gendlin admits, we do not control when a shift comes.

In addition to helping clients become "unstuck," focusing provides the experience of passivity. Often, passivity is viewed negatively within our Western culture and is associated with traits such as helplessness and dependence. However, focusing encourages qualities of passivity such as patience, receptivity, awareness, and acceptance. These qualities lead the individual to the experience of "being" rather than "doing." According to Bassoff (1984), people need a balance of passivity and activity to promote psychological growth, and focusing provides a means for a client to increase his or her passive capacity.

Another positive aspect of focusing is that it is a skill that can be learned and used outside the therapy sessions. This allows clients to develop independence, empathy, and unconditional positive self-regard. In some respects, focusing empowers the client to become his or her own counselor, or, reframed, the client claims responsibility for his or her own process of growth.

One problem with focusing is that some of the concepts used to explain the technique are difficult to explain and to comprehend. A counselor may have difficulty explaining what is mean by a "felt sense" or an "experiential effect." If clients have difficulty grasping these concepts or the implicit values of self-awareness and the mind-body connection, the focusing exercise may be unsuccessful.

APPROPRIATE AND INAPPROPRIATE USES

The research indicates that successful therapeutic outcomes occur most often among people who are already highly capable of experiential awareness. However, Gendlin (1981) claims that the clients who benefit most from focusing are those who initially have little experiential aware-ness. He believes that focusing is a skill that is essential to personal problem solving and mental health and should be taught to clients who do not already have these skills and awareness.

One specific population that often benefits from focusing techniques is "borderline psychotics, or generally people to whom voices and other 'weird' experience can happen" (Gendlin, 1969, p. 7). Focusing allows these individuals to be grounded in the present and helps them to shut out the "weird experiences." In contrast to the psychotic experiences, "feel-ing is a safe and different 'place' in oneself" (Gendlin, 1969, p. 7). Both Mcguire (1991) and Shea (1987) warn against use with clients who have fear or resistance regarding their body, for example, physical and sexual abuse victims.

Other therapists have defined, described, and implemented "focusing" in ways that diverge from Gendlin's rather precise meaning and pro-cedures. Although meanings and procedures may differ, the common goal of bringing a client into contact with his or her own experience remains constant.

Ivey (1994) asserts that focusing occurs during the advanced stages of the psychotherapeutic process. By "focusing," he means directing the client's attention and talk to one or more of the dimensions relevant to his or her experience. Cottone (1992) also discusses focusing in terms of queries intended to help the client become aware of his or her experience. He credits Yontef and Simkin (1989) with the classic gestalt focusing question, "What are you aware of (experiencing) now?" Cormier and Hackney (1993) present focusing as "used to encourage and facilitate introspection in such a way that problems can be clarified and conceptualized by the client. Focusing emphasizes present feelings toward either present or past circumstance" (p. 158).

Clearly, the meaning assigned to focusing is influenced by the author's theoretical orientations. They are presented here not so much to reveal inconsistency as to point out additional applications of focusing. In addition to facilitating a "felt sense," focusing also may be used to increase a client's awareness of his or her experience in the areas of thoughts, feelings, values, and the complex influences of family, community, and culture. Also, medical treatments that are dependent upon bodily awareness could make appropriate use of focusing. Focusing also could be appropriately used in research on consciousness, whether brain/autonomic based, ecologically based, or spiritually based.

RESEARCH

Research on the technique of focusing is limited because of the difficulty in measuring such subtle changes in personal awareness. However, there have been some encouraging findings. In a series of studies, Gendlin and his associates discovered that an individual's ability to refer to his or her own internal feeling process is related to therapeutic change. The Experiencing Scale was designed and used "to define the sorts of verbal behavior occurring in therapy interviews when a patient uses his freshly ongoing experiential process as a basis for what he says, thinks, and does in the interview" (Gendlin, 1969, p. 12).

In addition to Gendlin's findings, Bassoff (1984) has reviewed three independent studies. Davison concluded that individuals who were instructed in the technique of focusing displayed more self-expression than individuals who did not receive such instruction (Bassoff, 1984). Results from a study by Greenberg and Higgins found evidence that suggests that focusing instruction is related to greater change in awareness (Bassoff, 1984). Finally, a study at Case Western Reserve University compared focusers to a control group (traditional talk therapy) and concluded that focusers showed increased awareness of feelings but that the experiential nature of the problems did not change. However, 77 percent of the focusers reported a positive change in their perspective on the problem, while 55 percent of the control group reported the same positive effects.

During the 1970s, numerous research studies were completed on focusing, and most demonstrated a positive association with favorable change. Because of the nature of the change involved, direct demonstration and controlled studies are not possible, or, said another way, controlled studies are not the appropriate method of validation. Instead, the positive outcome of focusing in psychotherapy, in psychosomatic and somatic medicine, in consciousness studies, and in spiritual practice offers some confirmation of its efficacy. The philosophy of direct experience underlying focusing makes empirical research even more difficult and questionable. In the case of focusing, the method of inquiry most consistent with the underlying philosophical assumptions of the technique is reliance upon the perception of those who use focusing techniques. Gendlin continues to develop and communicate with others about focusing, its use, and its effectiveness. In fact, he invites communication: E. T. Gendlin, Department of Behavioral Sciences, University of Chicago, 5848 S. University, Chicago, IL 60637.

REFERENCES

Bassoff, E. S. (1984). Healthy aspects of passivity and Gendlin's focusing. *Personnel and Guidance Journal, 62*, 268–270.

Cormier, S., & Hackney, H. (1993). *The professional counselor.* Boston, MA: Allyn and Bacon.

Cottone, R. (1992). *Theories and paradigms of counseling and psychotherapy.* Boston, MA: Allyn and Bacon.

Gendlin, E. T. (1981). *Focusing* (2d ed.). New York: Bantam Books.

Gendlin, E. T. (1978). *Focusing.* New York: Bantam Books.

Gendlin, E. T. (1969). Focusing. *Psychotherapy: Theory, Research and Practice, 6*, 4–14.

Ivey, A. (1994). *Intentional interviewing and counseling* (3rd ed.). Pacific Grove, CA: Brooks/Cole.

Mcguire, K. (1991). Affect in focusing and experiential psychotherapy. In J. Safran & L. Greenberg (Eds.), *Emotion, psychotherapy, and change.* New York: Guilford.

Shea, J. (1987). *Religious experiencing: William James and Eugene Gendlin.* Lanham, MD: University Press of America.

Yontef, G., & Simkin, J. (1989). Gestalt therapy. In R. Corsini & D. Wedding (Eds.), *Current psychotherapy.* Itasca, IL: Peacock.

9

Assertiveness Training

Mary Ballou

BACKGROUND

Assertiveness is a quality of interaction and a skill unevenly distrib-uted in the U.S. population. Certain segments of the population are both trained and rewarded differently for assertiveness. Developing an atti-tude that one's own words are important and the skills to communicate them effectively is important to mental health, educational and voca-tional success, and social interaction. Cultural, class, and gender-based deficits join with some mental health issues in the list of arenas where assertiveness training (AT) might be beneficial.

Both the clinical reports and the outcome research seem to indicate that AT, although useful for some under certain conditions, is not the panacea initially claimed. In the 1990s, AT more often is seen as a strategy to be used in addition to therapy and with strong consideration of the contextual factors in a client's life.

Assertive behavior helps create equality in relationships. It allows an individual to exercise his or her personal rights without denying those of others. Many consider assertion an essential aspect of relationships, and it is a difficult skill that people can learn. AT offers people an opportunity to develop this important social skill.

AT involves role-playing, modeling, rehearsal, and homework. It also may involve cognitive restructuring, learning to replace certain beliefs with other ones. The therapist is able to demonstrate assertive skills to the client through role-play. Repeating this modeled behavior inside and outside the therapy session allows the client to rehearse assertive skills. The ultimate goal, then, is for the client to become comfortable with acting assertively.

Andrew Salter (1949) first wrote about assertiveness in *Conditioned Reflex Therapy*. Here, he discussed several techniques designed to "increase excitation," including the expression of contradictory opinions, using the pronoun "I," and accepting compliments (p. 97). Prompted by Salter's writings, Joseph Wolpe further explored AT in the 1960s. To Wolpe, assertive behavior is "the socially appropriate verbal and motor expression of any emotion other than anxiety" (1990, p. 135).

AT grew out of behavioral theory. Similar to behavior therapy's goal of learning new responses is AT's goal of acquiring assertive behaviors. AT also has cognitive components, illustrated by the use of cognitive restructuring. This focuses on helping people to identify and accept their personal rights, as well as the rights of others, while reducing cognitive barriers to assertive behavior. These barriers include excessive anxiety, guilt, and irrational beliefs (Cormier & Hackney, 1993).

AT has been recognized and widely accepted as an important behavioral intervention. It has two major goals: anxiety reduction and social skill training (Cotler & Guerra, 1976). Before attempting training, however, it is necessary for the individual or group to understand what assertiveness is, and to do so, an understanding of nonassertive and aggressive behavior also is necessary. Although social and situational aspects cannot be ignored, at an individual/ contextual level, assertiveness might be characterized as follows.

The nonassertive person denies himself or herself his or her rights and is inhibited from expressing his or her actual feelings. This person is often hurt and anxious because of his or her inadequate behavior. He or she seldom achieves his or her own desired goals because he or she allows others to choose for him or her.

On the other hand, the aggressive person usually carries his or her desire for expression to the extreme. He or she tends to choose for people and, so, minimizes their worth as persons. He or she usually gets his or her goals by hurting others. As a result, he or she usually suffers hatred and frustration generated by his or her actions.

Providing middle ground between these two behaviors is the assertive mode. The assertive person is self-enhancing. He or she expresses feelings honestly, has a strong sense of self-worth, and usually achieves his or her goals after choosing how to act.

Two concepts that determine the need for AT are situational nonassertiveness or aggressiveness and general nonassertiveness or aggressiveness (Alberti & Emmons, 1974). People whose behavior is usually adequate and self-enhancing can become nonassertive or aggressive in certain situations. These individuals may readily recognize their problem and voluntarily seek assistance. Without too much preparation or prompting, they may successfully initiate a more adaptive response.

In contrast to these are people who are unable to assert their rights or feelings or who are generally aggressive in every situation. In both cases, they are anxious in nearly all social situations, are extremely sensitive to criticism, and tend to feel rejected. Because of a severe lack of a sense of self-worth or an inability to respond honestly to an emotional event, they may need in-depth treatment by a trained therapist before or instead of AT.

Almost everyone can benefit from AT. However, researchers have identified certain groups for whom this training should be specially designed. One such group is men who have accepted the misleading notion that aggressiveness is "instinctive" to men. They dominate their environment and ride roughshod over people in order to accomplish their goals. Sex role socialization my predispose them to nonassertive behavior. When one's own needs are seen in the meeting of others' needs, self-assertiveness is difficult.

Another group for whom AT can be specially designed is blacks who fear that their assertiveness will be evaluated more negatively by white observers than would the same behavior displayed by whites (Cheek, 1976; Fleming, 1983). Black women who think that their assertiveness and ambition may not always be well-received by black male colleagues or spouses also can benefit from this training, as can Asian-Americans, who have been found to be lower in overall assertiveness than whites (Fukuyama & Greenfield, 1983). This subject is discussed more fully under the description of bicultural AT.

DESCRIPTION

Individuals who are more generally nonassertive or aggressive and who seek or are referred to a therapist for assistance need detailed assessment. Beginning in the initial interview, the therapist pays close attention to what is being said and how the information is given. Behaviors such as eye contact, body posture, voice tone, and gestures should be considered carefully. Questions should be asked to find out what the client sees as his or her problem, the extent of that problem, and what the client hopes to achieve.

Additional information for and about the client may be discovered by administering a battery of tests. Some examples of these are the Fear Survey Schedule (Wolpe, 1958), the Assertion Questionnaire (Wolpe & Lazarus, 1966), the Behavioral Assertiveness Test (Eisler, Miller, & Hersen, 1973), and the Alberti and Emmons Assertive Inventory (1974). These tests give the therapist more understanding of the client's difficulty and help the client to understand the characteristics of assertive behavior.

Extremely anxious clients may need other types of therapy before AT begins. Still others may need to be more aware of their tension and calmness levels. Using the Subjective Units of Discomfort Scale (Cotler & Guerra, 1976), clients identify their complete relaxation (represented by zero) and their highest state of anxiety (represented by 100). Using this scale to mark their feelings in daily situations, clients can then keep an Assertion Training Diary. In this, they record what happens to cause them anxiety, how they felt, and what goals might be set to change the situation.

Alberti and Emmons (1986) suggest that some clients need individual AT before attempting group AT. They also suggest that groups should not contain more than 5–12 members, should meet twice a week for one hour, and should continue for 6–8 weeks. Methods that have proved most effective for them are modeling, role-playing, covert rehearsal, coaching, and systematic desensitization.

A typical group program for AT contains the following steps:

1. An informational presentation on assertiveness starts the group.
2. Members of the group introduce themselves.
3. Background material is presented on nonassertive, aggressive, and assertive behavior.
4. Group organization is discussed.
5. A situation is role-played by a model(s).
6. The group discusses modeling behavior.
7. The group closes their eyes and visualizes modeled behavior.
8. A new situation is presented.
9. Group members engage in covert rehearsal.
10. Group members role-play, with coaching, if needed.
11. Therapist and group give feedback.

Step 8, presenting a new situation, can be structured to provide learning for particular group members' problems or for general application.

Typical situations that can be posed are starting a conversation with a stranger on a bus or in a meeting, asserting one's rights and needs with significant others (parents, spouse, roommate(s), boyfriend or girl-friend), learning to argue or assert one's opinion with a dominant or opinionated person, and stating one's requests for more resources to a boss to be able to accomplish an assigned task at work. Clients should be encouraged to keep a log or diary of what they encounter and how they handle it.

The social, cultural, and situational nature of assertive skills and reactions to them must be discussed extensively. Although persistence in the skills will bring progress, initial client attempts may not meet with success. Skills take motivation, practice, and appropriate use and selection. The therapist also should caution clients about possible negative reactions to their assertive behavior. For instance, people significant in clients' lives may respond with aggression, temper tantrums, or revenge. Although now acting in a more competent manner, clients may be seen by these people as less "sympathetic" (Epstein, 1980), less "kind" (Woolfolk & Denver, 1979), or less "likeable" (Keane, Wedding, & Kelly, 1983). Clients should be guided to anticipate situations that may cause such reactions and to recognize the needs of the significant person in such a situation. Encouragement should be given to clients to use conversational and complimentary comments to mitigate the negative impact of assertion (Wildman, 1986).

Women may be nonassertive because they think society will find their assertive behavior inappropriate and undesirable. Similarly, men may be aggressive because they fear that society will deem any expression of positive feelings as "feminine" behavior (Hess, Bridgwater, Bornstein, & Sweeney, 1980). Both groups must be given much encouragement and support to counteract these thoughts and to take pride in their new mode of behaving. Single-sex AT groups may be appropriate for these two groups to concentrate on specific areas of concern for each sex. Similarly, clients with psychiatric illness (Brown & Carmichael, 1992), adolescents at risk for substance abuse (Silverman, 1990), and victims of battering (Lantican & Mayorga, 1993) are examples of populations for whom AT may be appropriate.

BICULTURAL ASSERTIVENESS TRAINING

Bicultural sensitivity as developed in the 1980s and 1990s has expanded and broadened AT in ways important for all using it. If an assertive person is defined as one who finds an appropriate balance between passivity and aggression, then we must look more closely at who determines what is appropriate. This usually is determined by the values of the dominant culture. A client from a minority background may feel uncomfortable with assertive behavior as defined by traditional psychology. Bicultural AT addresses cultural tensions by encouraging awareness and dual modes of social behavior. This strategy does not limit a client to a single set of behavioral norms but attempts to increase his or her repertoire of assertive responses. Depending on the social situation, a biculturally assertive person can draw on the majority's and his or her own cultural values.

Bicultural AT is similar to a "majority" AT strategy in that it emphasizes building practical skills in a small group. Teaching and modeling assertive behavior is done by the leader (therapist), and group members role-play social situations and give feedback. They also provide support for each other in applying what they have learned. However, there also are important differences between the two strategies.

In bicultural AT, members and leaders usually are from similar minority backgrounds. In modeling and role-playing exercises, bicultural examples are used for social situations both within the minority community and in society at large. The therapist speaks directly about cultural variables involved in assertive behavior, and group members respond with their observations. During group discussions, members help each other find concrete ways to be assertive within their cultural norms. Much of this would not happen in a traditional AT setting.

Minority people need to know how to be assertive in a dominant culture. They need to find jobs, deal with employers, and locate needed resources. However, to be happy within their own culture, they need assertiveness strategies based on their own cultural norms. As Wood and Mallinckrodt (1990) state, "The same assertive behaviors that would be appropriate for a white client may exacerbate the problem for the ethnic minority client."

As discussed previously, blacks often have been penalized for assertive behavior. A bicultural AT group helps them to address the ways in which racism affects their ability to act assertively. Many Asian people retain their culture's emphasis on harmony and avoidance of direct confrontation. Role-play in a bicultural AT group can help increase comfort with behaving assertively when necessary in the dominant culture. Hispanic women, who may subordinate their needs to those of the family, can work together in a bicultural AT group to find ways to be assertive that will be acceptable to their families.

As in all AT, the needs of the individual always must be considered. Some minority clients may be acculturated to majority norms and would be more comfortable in a group that does not focus on ethnic background.

APPROPRIATE AND INAPPROPRIATE USES

AT has been employed with quite a few different populations. Potential clients might include the nonassertive person who has high levels of anxiety or guilt or deficiencies in social skills and the aggressive person who meets his or her needs at the expense of others (Cotler & Guerra, 1976). Since its association with the women's movement in the late 1960s and early 1970s, AT has been used with groups of women. Some behavior problems that may be dealt with effectively through AT are substance abuse (Rakos, 1991; Silverman, 1990), depression (Brown & Carmichael, 1992), and some anxiety behaviors, including nail biting and stuttering (Rakos, 1991). However, AT has been used effectively with other populations, as well. Some of these include the elderly and young children, whose rights are often infringed upon, medical patients, whose physical complaints may result from unexpressed feelings, and phys-ically or mentally disabled people, whose special needs are ignored by others (Rakos, 1991).

Alberti and Emmons (1986) found many appropriate settings for AT, including school, professional, and community settings. Wehr and Kaufman (1987) found that AT decreased anxiety in ninth graders; they believe it both desirable and practical in school programs.

Cormier and Hackney (1993), after reviewing the literature, state that AT is an appropriate technique for people who have a strong goal orientation and who are willing to participate in the helping process. They also report benefit to those people willing to change a discrete and limited number of behaviors. The most effective therapeutic use of AT was found to be with a group format, because it offers social feedback and the opportunity to practice assertive behavior.

Alberti and Emmons (1986) find that generally aggressive people in a group setting may react defensively to their anxiety and try to dominate or manipulate other group members. However, Rakos (1991) disagrees with this, believing that aggressive behavior can be effectively managed and reduced through AT.

Disagreement exists, as well, over the use of AT with another population. Many professionals recommend the use of AT with abused women, but O'Leary, Curley, Rosenbaum, and Clarke (1985) believe that data do not support the assumption that abused women are nonassertive. Indeed, they think battered women's nonassertiveness is quite functional, because these women understand that an assertive message may only increase the hostility of the batterer. If AT should proceed, the therapist must warn these women of potential hazards, teach them the distinction between aggression and proper assertion, and guide them to first use assertive behaviors outside the battering relationship. Cox and Stoltenberg (1991) state that supplementing AT with a discussion group helps battered women to understand how assertive behavior could aggravate their batterer and to develop ways of being assertive while protecting themselves.

RESEARCH ON EFFECTIVENESS

Numerous studies have attempted to determine the effectiveness of AT. Many of these rely on a self-report method to assess pre-AT and post-AT effectiveness. In a study done by Starke (1987), 30 cerebral palsy and paraplegic individuals reported on their assertion and acceptance of disability. Subjects in the AT group showed the most improvement as compared with a control group and a discussion group. In a study of peer pressure and assertiveness with undergraduates, Williams and Hall (1988) discovered that those students in the AT group showed significant improvement over the discussion group members in resisting peer pressure.

Lazarus (1981) found that AT as part of a multimodal therapy alleviates symptoms and prevents the relapse of mild depression. AT will not produce significant change in these individuals if used alone, only if used as part of a multimodal framework. Harrell and Strauss (1986) found that a combination of techniques was effective in helping visually impaired people to assert their wishes. People with impairments often are characterized by a sense of learned helplessness related to their disability that contributes to their lack of assertive behavior. As a result, such people may be overly aggressive or passive. AT was used to improve this population's assertive behavioral skills, and a discussion group was used to enhance its self-perceptions. The subjects' sense of control and communication skills both were found to be improved. These two studies indicate that assertiveness training alone is not effective with some individuals but, rather, AT in combination with other techniques.

A study on the effectiveness of booster sessions for AT was done by Baggs and Spence (1990). The subjects were women aged 20 to 65 whom the Assertion Inventory had determined to be nonassertive. All women completed AT and were assigned to monthly assertion training boosters, monthly placebo boosters, or no boosters. Those women who attended six monthly assertion training boosters showed improvement in assertiveness beyond the original AT group. Women in the attention placebo booster group only prevented relapse, which did occur in the no booster group. In 1986, Riedel, Fenwick, and Jillings noted significant improvements in depression after AT, and these results were better maintained when follow-up sessions were provided. Such studies suggest that the learning of assertive behavior is an ongoing process.

Given the measurement that exists, the typical group format of the training, and the behavioral definitions, it is curious that more control research does not exist. However, the self-report and few control studies do suggest that AT is most effective in group formats, along with other therapy, and when follow-up is provided. Clearly, contextual examination of the population and its relationship to larger issues of coping, control, danger, cultural norms, social standard compliance, and survival strategies must all be considered carefully before AT is carelessly prescribed or suggested.

REFERENCES

Alberti, R. E., & Emmons, M. L. (1986). *Your perfect right: A guide to assertive living*. San Luis Obispo, CA: Impact.

Alberti, R. E., & Emmons, M. L. (1974). *Your perfect right*. San Luis Obispo, CA: Impact.

Baggs, K., & Spence, S. H. (1990). Effectiveness of booster sessions in the maintenance and enhancement of treatment gains following assertion training. *Journal of Consulting and Clinical Psychology, 58*, 845–854.

Brown, T., & Carmichael, K. (1992). Assertiveness training for clients with a psychiatric illness: A pilot study. *British Journal of Occupational Therapy, 55*(4), 137–140.

Cheek, D. A. (1976). *Assertive black . . . puzzled white: A black perspective on assertive behavior*. San Luis Obispo, CA: Impact.

Cormier, L., & Hackney, H. (1993). *The professional counselor: A process guide to helping*. Needham Heights, MA: Allyn and Bacon.

Cotler, S. B., & Guerra, J. J. (1976). *Assertion training*. Champaign, IL: Research.

Cox, J., & Stoltenberg, C. (1991). Evaluation of a treatment program for battered wives. *Journal of Family Violence, 6*(4), 395–413.

Eisler, R. M., Miller, P. M., & Hersen, M. (1973). Components of assertive behavior. *Journal of Clinical Psychology, 3*, 295–299.

Epstein, N. (1980). Social consequences of assertion, aggression and submission: Situational and dispositional determinants. *Behavior Therapy, 11,* 662–669.

Fleming, J. (1983). Black women in black and white college environments: The making of a matriarch. *Journal of Social Issues, 39*(3), 41–54.

Fukuyama, N. A., & Greenfield, T. K. (1983). Dimensions of assertiveness in an Asian-American student population. *Journal of Counseling Psychology, 30,* 429–432.

Harrell, R., & Strauss, F. (1986). Approaches to increasing assertive behavior and communication in blind and visually impaired persons. *Journal of Visual Impairment and Blindness, 6,* 794–798.

Hess, E. P., Bridgwater, C. A., Bornstein, P. H., & Sweeney, T. M. (1980). Situational determinants in the perception of assertiveness: Gender-related influences. *Behavior Therapy, 11,* 49–58.

Keane, T. M., Wedding, D., & Kelly, J. A. (1983). Assessing subjective responses to assertive behavior: Data from patient sample. *Behavior Modification, 7,* 317–330.

Lantican, L., & Mayorga, J. (1993). Effectiveness of a women's mental health treatment program: A pilot study. *Issues in Mental Health Nursing, 14,* 31–49.

Lazarus, A. A. (1981). *The practice of multi-modal therapy: Systematic, comprehensive, and effective psychotherapy.* New York: McGraw-Hill.

O'Leary, K. D., Curley, A., Rosenbaum, A., & Clarke, C. (1985). Assertion training for abused wives: A potentially hazardous treatment. *Journal of Marital and Family Therapy, 11*(3), 319–322.

Rakos, R. F. (1991). *Assertive behavior; Theory, research, and training.* London: Routledge.

Riedel, H. P., Fenwick, C. R., & Jillings, C. R. (1986). Efficacy of booster sessions after training in assertiveness. *Perceptual and Motor Skills, 62,* 791–798.

Salter, A. (1949). *Conditioned reflex therapy.* New York: Farrar, Strauss & Giroux.

Silverman, W. (1990). Intervention strategies for the prevention of adolescent substance abuse. *Journal of Adolescent Chemical Dependency, 1*(2), 25–34.

Starke, M. C. (1987). Enhancing social skills and self-perceptions of physically disabled young adults: Assertiveness training versus discussion groups. *Behavior Modification, 11,* 3–16.

Wehr, S. H., & Kaufman, M. E. (1987). The effects of assertive training on performance in highly anxious adolescents. *Adolescence, 22*(85), 195–205.

Wildman, B. G. (1986). Perception of refusal assertion. *Behavior Modification, 10*(4), 472–486.

Williams, J. M., & Hall, D. W. (1988). Conformity to peer influence: The impact of assertion training on college students. *Journal of College Student Development, 29,* 466–471.

Wolpe, J. (1990). *The practice of behavior therapy.* New York: Pergamon.

Wolpe, J. (1958). *Psychotherapy by reciprocal inhibition.* Stanford, CA: University Press.

Wolpe, J., & Lazarus, A. A. (1966). *Behavior therapy techniques: A guide to the treatment of neuroses.* New York: Pergamon.

Wood, P., & Mallinckrodt, B. (1990). Culturally sensitive assertiveness training for ethnic minority clients. *Professional Psychology: Research and Practice, 21,* 5–11.

Woolfolk, R. L., & Denver, S. (1979). Perceptions of assertion: An empirical analysis. *Behavior Therapy, 10,* 404–411.

10

Journal Writing

Jan Youga

Journal writing as a strategy in psychotherapy encourages clients to keep a record of their personal thoughts, whether these be past experiences, current emotional states, or plans for the future. The entries then become a tool for self-discovery, understanding, and healing. Over time, the material can be reread, analyzed, reflected on, evaluated, or simply acknowledged and affirmed as an accurate reflection of self.

THE HISTORY OF JOURNAL WRITING

Throughout history, the existence of journals has indicated that someone recognized that the events being experienced in that specific time and place were, in some way, significant and worth noting. At first, the significance of the events was determined by their importance to the community in which the recorder lived. The earliest known journals were written by the Chinese in the first century A.D. and kept as historical documents (Lowenstein, 1987). This practice of journal writing as community record continued for centuries; thus, in 1620, we find William Bradford acknowledging the significance of the Mayflower landing by keeping a journal of the history of Plymouth settlement.

However, journals as a form of personal expression have a later history, beginning to appear during the Renaissance with the shift in philosophy that emphasized the importance of the individual over the community. Pepys' *Diary* (1660–69) serves as the most famous example from this period. His journal contained the official news on the "condition of the State," his "private condition," which was "esteemed rich, but indeed very poor," and current inventions, such as "engines to draw up water, with which sight I was very much pleased" (Pepys, 1967). He also included the gossip of the day concerning his own, as well as others', lives.

A more intimate form of personal journal writing began in the next century in France during the Revolution. The "Journal Intime" was "intense, self-preoccupied, confessional, passionate writing" (Lowenstein, 1987). George Sand's diary, a highly emotional account of her life that she wrote for publication is an example of the remarkable lack of inhibition promoted by this new form, and this freedom of expression seemed to open the floodgates, as it were, so that, in the nineteenth and twentieth centuries, numerous diaries, journals, and notebooks were published in Europe and the United States.

In the past several decades, journal writing has received considerable attention from women historians. Women's voices in literary traditions have been notoriously silent. So, when literary avenues were closed to women by the male-dominated publishing world or public writing was forbidden by husbands or guardians, many women turned to journal writing to record their experiences. The privacy of the form, the freedom of expression it allows, and the value it places on the individual's point of view have made journals a valuable tool for women to find their voices and affirm alternative (nonlinear, subjective) ways of understanding the world.

USES IN PSYCHOTHERAPY

Recently, journal writing also has received attention from psychotherapists as a supplemental tool to therapy. Historically, journal writing often began as a response to some outside force — environmental changes such as imprisonment or travel, moments of political or social crisis when the writer recognized the meshing of her or his personal life with momentous political events (*The Diary of Anne Frank*, for example), or at times of personal crisis (as in Vita Sackville-West's memoir of her love affair with Violet Keppel Trefusis). In other words, journals have been used throughout history as a kind of personal therapy — to cope with change, to vent frustrations or guilt, to try to make sense of a chaotic world.

It is not surprising, then, that therapists would come to see journals as a way of enhancing therapy, because the work accomplished in a journal can directly parallel the work of a therapy session. For the past 25 years, researchers have been suggesting journal writing as an effective strategy to use with certain clients or for particular disorders. Uses vary, but all proponents of the technique recognize the historical lessons: that journals allow the writer to work through the significance of external and internal events, that they are a means of self-expression, and that they can help the client to make sense out of a chaotic or fragmented world.

For therapists such as Ira Progoff, a pioneer in the use of journals to enhance psychotherapy, these historical lessons translate into specific forms of journal entries: personal history recorded in a daily log; conversations with people, events, or society; and the recording of dreams. As the title of one of his books, *The Well and the Cathedral* (1977), suggests and as Progoff discusses in his book *At a Journal Workshop* (1992), the client is like a well connected to "an underground stream," the collective unconscious, as it were. The purpose of the journals is to tap into that stream as a source of connectedness through time to other human beings, to achieve a wisdom that is "transpersonal." The client then can draw on this well of strength to rise, like a cathedral, above the surface of the mundane, disturbing, or chaotic events of the personal life. Progoff's method focuses on enhancing personal growth through a feeling of connectedness and through "qualities of poetry and spirit." Although the language he uses to explain his method is highly imaginative and figurative, the actual journal assignments are intensely structured and rigorous, a regimen he claims achieves the goal of greater self-awareness.

In addition to the general goals of personal growth and self-discovery, journals also have been used to give structure to the more specific task of problem solving or task completion. For example, in solution focused therapy (Nunnally & Lipchik, 1989), journals were used to focus the client's attention on the problem, heighten the dramatic impact of the problem and the change the solution might bring, clarify directives, and send messages to absent family members. In task oriented therapy (Quinn, 1987), journals have been used to monitor progress in taking responsibility for work to be done and completion of the task. The goal here is to enhance the client's performance of a task or progress toward a desired behavior.

Journals also have been used as an aid to monitoring adjustment during key times in the therapeutic process, particularly during the opening assessment, during times of evaluation, and at termination (Kelley & Williams, 1988). If successful, the termination journal essentially steps in to fill the role of the therapist as the client's tool for working through future difficulties. Clients learn to mimic in their journals the questioning, probing, and problem solving of therapy sessions, thus, increasing their ability and confidence to work through problems and to continue personal growth on their own.

Finally, journals have been used with specific disorders: to cure insomnia (Kupych-Woloshyn, MacFarlane, & Shapiro, 1993), posttraumatic headaches (Hickling, Blanchard, Schwarz, & Silverman, 1992), anxiety (Marks, 1991), panic attacks (Beitman, Basha, & Trombka, 1987), depression (L'Abate, 1991), sexual abuse (deLuca, Boyes, Furer, Grayston, & Hiebert-Murphy, 1992), and eating disorders (Zimmerman & Shepherd, 1993; Rabinor, 1991). In addition, journals have been used as part of couples, family, and group therapy in which the individual client's writings become the basis for group discussions (Zimmerman & Shepherd, 1993; Quinn, 1987). Sometimes, journals have specific limitations or formats, as when clients record only their dreams (Freeman & Boyll, 1992) or do guided letter writing (Rasmussen & Tomm, 1992).

In all of these cases, the journal becomes a tool for recording the client's mind at work with the intention of using the entries to promote further growth and progress in therapy.

APPROPRIATE CLIENTS

Although journals may be beneficial in all of these areas, from Progoff's general claim of increased self-awareness to the work done with specific disorders, the effectiveness of the journal as a technique is dependent on the ability of the client to use it. Unlike other more therapist-directed activities, journals rely on the independent work of the client. Even in interactive journals, something must be written before the therapist can respond and begin the interaction.

In addition, the quality of the content needs to be such that the exercise is worthwhile. This is not to say that the journal must be well-written; in fact, the therapist should make it clear that the quality of the writing is irrelevant, that this should be a freeing activity of self-expression. However, the purpose of the journal is to capture the client's thoughts and feelings, and those expressions of self must be coherent and relevant enough to further the therapy. Although writing that reveals the client's inability to be coherent and relevant may prove to be a valuable diagnostic tool for the therapist, if the client cannot move beyond this, some other intervention technique might prove more helpful.

In other words, journaling is a linguistic activity; it demands that the client translate emotions, thoughts, and experiences into words. The more natural an activity this cognitive process is for the client, the more valuable this technique will be and the more self-directed and creative the client will be in using it. If journaling is a struggle for the client because of worrying about what and how to write and if sessions around journals become a constant plea for more direction, the freeing nature of this activity will be lost and, perhaps, even replaced by feelings of guilt or obligation.

In addition to possessing an ease in writing, the best clients for this activity are those who are already somewhat reflective. For such people, "thinking on paper," with the accompanying analysis, evaluation, and insights that are part of that process, will come easily. These thoughts then will naturally lead to material for discussion in sessions and faster progress, because a good deal of the processing of insights gained in therapy will be accomplished by the client outside of therapy.

Although not an essential quality, journaling also is aided by the intellectual or creative ability of the client. Interpreting dreams, recreating experiences so as to capture their emotional impact, logically working through problems and trying out solutions, gaining access to one's emotional state, writing letters to relatives, and monitoring emotional or behavioral progress all take a certain level of intellectual and emotional engagement as well as, in some cases, imaginative ability. Journaling may demand a level of mental gymnastics that many clients would find daunting.

Finally, the client must have a certain grasp on reality and be able to distinguish the interpretation of events from the events themselves and imaginative exercises from daily experience. Journaling also requires that the client be able to focus on the writing activity long enough and with enough concentration so as to complete the task in a productive way.

Although these verbal, intellectual, and reflective skills aid in journal keeping, even clients who are not predisposed to journaling still may find more carefully defined writing tasks helpful and may even find journaling a way to develop their self-awareness and reflective abilities. Therapists can tie writing tasks to general or specific therapeutic goals. For example, a client who needs to work on feeling empathy for others and is in the process of resolving a conflict with a specific person may be given the writing task of speculating on how the conflict appears to the other party so as to both increase the client's empathy and work on conflict resolution. The therapist also may suggest journal assignments that do not demand imagination or self-direction. For example, a therapist may suggest using a journal that is focused on listing or on monitoring one specific activity. The journal, then, is used as a form of directed record keeping.

CAUTIONS

Writer Gene Fowler (1992) said, "There's nothing to writing. All you do is stare at a blank sheet of paper until drops of blood form on your forehead." Although journal writing can be a safe, freeing experience, even if painful memories are revisited, it assumes that the act of writing itself is not painful and stress-producing for the client. For people who write well and easily, the idea that writing might be painful can be difficult to understand, but "writing anxiety" (Daly & Miller, 1975), as it is called, can be a paralyzing fear.

For some people the act of committing self to paper is the equivalent of sweating blood. The basic caution, then, in suggesting this strategy is to be certain that the writing itself will not hamper, rather than enhance, the client's ability to think and process. In cases of serious writing anxiety, encouragements such as "No one will see this" or "It doesn't matter if the writing is any good" do not help. Once something is written, there is always the danger of someone else finding it (and a therapist cannot keep that from happening), and the lack of quality is often the very aspect of writing that disturbs anxious writers the most. Studies in writing anxiety also have shown that some of the worst cases may be found among clients who seem the most likely to enjoy and benefit from journaling and who do not exhibit the characteristics associated with apprehension, such as a lack of confidence in self-expression (Daly, 1979). Hopper (1988) suggests that anxious writers may be highly verbal individuals whose competence simply breaks down when the writing is personal and will be shared.

The concrete nature of the written word also can make it a threatening strategy for someone in a particularly fragile state. Putting something into words often makes events and emotions seem more real. Writing creates a document that says, "This is my life. This really happened to me." When these experiences are being discussed with a therapist, support is readily available, but when clients are journaling between sessions, they may find themselves facing the reality of a trauma alone. Some clients, especially those who happen to be good writers, may be very skilled at recreating past events, imagining conversations with people who have played significant roles in their lives, or capturing the pain of their present state. When going through this emotional white water for the first time, clients may need a guide so as not to wreck upon the rocks. Private journaling offers no such guidance. Therapists, therefore, need to anticipate the effects that journaling may have on a client and be prepared to offer help in the form of careful instructions, cautions, or even telephone contact if this activity becomes a source of pain.

Although physical handicaps to writing often can be overcome with sophisticated computers, for many people, the act of writing, no matter what equipment may be available, is still a laborious task. Whether this is because of poor writing training in school or a lack of verbal processing skills, writing is not an aid but a hindrance to thinking. Watching clients' labored efforts to construct sentences and seeing them worrying over mechanics, expression, or even penmanship will quickly dispel the notion that this method will help them to think more clearly or sort through experiences. The energy that should be focused on thinking is, instead, exerted on writing as a physical — and strenuous — exercise, which, when shared, is often punctuated by exasperated questions such as, "Can't I just talk to you about this?"

For some clients, then, journaling will prove a natural, beneficial activity that complements their own ways of processing and perhaps even builds on their linguistic strength and writing talent. For others, the activity will have more limited value but still may help them work through specific tasks. However, there will be times when the benefits of this strategy will not outweigh the effort it would take to use it, and in some cases, this method actually may prove harmful to clients. Therapists, therefore, need to use caution in suggesting it and be prepared to offer help and guidance in its use.

APPROACHES TO JOURNAL WRITING

Once it is determined that the client could benefit from journal keeping, there are two basic approaches the therapist can take: the private journal and the interactive or dialogue journal.

Private journals may begin without the intervention or, even, the knowledge of the therapist if the client is someone who naturally uses writing to process. In dealing with a highly verbal client, the therapist simply may discover at some point in the therapy that this tool has become a part of the client's personal way of remembering what has transpired and preparing for the next session. Clients accustomed to preparing for business or committee meetings, for example, may carry this skill into their therapy. Therapists also may discover that they have inadvertently initiated journaling; a simple suggestion, such as, "Keep track this week of . . ." or "Try to remember . . . ," may be interpreted as an invitation or even a command to "write down" these thoughts. However it starts, once the client is using journals, the therapist simply can tap into this ongoing process by suggesting "homework" for the client or using what the client has written about as a starting point for a session. Therapists also may find that if the client is using this technique effectively, no intervention is needed at all.

End of session suggestions for monitoring thoughts before the next meeting can easily become an actual request for the client to try journaling. Clients may also provide this opportunity by expressing difficulty remembering all that has happened since the last session, expressing a need to work things out, or feeling a desire to imagine options or outcomes.

Although most clients would have some sense of what journals are and how to use them, therapists should be prepared for some very practical questions about "how to." Although there is no right answer, the therapist can help the client by simply acknowledging that there are decisions to make and that those decisions can be significant. For example, the personal choice about how and where the journal is kept may be influenced by the privacy of the client's home environment; computer disks may not be a traditional journal medium, but the use of code words to access a file and the ease with which they can be concealed may make them ideal.

The therapist also should be prepared for the simple question, "What do I write?" Although "Anything you want" may seem like an answer that would create the least anxiety, it also may present an overwhelming set of options with no safe boundaries. Because the idea of journals most likely will come from something in therapy that could benefit from written reflection, therapists can start with a suggestion that will meet that need. If journaling proves beneficial to the client, further instructions probably will not be necessary. If they are, the therapist can suggest one or several "assignments" about which the client might write, based on what transpired during the session. General instructions such as "keep track of" or "try to remember" or "respond to" are good places to start.

Private journals are intended for the client's eyes alone. If this is the ground rule on which the journal is established, the therapist needs to respect this and not request to see the writing. If the client offers a particular entry to the therapist, a suggestion to have the client read it aloud might be better than to have the journal be in the hands of someone else. If the client repeats the request to share what is written, then the nature of the journal has changed, and the therapist might suggest that the writing become a dialogue journal.

Dialogue journals are a more direct way of continuing the conversations of therapy between sessions. In this technique, the client is writing directly to the therapist or with the understanding that the therapist will read the journal and respond to it. How often and how much of the journal is exchanged, as well as the medium of response, varies according to what is judged best for the client. For example, if the client is working on a specific task, she or he may be responding directly to "prompts" or exercises from the therapist, and the next session will be spent discussing the recorded progress. If the journal is less controlled, the client may be encouraged to use entries to explore various areas of concern and to share in session the one entry that seems to need the most attention.

The dialogue also may take place in writing, with the client actually turning over the journal to the therapist, who responds with written comments and questions. This can be a tangible way of taking the helpful "voice" of the therapist home and continuing therapy outside the sessions, and the progress that might be made through this exchange should not be underestimated. However, there are drawbacks to written comments. First, they are time consuming, because they must be legible, thoughtful, and unambiguous; they should not create more problems than they help to solve. The therapist would have to develop the proper voice and style to use in making such comments and learn to adjust them for each client's needs. Second, most people have a desire to keep their journals in some form of a notebook. When this notebook is in the hands of the therapist, the client's journaling stops. Although two journals may be kept, of course, one of the most valuable aspects of the dialogue journal is the therapist's ability to reread the dialogue, noting such things as progress, recurring ideas and images, unanswered questions, and shifts in tone or concerns, all of which are more difficult to spot if the line of the exchange is interrupted.

The "public" nature of dialogue journals may make them less revealing; writing always becomes more self-conscious when it has an audience. The trade-off is that the therapist will gain an opportunity for monitoring progress and identifying issues. Examining both what the client chooses to write about and how those ideas are expressed will always provide clues to the thought processes and priorities of the writer. Through questions, comments, and personal responses, the client's thoughts can be probed, evaluated, questioned, affirmed, and shared. For some clients, having an audience will give their writing more purpose.

POTENTIAL BENEFITS

Numerous benefits have been cited both by researchers and by journal users seeking help for a wide variety of problems.

Controlling the Chaos

Writing is a form of order. Random, sporadic thoughts can be put into recognizable and meaningful symbols ready to be examined and interpreted. Even if it is only to discover their incoherence, reflecting on written words has the power to reveal meaning. When the words are not random but actually capture some experience or thought, the writing may make the idea seem more manageable. When the problem can be explained, the event can be recorded, the fear can be named, it can seem less threatening.

In addition, writing has the power to objectify the thought or externalize the experience so that the client can gain some perspective on it. The cognitive process of putting events into words rather than directly feeling them creates some distance. The emotion becomes something that can be examined, even revised for accuracy, and this analytical process can create a safe space for reflection.

Taking Action

Writing is an activity, something that involves willful and deliberate action. For clients who are unable to act in some arena of their lives, writing can be a substitute for or a practice session in acting. By imagining and creating worst-case scenarios, planning and trying out strategies, envisioning themselves taking the necessary steps toward recovery through the act of taking up a pen and making these events happen on paper, clients may gain the confidence to carry these actions through into their lives.

Continuing Therapy

Most therapy is limited by time constraints, but the client's life, discoveries, flashbacks, and questions are not. The journal provides an outlet for these thoughts and allows the client to capture them as they occur, with all the depth of emotion and the clarity of insight that accompany them. These entries then may be shared in the way they were experienced with the additional insight that may have occurred since.

Also, when eye contact or the therapist's presence increases the client's difficulty in speaking about certain events or personal revelations, the journal creates a safer space in which to speak. Journals also can be a place to work out difficulties with the therapist and keep communication lines open so that productive counseling can continue. They can serve as a place to discuss the therapy itself and the client/therapist relationship and to make requests for change in a nonconfrontational way. Of course, if this use of the journal were to become a pattern or continue for a long period of time, it would probably signal a need for some change in the therapist/client interaction. The therapist would need to discover why the client was feeling uncomfortable or a lack of trust and address this issue directly. Occasionally, however, the journal may provide a safe place to approach a difficult topic.

Taking Control

Because the therapist is the one in a position of power and the one to whom the client is looking for help, if not answers and solutions, the client can easily become passive, relying on the therapist to determine direction, ask questions, and probe for significance. While designing an appropriate plan is the job of the therapist, fostering submission and dependency is not. Encouraging clients to ask questions and to probe on their own will help them to take control of their own healing as well as giving them the tools to monitor their healing process throughout their lives. Journals can serve as a practice place for developing these tools.

Increasing Self-esteem

As mentioned earlier, historically, women often used journals because their more public voices were silenced. The journal became not only an outlet for their thoughts but also a way of validating their ideas and themselves as people. When self-esteem is low, one's own voice is often lost, as if nothing the client could say would be worth listening to. Journals can be a valuable tool for affirming the worth of clients and encouraging them to value their own ideas and to give voice to their concerns.

Working through the Past

Because some therapy involves resurrecting and then exorcising demons from the past, creative journals can be a valuable aid in this process. Clients can be encouraged to describe an event from the different points of view of the people involved, actually taking on their voices, and recreating conversations. They can rewrite experiences in a way that expresses what they wish had happened or what they wish they had said. They can write letters, realistic obituaries, birth announcements for aborted children, or prayers and meditations. This kind of creative activity can be very freeing, especially when the client is hampered by guilt or someone else's interpretation of reality.

Bridge to Termination

Using journals to help clients develop their own tools for healing can be the perfect bridge to terminating therapy. Journals provide written proof of the client's progress, strengths, weaknesses, and strategies for coping. Past struggles and successes as well as the therapist's advice are all contained in one place and available for future reference. Past recordings, then, become reminders of what was accomplished and learned during therapy, and the habit of using the journal becomes a method of conscious healing.

RESEARCH

Proving the effectiveness of journals in producing change is very difficult because of the variety of ways in which journals can be used, from the very personal re-creation of a past event to the very objective recording of task completion. In addition, the particular constraints the strategy imposes simply because it involves writing and because of the differences among clients, counselors, and their interactions further complicate the research questions. Still, despite the variability of the research and issues about methodology, there is some evidence for the effectiveness of journal writing as a strategy in therapy.

Using five case studies of schizoid disordered patients who were unable to maintain verbal interaction with their therapists, Oberkirch (1983) found that patients could continue therapy in written form. They were successful in writing their secrets, sharing this writing with their therapists, and reacting to their therapists' responses. The process not only strengthened the therapeutic relationship but also allowed for therapeutic progress to be made.

In a correlation quasi-experimental study on the effectiveness of journaling, Pennebaker and Beall (1986) worked with four groups, three assigned to three treatment conditions and one serving as a control group. The study used heart rate, blood pressure, a self report, and the number of visits to health and counseling centers as its measures. The findings revealed that through writing about traumatic events, the subjects showed statistically significant improvement in physiological reactions and a long-term decrease in health problems. Similarly, when college students wrote about their thoughts and feelings in transitioning into the college environment, their visits to health care facilities significantly decreased when compared with a control group (Pennebaker, 1990).

In addition to empirical research in this area, the effectiveness of journal writing has been cited by therapists drawing on their clinical experience and by clients who have found it a helpful technique. Their unequivocal endorsement of journal writing as a tool for exploration, discovery, clarification, growth, and resolving issues is powerful. Although one must bear in mind that only the advocates are apt to sing the praises of the strategy, rather than negating its worth, this advocacy might be interpreted as a clear signal of the technique's usefulness for certain clients in certain situations.

Furthermore, as was noted at the beginning of this chapter, journal writing has a long history, testifying to its endurance as a creative tool for processing, coping, and growing. Recording and analyzing one's experience, including wonderings, yearnings, and turmoils, have been a part of human history and central to the experience of many individuals for centuries — a compelling indication of journaling's reliability and validity for many. Finally, there is the intuitive fit between some clients and this particular strategy that attests to its effectiveness as a therapeutic device.

More empirical research in journaling is needed with additional populations, covering a wider range of questions and using different measures. Concerns such as which clients would find it most helpful, at what points in therapy, and with which experiences need to be addressed. In addition, research is needed to determine under what circumstances journaling might prove useless or even harmful. However, given its history, its endorsement by clients and therapists, and the initial studies in this area, there is sound support for journaling as an effective therapy strategy for some clients.

REFERENCES

Beitman, B. D., Basha, I. M., & Trombka, L. H. (1987). Panic attacks and their treatment: An introduction. *Journal of Integrative and Eclectic Psychotherapy*,

6(4), 412–420.

Daly, J. A. (1979). Writing apprehension in the classroom: Teacher role expectancies of the apprehensive writer. *Research in the Teaching of English, 13*, 37–44.

Daly, J. A., & Miller, M. D. (1975). Apprehension of writing as a predictor of message intensity. *Journal of Psychology, 89*, 175–177.

deLuca, R. V., Boyes, D. A., Furer, P., Grayston, A. D., & Hiebert-Murphy, D. (1992). Group treatment for child sexual abuse. *Canadian Psychology, 33*(2), 168–179.

Fowler, G. (1992). In J. Kaplan (Ed.), *Bartlett's familiar quotations* (p. 678.19). Boston: Little, Brown.

Freeman, A., & Boyll, S. (1992). The use of dreams and the dream metaphor in cognitive-behavior therapy. *Psychotherapy in Independent Practice: Current Issues for Clinicians, 10*(1–2), 173–192.

Hickling, E. J., Blanchard, E. B., Schwarz, S. P., & Silverman, D. J. (1992). Headaches and motor vehicle accidents: Results of the psychological treatment of post-traumatic headache. *Headache Quarterly, 3*(3), 285–289.

Hopper, V. (1988). *Apprehensive student writers: Are they all avoiders?* Master's thesis, Illinois State University.

Kelley, P., & Williams, B. (1988). The use of assigned writings as an adjunct to therapy with individuals, couples, and families. *Journal of Independent Social Work, 3*(1), 23–38.

Kupych-Woloshyn, N., MacFarlane, J. G., & Shapiro, C. M. (1993). A group approach for the management of insomnia. *Journal of Psychosomatic Research, 37*(Suppl. 1), 39–44.

L'Abate, L. (1991). The use of writing in psychotherapy. *American Journal of Psychotherapy, 45*(1), 87–98.

Lowenstein, S. (1987). A brief history of journal keeping. In T. Fulwiler (Ed.), *The journal book* (pp. 87–97). Portsmouth, NH: Boynton/Cook.

Marks, I. (1991). Self-administered behavioural treatment. *Behavioural Psychotherapy, 19*(1), 42–46.

Nunnally, E., & Lipchik, E. (1989). Some uses of writing in solution focused brief therapy. *Journal of Independent Social Work, 4*(2), 5–19.

Oberkirch, A. (1983). Personal writing in psychotherapy. *American Journal of Psychotherapy, 37*(2), 265–273.

Pennebaker, J. W. (1990). *Opening up.* New York: William Morrow.

Pennebaker, J. W., & Beall, S. K. (1986). Confronting a traumatic event: Toward an understanding of inhibition and disease. *Journal of Abnormal Psychology, 95*(3), 274–281.

Pepys, S. (1967). The diary. In G. K. Anderson & W. E. Buckler (Eds.), *The literature of England* (pp. 443–452). Glenview, IL: Scott, Foresman.

Progoff, I. (1992). *At a journal workshop.* Los Angeles, CA: Jeremy P. Teacher.

Progoff, I. (1977). *The well and the cathedral.* New York: Dialogue House.

Quinn, W. H. (1987). Written language as a context of therapeutic change. *Journal of Strategic and Systemic Therapies, 6*(2), 57–66.

Rabinor, J. R. (1991). The process of recovery from an eating disorder: The use of journal writing in the initial phase of treatment. *Psychotherapy in Private Practice, 9*(1), 93–106.

Rasmussen, P. T., & Tomm, K. (1992). Guided letter writing: A long brief therapy method whereby clients carry out their own treatment. *Journal of Strategic and Systemic Therapies, 11*(4), 1–18.

Zimmerman, T., & Shepherd, S. D. (1993). Externalizing the problem of bulimia: Conversation, drawing and letter writing in group therapy. *Journal of Systemic Therapies, 12*(1), 22–31.

11

Divorce Mediation

Mary Ballou

Divorce often is an emotionally turbulent time as each spouse experiences anger, resentment, and, possibly, the remnants of love and tenderness. It also affects each partner differently, for example, Sibbison (1988) found that the post divorce parent with custody (mostly women) had a 73 percent decrease in their standard of living, while the other parent (mostly men) had a 42 percent increase. Many separating couples would like to avoid the destructive, competitive battles and unequal outcomes that often occur in the adversarial divorce process. Traditionally, they have lacked an alternative that personalized the legal dissolution of their marriage. Divorce mediation has evolved as just such an alternative. An approach aimed at the resolution of financial and emotional concerns, divorce mediation stresses rational cooperation in the hope of minimizing conflict. It is a useful intervention tool because energy is focused on solving the practical problems normally related to the termination of marriage. Such a cooperative method discourages the destructive and nonproductive thinking typical in adversarial divorces (Shapiro & Caplan, 1983).

Divorce mediation is a form of conflict resolution in which an impartial third party (or parties) works with the two disputing partners in order to identify, discuss, and ultimately resolve the dispute (Emery & Wyer, 1987). The two traditional means of reaching divorce settlements, litigation and negotiation between the parties' lawyers, differ from divorce mediation in several important ways. Mediation is based on an assumption of cooperation rather than competition. The communication in mediation takes place between the separating couple and an impartial party (or parties), not between lawyers advocating each of their clients' rights, views, and so on. In mediation, the separating couple sets their own goals and makes their own decisions about their personal settlement (Emery & Wyer, 1987). This differs greatly from the past, when divorce was a battle to be won by the best attorney, working to gain the most for his or her client in the areas of finances and custody (Emery & Wyer, 1987).

BACKGROUND

Divorce mediation is a process of direct negotiations between spouses at the termination of a marriage (Shapiro & Caplan, 1983). It is through this process that a couple develops a written agreement that addresses division of property, financial considerations, child custody, and spousal and child support. The intent is to provide the couple with objective guidance through a structured problem-solving process. Mediation focuses on resolving future oriented issues, as opposed to divorce counseling, where therapy is intended to resolve past conflicts.

The goal of divorce mediation is to reach a mutually acceptable marital settlement agreement. All issues involved in the dissolution of the marriage are negotiated in good faith. Therefore, it is essential that each spouse share all pertinent information. During the mediation sessions, the mediator(s) assists the husband and wife in forming the agreement. It is the job of the mediator to facilitate an agreement that is as fair as possible to all involved. In this process, the mediator is able to address individual and interpersonal difficulties, but the formation of a fair agreement remains the primary goal (Emery & Wyer, 1987).

In order to form a fair agreement, all parties must understand the difference between arbitration and mediation. In mediation, the decision-making power is shared by the two parties, while in arbitration, that power lies solely in the hand of the arbitrator (Friedman, 1993). To share this power, each spouse must work from a sense of fairness and openness. They cannot, and should not, expect the mediator to tell them what is fair or to tell them what to do. The goal of mediation, unlike arbitration, is not to merely settle a dispute; rather, it is to settle matters between the parties in such a way that each participates in finding and agreeing to the solutions.

Professionals from both the legal and the mental health fields have been seeking a way to alleviate some of the pain and pressure involved in traditional divorce. Mediation is a valid solution, but there is disagreement as to who should mediate. Does mediation belong in the domain of attorneys or of mental health professionals? Originally, friction between these two groups centered around whether or not mediation should exist. Now the main focus has become which profession should provide the service. It has been argued that mediators from the mental health field are unskilled in financial and legal matters and verge on engaging in the unauthorized practice of law. The argument against attorneys who mediate is that they are untrained in the psychology of divorce (Emery & Wyer, 1987). Regardless of the arguments, both professions are acting as mediators and are legally free to do so.

Both legal and mental health professionals need to see the similarities in their professions and to realize that divorce mediation is an equal opportunity area for both. Mediation is a skill available to the mental health professional knowledgeable in the law. It is also a skill available to the matrimonial lawyer knowledgeable in interviewing and counseling skills. Each profession is only as useful as their clients allow them to be, and each requires an understanding of the other's profession in order to function properly (Steinberg, 1985).

An alternative to choosing either an attorney mediator or a therapist mediator is having a lawyer-therapist team. Divorcing couples who wish to use mediation to settle their disputes can hire an interdisciplinary team. The lawyer can handle the legal matters, while the therapist can tune into the emotional aspects. Together, they help the process toward settlement move more smoothly and freely (Mosten & Biggs, 1985). For purposes of discussion in this chapter, the singular term "mediator" is used. However, the team of lawyer and mental health professional may be implied in all uses.

Although the mediated agreement is not a legal document until it has been reviewed and accepted by the courts, it remains a faster and more cost-effective process than adversarial divorces handled by attorneys. Research indicates that couples comply more with their self-created agreements. Also, these couples are more open to mediating future disagreements or changes of circumstances (Folberg & Milne, 1988).

In its usual presentation, divorce mediation applies only to heterosexual relationships under legal contract. Mediation as presented through the description of divorce mediation is, however, a strategy appropriate for dispute resolution for many kinds of relationships and types of conflicts. Some of these include homosexual unions, familial arrangements (such as siblings owning property together), and extended family responsibilities (such as grandparents raising grandchildren). Laws may exist governing property and custody of minors, but the significance of what people mean to one another and how they have functioned in these relationships (in other words, the social and emotional aspects) are left without attention if merely legal avenues are pursued. Seeking a nonadversarial, cooperative, and fair resolution to disputes is needed in many forms of interpersonal relationships. The mediation process, if not the legal precedent, described in this chapter applies to them as well.

DESCRIPTION

Folberg and Milne (1988) define a mediator as someone who "should protect the objectivity of their role and strive to provide information in a way that allows the parties to make informed agreements, but does not bias the decision-making process or negate the autonomy and traditions of the family" (p. 390). His or her role is to guide the couple through the negotiation process in order to find viable, mutually agreed upon solutions. The mediator does not make decisions for the couple. Indeed, "The principle behind mediation rests on the parties making the decisions for themselves" (Friedman, 1993, p. 147). The mediator facilitates the decision making of the two individuals. He or she does not impose his or her own ideas on the process or resulting agreement.

The mediator is a neutral third party who attempts to balance the negotiating process by establishing and enforcing rules that direct the couple toward an amicable and fair solution. The mediator uses a conceptual framework made up of four basic building blocks aimed at creating an atmosphere of emotional safety (Erickson & McKnight Erickson, 1988). First, the communication dialogue must be open and honest, free of blame and faultfinding and also free from disparaging remarks. From the initial session, the couple is guided to communicate in an assertive, affirmative manner without coercive statements. The mediator minimizes negative remarks by redefining the issues in such a way that the couple must work together and mutually resolve the problems. The couple is also instructed to focus on the future and not the past, helping them to rechannel negative emotions into a more creative direction. If these prerequisite communication patterns cannot be achieved, mediation is not possible.

Second, cooperative resolutions must be developed on a foundation of trust and mutuality. However difficult this may be, it is mandatory that trust be created and maintained throughout the process. Mediators frequently attempt to help rebuild trust by having the couple resolve minor conflicts and by including all the issues that either spouse experiences as part of the mediation agenda. This would include such issues as unpaid labor in service of family maintenance and refusal to engage emotionally within the marital relationship. Such issues usually are not considered in divorce settlements of property, income, and custody. Naming these issues as part of the proposed mediation is important for trust building and for the thoroughness of the mediation process.

Homework assignments between sessions can be a tool instrumental to this rebuilding process, and progress then can be seen at each session. By encouraging mutuality and not individualistic attitudes, the mediator encourages the couple to attack their problems, rather than one another.

Third, the mediator influences the couple to practice productive bargaining procedures. He or she directs the couple away from positional and toward more cooperative bargaining. Erickson and McKnight Erickson (1988) state that "Couples do not understand that once they take a position they have locked themselves into achieving their interest through one, and only one, mechanism. Unfortunately, the mechanism they have chosen allows for only one side's interest to be met, usually to the detriment of both" (p. 19). The mediation process stresses the construction of a standard of fairness that is acceptable to both parties. This standard helps the couple to create options that benefit both of them rather than only one individual.

The fourth building block is evaluation of the couple's long-term goals. The mediator must look after the interests and needs of both parties. This is demonstrated by his or her emphasis on compromise. As all three parties (mediator and two spouses) evaluate the alternatives for the final agreement, the couple is helped to find a middle ground that will satisfy each of their long-term goals.

The actual process of mediation is a set of stages that has specific goals, tasks, and skills that must be completed before the conclusion of mediation. The mediator's role, functions, and responsibilities change with each stage. Introduction, the first stage, establishes rapport with the couple and develops structure and trust. The mediator seeks relevant information about conflicts, goals, and expectations. Specific topics addressed are motivation to use mediation, background of events leading up to the conflict, the couple's interactions and communication, and the couple's emotional state (Folberg & Milne, 1988). During this stage, most communication flows through the mediator, who reframes the statements in a more neutral voice. Participants move to the next stage only after obvious and subtle issues are brought to light.

The second stage is one of fact finding and isolation of issues. The mediator helps the couple decide where conflict lies and which issues need to be resolved. The mediator then summarizes, prioritizes, reflects, and clarifies these issues. The mediator's definition of issues and their inclusion into the mediation agenda must be inclusive of both parties and, at times, instructive. Couples do not always have the language or conceptual clarity to frame their felt issues. Mediators should walk a careful line between instruction to explore and pushing the mediator's own interpretation. Yet, subtle issues of power, control, and social organization and the way they are played out in the relationship and decision making must be explored. Intrapersonal and interpersonal dimensions are identified for both individuals and are confirmed on an individual or collective basis. Stage two ends when the mediator fully understands the marital conflicts as well as what each person wants and will accept. This stage usually takes several sessions to complete.

The third stage is the creation of options and alternatives. The mediator helps the couple invent realistic and workable options. This is the most creative and active stage of mediation, when ideas are exchanged and developed. Once alternatives are derived, mediation proceeds to the fourth stage: full exploration of the derived options.

This stage involves negotiating and making decisions about options. It stresses cooperative effort on the part of the couple to reach their final decisions. It includes as many of the identified issues as possible, even those that fall outside the usual legal areas. For example, parenting styles and methods of discipline might be a mediated issue. The mediator changes his or her activeness and, consequently, changes the communication pattern. The couple now speaks to one another, and equality of communication is stressed. The mediator encourages the couple to make their decisions using a viewpoint that includes the best for both and that rests on equitable inclusion of dimensions and distribution of resources, debts, and any ongoing responsibilities. Before moving on to the next stage, the questions of whether all the decisions have been made and if they are inclusive and fairly fitting must be affirmed.

The fifth stage involves clarification of the couple's decisions and the writing of the agreement. All terms are clearly stated in the document. At this point, most participants seek verbal reassurance from the mediator that they have produced an agreement that satisfies both individual and collective needs. The signing of the agreement is quite symbolic, because it represents cooperation and closure.

In the sixth stage, the marital settlement agreement undergoes legal review. Often, each spouse submits it to his or her individual lawyer for checking. If the mediation has involved a lawyer, this may not be done if each spouse agrees. Finally, the agreement is submitted to the local court for review and acceptance. The seventh stage begins implementation of the agreement, with the couple trying to live within its terms. The mediator no longer plays a direct role, unless follow-up encouragement or renegotiation (because of changed circumstances) is needed.

APPROPRIATE AND INAPPROPRIATE USES

The willingness of the couple to mediate rather than use the adversarial process is key to knowing for whom mediation is most appropriate. There are several questions the mediator should consider prior to accepting a couple for mediation:

Do they want a divorce?
Do they have sufficiently equal abilities to negotiate for themselves?
Are they able to put aside (i.e., hold for other arenas) most of their anger and
    frustration so they can mediate together?
What is the couple's motivation to mediate?
What is their style of communicating?
Are they flexible?

Evaluation of answers to these will determine the couple's readiness to the mediator (Blades, 1985).

The fact that a couple chooses mediation does not necessarily mean that it is the best solution for them. In divorce disputes where a great imbalance of power exists or one spouse defines himself or herself only in terms of the relationship, mediation usually is impossible. Such an imbalance may happen if one spouse normally handles all decision making, including financial matters, while the other spouse normally accedes to this arrangement. A similar imbalance may occur if one party lacks the ability to go about his or her own life. For example, if one spouse is severely disabled and the other spouse provides most of the supportive care, separation and divorce so greatly change the disabled spouse's life that he or she may not be immediately ready to work toward a cooperative settlement of property and other issues. Another example is if a divorce would cause one spouse to lose essential benefits, such as health insurance. In all of these examples, mediation cannot work if both spouses cannot learn to assert their own needs and be part of making decisions. Other avenues for property and custody settlement should be considered.

In cases of spouse abuse and child abuse (or neglect), the police or the courts must be notified (by the mediator, other service providers, or offended party) before any thought can be given to mediation. Cessation of harm to the abused spouse or child must be agreed to by the offending party. The abuse issue must be dealt with by both spouses before mediation can begin or continue. Otherwise, the threat of coercion will negate the possibility of a fairly negotiated agreement.

If one spouse withholds information (e.g., about parenting intentions, relational conflicts, and, particularly, assets) from the other spouse and the mediator, then the process will not work. Any forthcoming agreement would not be based on full disclosure and, therefore, would not be binding either legally or morally. The betrayed spouse would still have recourse through the courts. Most importantly, however, the openness and fairness upon which the mediation is based would be violated. There simply would be no point for any of the parties, including the mediator, to engage in discussions based on lies or significant omissions. As previously stated, this intervention is about cooperation, not about winning. However, a mediator must be alert to this competitive/winning stance, because it is so much a part of our culture.

Other situations exist where mediation might not be the best answer. One is when there is severe psychopathology on the part of one or both of the divorcing partners; another is when there is low intelligence in one or both partners. In both situations, independent psychological judgments and legal determinations need to be made before mediation can begin (Emery & Wyer, 1987).

Divorce mediation involves a complicated array of skills and procedures. These are, however, already existent somewhat separately within the training of lawyers and mental health counselors. The point of view and set of goals from which mediators work is the dimension that is new to both professions. Therefore, lawyers and counselors need to not only work together and share in each others' skills but also hold in mind and guide their practice by a different set of values and assumptions. Clearly, for the complexity, for the interdisciplinary collaboration, and for the new value set, divorce mediation calls for further formal training.

RESEARCH ON EFFECTIVENESS

Divorce mediation is a relatively new intervention. Empirical evidence is limited, and available data are difficult to interpret because of many potential biases in self-report and sample selection. However, the data do suggest that couples who used mediation were satisfied with their agreements. Pearson and Thoennes (1988) found women did not differ from men in satisfaction with divorce mediation, especially in regard to division of property and child support and custody issues. Emery and

Wyer (1987) found in their study that parents thought that their divorce mediation had a positive effect on the children.

Folberg and Milne (1988) reviewed the outcome research published to date on divorce mediation. Two findings typical of the area follow. Pearson and Thoennes found in a longitudinal study in 1982 (Folberg & Milne, 1988) that couples 6 to 12 months after their final agreement thought mediation provided a positive outcome. These couples also reported cooperative relationships and satisfaction with the process of mediation.

Kelly, Gigy, and Hausman, in a comparison study, investigated the effectiveness of mediation as an intervention to reaching divorce agreement (Folberg & Milne, 1988). In contrasting mediated and adversarial agreements, the researchers found little variation in satisfaction with both methods of divorce settlement. The respondents' perceptions of their spouses, however, were one of the few differences that did exist. Those people who participated in mediation seemed to view their spouse ultimately as more honest and fair-minded. Overall, the findings suggest that mediation has the ability to affect the quality and future of the spousal relationship.

Initial research data are encouraging, but caution should be used when assessing the available research. Follow-up assessments were often within six months of the couple's settlement and, therefore, may have been too early to measure the levels of satisfaction accurately. In addition, data were gathered through the self-reporting measure, which may have resulted in biased findings. As with many applied strategies, research is to do. The subjectivity of the process stands against objective measurement. Each divorcing couple has individual conflicts and issues that require unique negotiating methodologies. Though the goal for each mediating couple generally is similar, the postmediation relationship may determine the success of the agreement. With these applied realities in mind, further research may wish to concentrate on the influence of the mediator as well as the techniques employed during the negotiating process. Pearson and Thoennes (1988) report initial findings confirming these variables. Additionally, rather than just self-reports of outcome, evaluation would be enhanced by comparative studies using matched pairs of divorcing couples under mediated and adversarial legal process and rated by judges and forensic psychologists.

CONCLUSION

Given that about 50 percent of marriages end in divorce, and because of the upset for all involved, divorce mediation holds tremendous promise for divorcing couples, because it may allow them to actively participate in the construction of a mutually satisfactory and enduring agreement. A couple's postdivorce relationship seems to benefit from this cooperative setting, because it fosters an equal contribution from each spouse. It may alleviate many stresses for the couple and those around them, especially children. Yet, research has not supported all of the enthusiastic claims. More careful evaluation and comparative studies over time will be required to fully explore this intervention.

REFERENCES

Blades, J. (1985). *Family mediation: Cooperative divorce settlement.* Englewood Cliffs, NJ: Prentice-Hall.

Emery, R., & Wyer, M. (1987). Divorce mediation. *American Psychologist, 42*(2), 472–480.

Erickson, S., & McKnight Erickson, M. (1988). *Family mediation casebook: Theory and process.* New York: Brunner/Mazel.

Folberg, J., & Milne, A. (Eds.). (1988). *Divorce mediation: Theory and practice.* New York: Guilford.

Friedman, J. (1993). *A guide to divorce mediation: How to reach a fair, legal settlement at a fraction of the cost.* New York: Workman.

Mosten, F. S., & Biggs, B. (1985). The role of the therapist in the co-mediation of divorce: An exploration by a lawyer-mediator team. *Journal of Divorce, 9*, 27–39.

Pearson, J., & Thoennes, N. (1988). Divorce mediation research results. In J. Folberg & A. Milne (Eds.), *Divorce mediation: Theory and practice.* New York: Guilford.

Shapiro, J., & Caplan, M. (1983). *Parting sense: A couple's guide to divorce mediation.* Dayton, OH: Greenspring.

Sibbison, W. (1988). *Massachusetts divorce: A consumer guide.* Greenfield, MA: W. Sibbison.

Steinberg, J. L. (1985). Through an interdisciplinary mirror: Attorney-therapist similarities. *Journal of Divorce, 9*, 9–13.

12

Feminist Community

Elaine Leeder

A feminist, community based approach to psychotherapy is one that views individual and family problems as socially constructed and that works at intervening at a level that involves others besides the therapist and the client. Individuals and families come to seek help, thinking that they are unique, but, more often than not, their problems are similar to those around them. Divorce, family violence, arguing, financial problems, and poor communication all are part of our social fabric. Yet, we and our clients often think we are alone in our pain. A feminist, community approach understands that we are all influenced by social, political, and economic forces. These forces influence who we are and teach us how to solve problems.

As products of our economic and political system, we are presented ideologies and values that we take as given. For example, we come to believe in the value of nuclear families and the importance of upward mobility, of being part of a couple, of having children, of hard work. These values keep our capitalist economic system in place and often lead to social and psychological problems. Nonetheless, when we try to solve these problems, we look to individual solutions, as the individualized social order has taught us to think. A community based approach questions these assumptions and tries a more broad based solution.

Practicing feminist therapists believe that social and cultural perspectives must be taken directly into consideration when working with clients. A purely intrapsychic explanation of behavior is both narrow and contrary to feminist analysis. Feminist therapists recognize that a client's life experience reflects society's institutionalized attitudes and values concerning gender roles. They take a political and community stance when working with clients.

A feminist community approach argues that social and psychological problems really can be boiled down to issues of power and control. In any kind of individual or family problem, such an analysis asks questions like "Who is in charge here?" and "How are decisions made?" Power is the ability to get someone to do something that someone would not ordinarily do, as well as the ability to mobilize resources. If people have power, then they can do what they like. Most of us have power in some circumstances but not in others. There are some people who generally have more power than others.

Clients often think they do not have power in their personal lives. Therapists have more power and need to be aware of how they use that power. This is far more easily realized by introducing community or family members into the therapy, rather than continuing in the atomized and isolated mode in which most psychotherapy is done.

In thinking about power, therapists must also consider race, class, ethnicity, sexual orientation, gender, and other social variables. Therapists also must consider the privilege they have as a result of whether or not they are white, middle class, male or female, heterosexual, or of an ethnic group that is accorded more status than others. With power comes the privilege of education, ability to choose a life style, access to travel, and a general sense of freedom. These are not available to others with less power. Often, these are not taken into consideration in approaching therapy. Yet, they are crucial in determining just how much therapists can change or adapt.

A community structure to intervene in a family system offers many different approaches. In this chapter, the process of feminist, community based therapy is described. This model might well be defined as an approach that takes into account multiple issues, including those of power, race, class, ethnicity, gender, and sexual orientation, and attempts to help a client system change through the creative involvement of community and family members in the therapeutic intervention strategy. Examples of how such an approach might be utilized in analyzing a problem are given. Intervention in varying types of family dynamics is also described.

ORIGINS OF COMMUNITY INTERVENTION

The community based approach to psychotherapy has been used for quite awhile. Social workers long have been identified with looking at environmental, familial, and community factors in individual problems. In psychiatry and psychology, community based mental health has been an important professional discipline since the 1960s. The main idea was that problems of mental health can be looked for not in single factors but, rather, in the permutations and combinations of many interacting factors, ranging from individual biological differences to environmental changes to the interactions among individuals. Since then, the community therapy orientation has reflected the emerging awareness that treatment and prevention of mental illness are social problems involving many factors that cannot be controlled and manipulated within the patient-doctor relationship alone. The society must be taken into consideration, rather than just an individual's problem, as the key to restoring mental health.

If a "cured" poor person is sent back to a poor neighborhood, conditions can undo all the good that has been done. If a battered woman is sent back to an abusive home, no matter how strong she has been helped to become, nothing has been done to really change the situation. The community based approach understands all this and realizes that treatment, if it is to be truly effective, must influence all aspects of a client's life.

Understanding that cultures and subcultures determine value systems and behavioral boundaries and expectations is also important. The community based mental health approach focuses on the social unit to understand the behavior of an individual within it. A community in which there is massive social change can produce mental health problems that are based in the community rather than in the individual. One example is the blindness of elderly Khmer women because of atrocities they witnessed during the Cambodian civil war. Another example is the silence of an entire generation of Holocaust survivors, who could not speak of the brutality they experienced during World War II. This experience led to a generation of mental health problems for them and their surviving children. Another example, perhaps closer to home, is the development of eating disorders among young women who are following the cultural script of wanting thin bodies in order to feel attractive.

Social class is another variable that has been taken into consideration when doing a community approach to treatment. A therapist would need to consider that there are strengths within the lower classes and that these should be respected and worked with, rather than undervalued and seen as problems. For example, those of the working class often have a strong work ethic and sense of responsibility to family and friends. There is also a sense of "street smarts" or a knowing about how to survive and cope with the world that is a quality that can be enhanced and developed as one works with such clients. Therapists often are unconscious of the class biases they might hold. There are negative images they might carry toward people from classes lower than their own. There is also a positive bias that often is held toward clients who are of classes higher than that of the therapist. Often, therapists think more highly of clients with more money than those with less.

Ethnicity is also an important consideration when using a community approach. Ethnicity is a collective identity that is shared by a group of people, whether or not they share a specific physical space. It is a sense of "we-ness" that comes from sharing a history, a value system, and a sense of how to do things that is passed on from one generation to another. Truly understanding what that ethnicity means to a client allows a therapist to thoroughly enter that client's life.

Once he or she enters this world, the therapist can enhance functioning by utilizing strengths exhibited by that ethnic group. For example, with some Asians, the therapist must understand from which ethnic group the client comes and then work with the concepts of ancestor worship and filial piety and learn how to employ these in the therapy. I once had a client who was Chinese, and after she finished her therapy on sexual abuse by her father, she held a Chinese ritual to speak to this now dead man and lay the spirit and issue to rest.

Race is another variable that has been taken into consideration in community treatment. A community approach understands that race clearly affects an individual's worldview and influences an individual's value system. The therapist looks at the strengths within the different races and tries to enhance those, rather than focus on the problems and negatives. For example, when working with African-American clients, the therapist would focus on the importance of the extended family or the role of the church in building support for a client. A community based therapist also would work on the role that racism has played in a client's worldview and life experience.

All of the above factors are part of the community approach to mental health, which is itself rooted in social work, psychiatry, and psychology. Another important root of this approach is the second wave of the feminist movement, which began in the late 1960s. This social change effort, which took much of its early beginnings from the earlier civil rights movement, worked to situate gender as an equally important consideration. Feminists argued that the second-class status of women, as well as the socialization that perpetuates inferiority and resultant powerlessness, led to mental health problems that were socially constructed and not individually caused. To that end, feminists created treatment approaches, research projects, and theoretical explanations for women's conditions. As a result, feminist psychology and feminist therapy have become important influences in contemporary mental health care. In these fields, such important questions as "How is women's psychology different from men's?," "What is a woman's way of knowing?," and "What is a woman's experience?" are asked and appropriately addressed in treatment.

Family therapy is another important historical and theoretical antecedent to this type of work. The work of Bowen (1978) and others led to an understanding that one must involve families in the treatment of individual problems. There is an important awareness that has developed out of realizing that families often can be the source of the problem and can be a valuable resource in seeking a solution. Unfortunately, some family therapists still have a narrow definition of the individual and do not see that community and family must be broadly defined to include others outside the nuclear family.

HOW DOES ONE DO THIS INTERVENTION?

Certainly, there are as many ways to do community based intervention as there are therapists who do it. There is no one agreed-upon form or dogma. The principle that underlies the practice is to break the isolation and involve as many interested and concerned parties as may be needed in any situation. In some situations, it might mean bringing in concerned family members; in others, it might be neighbors, friends, and representatives of community agencies who should be involved. This model has developed out of years of practice and honing. It is presented as a paradigm and not as a definitive way of doing things. It should evolve through an interaction between each therapist's skills and each client's needs.

When a client presents to a therapist, issues must be prioritized. This is done by first identifying the most serious concerns and then devising a concomitant treatment plan. It often is best to find out if there are other family members who are involved in the situation. Sometimes, it is best to see just the presenting client the first time, or if there are others who are willing to come (e.g., a spouse), include them.

It is hard to provide exact guidelines about when or where to use this intervention strategy. It is best to consider it as a viable alternative, along with other models. There are no hard or fast rules about its use. Instead, it is provided as one possible consideration in an array of possibilities.

In a community approach, the model involves treating the identified client and the affected family members and bringing in other concerned family members or community members who might help to change the dynamics. Emphasis is placed on helping clients build positive relationships with people who are not necessarily blood relatives. Perhaps there are healthy role modeling adults in the community who could be called upon to become a resource. A real community approach means finding people who become the "family of friends" one might not have had before. It means being creative in finding people who can intervene on the client's behalf and with whom a positive relationship can be built. These outside community and family members become role models for developing healthy relationships within the family.

The model can be used with various types of problems, such as with families and couples in which there is violence, as well as with psychotic patients and their families. The ideas for work with violence are presented here.

COMMUNITY INTERVENTION IN
TREATMENT OF BATTERING

This model of treatment involves engaging the perpetrator, the victim, the couple, or the family system and including community involvement of some sort. Within the course of treatment, each part of the family is treated through a three stage process: engagement, development, and termination. The sequence of events and who is seen at which interval is dependent on the individual situation and based on the counselor's initial assessment of risk and seriousness of injury to the victim (Leeder, 1988).

Because safety is the first order of business in treating violence in families, it is *imperative* for the therapist to determine who is at risk and the likelihood that serious injury might occur. A safety contract must be negotiated early in treatment. If violence is likely, the therapist should first involve the appropriate community agencies, including the police, the courts, and child protective services or adult protective services. The therapist is an agent of social control who says that violence will not be tolerated. If there are appropriate community resources available for the victims, such as a group for victims of child abuse or a program for battered lesbians, then the therapist may have to involve these agencies while psychotherapy continues. The therapist remains in touch with all the appropriate agencies and holds case conferences to coordinate efforts. This keeps the plan for a community approach the main focus of treatment. This model is definitely *not* appropriate for situations in which there is significant danger to the victim or if the perpetrator is uninterested in obtaining help of some sort.

It is the contention of some that violence in the family is caused by the breakdown of human connection (Leeder, 1994, p. 193). Often, it develops as a result of trying to reclaim that human connection that has been lost. The abuser is engaging in a desperate act of trying to get closer but by using force. Unable to communicate and to connect, the abuser uses the last resort, violence. It is also the need to assert power and control, when the abuser feels out of control and powerless. If violence is seen as an effort at human connection, then there are other means that a perpetrator can learn in order to make a healthier bond with others.

Ellyn Kaschak (1992) has suggested that violence is a socially transmitted disease. However, it also holds the potential of being a socially transmitted treatment, but the treatment cannot be atomized and isolated modalities. This keeps the family isolated and individualized instead of making the problem a community problem. It perpetuates the isolation of the nuclear family through isolated treatment approaches and colludes with the social order that has as its foundation the privatization of the family (Leeder, 1994, p. 194). Including family members who are not abused or supportive community members who want to help deprivatizes the therapeutic relationship. Violence is a community problem, too, and it is the community's responsibility to do something about it. There is a socially transmitted treatment available: use of the community.

The feminist, community based approach involves including people who might not otherwise be considered in therapy. A neighbor, a grandmother, a few cousins, or a few friends might be invited into the therapy. These people would be given enough information to understand the dynamics and offered some suggestions as to how they might be helpful in changing what is happening. A neighbor might become the person to whom the victim turns when the tension mounts at home. The cousins might come over and "cool out" the perpetrator or provide support to the victim in calling the police or tell the perpetrator it is time to take a "time out." Instead of the family being alone in crisis, others become involved in a way that lends support and social control. These people say, by their presence, that violence will not be allowed and that they will see to it that safety is maintained.

Nonabused or nonabusive family members also might be invited into the sessions. These people are often inadvertent victims. Boys who witness violence are more likely to become abusers later in life, and girls who view it are more likely to become victims themselves when they grow up (Jaffee, Wolfe, & Wilson 1990). This does not mean, however, that all children who view abuse become abusers or victims. In fact, in one study (Kalmuss, 1984), 94 percent of the adults who had witnessed abuse at home were not involved in abuse in their present families; Kaufmann and Zigler (1987) found that two-thirds of their sample of abused children became adequate parents. A community based approach enhances the likelihood that they can overcome what they saw as children.

CASE EXAMPLE

The following case example illustrates the point about how family members are aware of and influenced by the violence. A family of four, in which the mother was regularly battered, is treated.

Harry came to treatment because the courts referred him because of the abuse he was inflicting on his wife, Sylvia. Sylvia asked to come in for the initial session because she wanted to be supportive of his treatment. In the first session, the lethality of the situation was determined, and a safety plan was devised. This plan included Sylvia phoning her nearby sister if the abuse began.

Harry agreed to the safety plan, saying he would leave the house if he felt himself about to become violent. He agreed to join a group for men who batter. It was agreed that Harry and Sylvia would be seen individually. The children would be seen separately, until such time as the family felt it was safe to come in together.

Harry was seen weekly for six months. He discussed his history of abuse (as a recipient and as a perpetrator) and his own skills for anger management. His gender role expectations and his family background of abuse were examined.

Through these discussions, as well as a concurrent group therapy, Harry learned that violence was his choice and that he could choose to not abuse. The probation officer stressed the legal consequences of Harry's abuse. His communication skills and identification of his feelings were also worked on.

Sylvia was also seen individually for these six months. Everything in the individual sessions was confidential, although they were encouraged to share their learning with each other. Sylvia learned that the violence was not her fault, that she had a right to live violence free, that she need not be Harry's emotional caretaker, and that she had a right to an independent existence. Communication skills and assertiveness were also worked on. She learned how to say no and to call upon others to break the privatization of her family in order to obtain the safety she needed.

After the first few months, the two children, aged 14 and 12, were brought into therapy. This happened when it seemed that the arguments had diminished and when Sylvia said she felt safer at home. The first session included all family members; then, the two children were seen together without the parents. Because the children were fearful in their father's presence, it was determined to work with the children separately. In those sessions, the children said that they knew when Sylvia had been abused. They were relieved that there was now intervention, and they both wanted to help in any way. The boy had become aggressive in school, and the girl had become sexually active recently.

Harry did not hit any of the children, although there was an aura of intimidation and fear pervading the home. The children felt sorry for Sylvia but also felt that she was a "wimp" who let him run the show. The children were seen on a monthly basis. They were helped to verbalize their feelings, first to the therapist and then within the family. How to handle the abuse should it occur again was worked on.

In the third month of treatment of the family, Harry came home drunk and hit Sylvia again. This time, the son ran to his aunt's home, and the police were called. Harry's probation officer was notified the next day. Harry spent four weekends in jail.

Afterward, treatment resumed. Sessions included all the family members, Sylvia's sister, and Harry's favorite buddy. Initially, Harry resisted, but the family had found its strength and insisted that they were still afraid and wanted added help. A safety plan was agreed upon that now included the friend, who would serve as a buddy to whom Harry could turn.

Harry joined Alcoholics Anonymous as well. He verbalized a lot of anger at the system for forcing him into group therapy, substance abuse work, and family therapy and for being made the fool in the community. He was informed that this was the treatment approach. Incarceration was the alternative.

At this point, a family therapy model was utilized. The five family members attended: Harry, Sylvia, the two children, and Sylvia's sister. The buddy was seen as someone to be called upon in case of trouble. The children and wife now felt comfortable telling Harry how it felt to live in a house of terror. With the presence of the therapist, an aunt available to help, and the court system behind them, the family felt able to be honest with Harry.

After hearing all that the family had to say, Harry apologized for what he had put his family through. He explained his own childhood upbringing, including his own experience of child abuse, and tearfully promised to stop the violence and intimidation tactics.

After that session, the family seemed to settle down. There was no more violence, and arguments were settled in a minimal amount of time. The children and Sylvia came to treatment sporadically, although Harry continued for six more months on an individual basis. The family is seen once a year for follow-up. The safety plan is still in place, with the probation officer monitoring the violence. Harry, Sylvia, and the children know they can call the therapist at any time and that a "tune-up" session can be arranged immediately. Sylvia is working part-time as a clerk, and Harry continues in Alcoholics Anonymous. After four years, Harry exhibits no violence, and the children have settled down behaviorally.

This case example illustrates all that is necessary in a community based approach: concern and limit setting by the therapist, employment of all possible community agencies, involvement of concerned friends and community members, and involvement of the nonabused and non-abusing family members. In this case, the perpetrator was shown that violence was not allowed and was provided with a support system from which his behavior could be monitored and changed. All the elements were present and, thus, a limited success was achieved. It was limited because, although one may be able to stop the violence in an abusive relationship, it often is impossible to stop the emotionally abusive components of the dynamic. Violence is controllable because it can be contained through social controls. Emotional abuse is harder to define and much harder to stop.

APPROPRIATE AND INAPPROPRIATE USE OF THIS MODEL

The community approach is not necessarily appropriate in all situations. If a client is in a potentially lethal situation, bringing in family and community will *not* work. The therapist constantly must assess whether the client is in danger, even if the client is not verbalizing any fear. This can be done by nonverbal assessment, by asking others around the client how dangerous the situation is, or by just maintaining a cautious approach and not bringing in outsiders until the therapist has determined that it is safe to do so. The safety of the client is of first order and should not be threatened because of the therapist's personal need to use any type of intervention.

Another situation in which this type of work is inappropriate is with people who are having economic or social problems that can be handled more appropriately by an advocacy approach. There are times when clients are experiencing difficulties in their lives that are caused by matters that are not intrapsychic or based in relationship problems. When a client's situation is based on social systems problems, taking on a position of advocacy for the client is far more effective. For example, a client who is experiencing racism on the job or sexual harassment should not necessarily be handled in this way. Rather, involvement with appropriate agencies, encouraging the client to deal with the matters legally, and giving advice in how to handle the matter might be more appropriate. The community approach is far more useful in situations in which the clients need support in changing dynamics interpersonally. Eventually, this might lead to some kind of social change but not immediately.

A feminist, community based approach is appropriate only for certain kinds of change, only at certain points, and only for particular kinds of clients. The kinds of change for which this is relevant are ones when the client is highly motivated and for clients whose problems are environmentally based, rather than purely intrapsychic.

The approach also is not useful right at the beginning of therapy, before the client has built trust with the therapist. It is better used in the middle of the treatment, rather than early into the intervention.

Clients for whom it is not relevant are those whose problems are basically historical in nature. If a client is now an adult but was sexually abused by a parent as a child, for example, this approach is not the treatment of choice. It also is not appropriate for clients who have biologically based mental problems or for those for whom individual therapy or group therapy seems to be effective.

RESEARCH NEEDS

Research supporting the use of the particular model described here has not been done. Hence, the model must be seen as opening possibilities for additional strategies. It is included here because it is one of the few to address the fact that individuals are not autonomous and isolated as they may seem in the consulting room and lab. In the lived experience of individuals, interactions with other individuals; families; groups; and cultural, social, and economic systems are critically important if psychological strategies and interventions are to be relevant and important.

Although the particular strategy presented here has not been evaluated through research, other community based interventions are being researched and are presenting researchers with demanding and expanding methodological issues. In fact, current efforts (Tolan, Keys, Chertok, and Jason [1990] and Robson [1993]) in community oriented fields are beginning to embrace existing and develop additional research methods that can address interactions among multiple levels and systems. Indeed, it seems that, in the end, important research may stem from interdisciplinary efforts at evaluation.

REFERENCES

Bowen, M. (1978). *Family therapy in clinical practice*. New York: Jason Aronson.

Jaffee, P., Wolfe, D., & Wilson, S. (1990). *Children of battered women*. Newbury Park, CA: Sage.

Kalmuss, D. S. (1984). The intergenerational transmission of marital aggression. *Journal of Marriage and the Family, 46*, 11–19.

Kaschak, E. (1992). *Engendered lives: A new psychology of women's experience*. New York: Basic Books.

Kaufman, J., & Zigler, E. (1987). Do abused children become abusive parents? *American Journal of Orthopsychiatry, 57*, 186–192.

Leeder, E. (1994). *Treating abuse in families: A feminist and community approach*. New York: Springer.

Leeder, E. (1988). Enmeshed in pain: Counseling the lesbian battering couple. *Women and Therapy, 7*(1), 81–99.

Robson, C. (1993). *Real world research*. Cambridge, MA: Blackwell.

Tolan, P., Keys, C., Chertok, F., & Jason, L. (Eds.). (1990). *Researching community psychology*. Washington, DC: APA Press.

13

Ecological Strategies

Jane Fried

"Ecological" has been described as a "fundamental metaphor in community psychology" (Levine & Perkins, 1987, p. 77). The ecological approach is a perspective about the process by which problems develop and suggests a wide range of approaches to solving them, rather than a specific set of strategies. The terms "metaphor" and "community" indicate that this approach diverges significantly from traditional, scientific psychotherapy. A metaphor is a comparison between two phenomena that are similar but not exactly alike. Metaphors are intended to expand a person's understanding of a situation by suggesting similarities with another situation. Metaphors suggest the use of intuition and familiarity with context of full understanding. They do not imply precise correlations between objects. They encourage listeners to develop different understandings of their significance in order to enrich the total comprehension of the phenomenon. For example, the Tower of Babel can serve as a metaphor for work situations in which people are unable to understand each other's values, language, and goals and, therefore, are unable to accomplish their tasks.

Ecology, in its original sense, is a biological term that describes interactive systems or organisms that occupy a particular physical space or environment. Prefixes such as "human" or "social" indicate the study of people in a particular environment and their interactions with each other and with the larger social, physical, and organizational structures that shape their lives. Doe (1990) suggests that four different levels of environment must be examined to paint a complete picture of an ecological system: the microsystem, which examines a person's level of defense against an emotional problem; the macrosystem, the physical setting in which the problem occurs; the excosystem of social and cultural beliefs that contribute to the existence and perpetuation of the problem; and the mesosystem, which is a description of the interactions among the other three. These systems and their interactions also have been described as nested within each other (Kelly, 1987) and exerting cycles of mutual influences (Stokols, 1992). The ecological approach assumes that the individual is to be understood in context.

The ecological approach focuses on context, process, and interactions. Although problems may be presented by an individual to a counselor, the problems are not assumed to originate "in" the individual or to be most effectively treated through conversations with an individual, although these may occur as part of a broader range of treatments. The ecological approach diverges from the traditional individual approach in that it is prevention oriented, assumes that the social context, including cultural factors, is relevant to mental illness and mental health and assumes that community based interventions often are more effective in enhancing mental health than individualistic approaches (Kelly, 1990).

Ecological approaches to counseling challenge traditional approaches on many levels, ranging from problem definition to level and type of intervention to description of desired outcomes. For example, a single mother who is African-American and lives with her mother and her brother may seek counseling because she thinks her son is out of control, spends too much time on the streets, and is chronically truant. She blames him for his misbehavior. An ecological psychologist might help the woman reframe the problem. Rather than blaming her son, the mother would be encouraged to identify the strong, responsible men in her community who might give her son some support for staying out of trouble and returning to school. Parents who are recent immigrants from Southeast Asia and are frustrated by the increasing Americanization of their children, including their declining respect for authority, might be encouraged to form a support group led by parents who immigrated to the United States a generation earlier and made a successful transition. The group approach, guided by elder members of the community, might be more effective than individual or family counseling. An Anglo-American male who has been out of work for six months and is depressed would be taught to think about his problem in the context of the global economy as well as in personal terms. His therapy could include discussing his own feelings about self-worth and the relationship between earning power and personal value. It also could include retraining for available jobs or participation in a job search training program. A Latin-American woman who suffers from "ataques de nervios," which she experiences as externally caused and debilitating, might be exposed to some insight therapy in order to understand the emotional causes of this psychosomatic problem. She also might be encouraged to explore her own culture and the roles it establishes for women so that she begins to understand the relationship between her "ataques" and her feelings of powerlessness. One possible intervention would involve training in culturally appropriate assertiveness so that she could feel more empowered, yet, remain involved in her own culture.

Traditional Euro-American approaches to counseling would involve meeting with each person described, trying to help the person achieve insight into the problem, and, then, if appropriate, taking action to begin solving it. Ecological approaches at their best define problems within the cultural, economic, family, social, age, and gender related contexts, then try to determine where and how to intervene in order to change the circumstances that provoke or exacerbate the problem. After listening to the person who seeks counseling, the counselor might continue meeting with that person, but she or he might also suggest that the person join a group, talk to a priest, move to a shelter, ask to meet with the rest of the family, help a family member find a job, provide some relevant reading material, or consult with a traditional healer. These and other approaches might be used in a wide range of combinations designed to alleviate the problem and may or may not involve what has traditionally been considered counseling — a therapist sitting in an office speaking with a client about a problem.

AN ECOLOGICAL INTERVENTION

One problem that is quite amenable to ecological interventions is intimacy violence, physical abuse that occurs between people who are involved in an intimate relationship. If such a situation developed between two college students, and a male was abusing a female, the female (Ellen) might seek help through the college counseling center. She would arrive for her appointment hoping that nobody she knows would see her in the waiting room. She might have fabricated a story ready to tell any friend, something about needing help with study skills or being stressed out over school. As part of her intake assessment, the counselor would begin to think about the individual help that Ellen needs as well as the environment in which the problem has arisen. She or he would ask about the cycle of beating, what the two argued about, and conditions that typically precede arguments and beatings (like excessive drinking or conflicts that her boyfriend [Tom] was experiencing elsewhere). She or he would ask about Ellen's family background, including the ways her father treated her mother and how both of them treated the children. She or he also would be aware of the literature on recent increases in relationship violence on college campuses and the connections between U.S. ideas about masculinity and femininity and interpersonal abuse and control. Finally, the counselor would ask Ellen how she felt about the beatings and try to assess her ideas about the relationships between conflict and intimacy in male-female relationships and make a judgment about the level of Ellen's communication skills, particularly assertive communication. All of these issues would help the counselor develop a picture of Ellen's family history, her level of self-esteem, her images of loving relationships, and the environment that shaped all of her ideas about these things.

ASSESSMENT DATA

During the intake, the counselor would solicit information from Ellen about her own behavior, Tom's behavior, and their relationship. She might inquire about behavior patterns, the campus context in which the behavior occurs, Ellen's and Tom's family backgrounds, and their ideas about male-female relationships. As a college counselor, she or he also would be aware of broader student behavior patterns on campus, including police reports on cases of intimacy violence as well as students' ideas about male-female relationships that might be discussed in many counseling situations. Ellen reveals to her counselor that Tom typically hits her after the two have been drinking, when he thinks she has been flirting with his friends, when he is getting frustrated because she is spending too much time with her female friends, or after his team has lost a game. Ellen is particularly aware of these antecedents and pays a lot of attention to Tom when she knows he is getting ready to explode. She has been aware of the patterns intuitively but never became conscious of her awareness until she describes the pattern to her counselor.

Ellen's description of her parents' relationship also gives the counselor information about the sources of Ellen's ideas of intimacy and family life. Her father never hits her mother, but they fight a lot. When her father yells at her mother, he calls her terrible names and tells her how stupid she is. Her mother is very loving toward the children but rarely holds her ground in disciplining them. The father spoils the kids sometimes and beats them other times. Her mother never stands up to her father in arguments and cries a lot. She is an expert at predicting when he is going to explode, as are her children. Ellen's level of communication ability is not really known yet, but some clues are available. She tries to avoid conflicts and confrontations. In this, she is patterning herself after her mother. In her college environment, she makes up stories to cover up problems and tries to present herself as socially acceptable. This also is typical of women her age, who tend to focus on maintaining relationships and managing conflict rather than confronting differences directly (Gilligan, Lyons, & Hanmer, 1990). Ellen may very well care more about maintaining her relationship with Tom than she does about her physical safety. She also cares a lot about her friends' opinions of her and is, therefore, embarrassed that they know about the fighting.

In addition to reviewing Ellen's personal experiences and perception, the counselor considers the situation in the context of Ellen's life circumstances. She is a child of an upwardly mobile, middle class, white U.S. Protestant family consisting of two parents living with their two children in the suburbs. Male college students with similar backgrounds have expressed their frustration with the limited economic opportunities they face compared with their fathers' and grandfathers' generations. Many blame their loss of opportunity on competition from women and people of color in the job market, although many young men take the presence of these people for granted and simply believe that all the good opportunities are over (Howe & Strauss, 1993). Men in this group express anger toward those whom they perceive as interfering with their opportunities, and those who cannot put their anger to productive uses may turn on vulnerable people in their own lives in destructive ways.

Images of masculinity and femininity historically have been rigid and nonoverlapping in the United States. Men are supposed to be physically strong, emotionally nonexpressive, self-contained or autonomous, and dominant. Women are supposed to be the polar opposite — physically less strong, emotionally expressive, relationship oriented, and submissive (Gilligan, 1982). Although these images have changed somewhat since the 1950s, they are still powerful and are quite obvious in media portrayals of men and women. U.S. ideas about mental health often are considered synonymous with stereotypic ideas about masculine behavior and attitudes (Bem, Martyna, & Watson, 1976; Block, 1973; Broverman, Vogel, Broverman, Clarkson, & Rosenkrantz, 1972). Men are expected to have everything under control and to take care of situations and people when they are in charge. Taking care of things means managing on a physical, rather than an emotional, level. For many, feeling out of control is very threatening. Many men seem to associate feelings of vulnerability and emotional connectedness with being out of control. These men who cannot control their women often feel out of control. Because people tend to absorb their ideas about sex role behavior from the culture, mediated by families and the mass media, both Tom and Ellen have probably absorbed U.S. ideas about masculinity and femininity. These beliefs seem to be reflected in their behavior toward each other. Many people at their age (between 18 and 22) tend to relate to members of the opposite sex stereotypically, operating from social conditioning rather than individually developed beliefs because the level of experience in intimate relationships is relatively low (Chickering & Reisser, 1993).

INTERVENTION POSSIBILITIES

Although the counselor conducts the intake interview in a fairly traditional, one-to-one setting, her response to the situation is complex and involves a number of ecological interventions.

First, she will listen to Ellen and establish a trusting relationship with her through a use of Rogerian, active listening techniques. However, as a feminist who believes in equalizing power in therapeutic relationships, she might be more self-disclosing than a traditional therapist. This would not involve discussing experiences from her own life as much as sharing her reactions to Ellen's experiences of abuse, saying how she would feel if a partner treated her that way. Her reaction would provide a point of comparison for Ellen and would demonstrate that there is a way to be a strong and caring woman, overcoming the conflict between caring and strength that might exist in Ellen's mind.

Second, the therapist might suggest that Ellen go home and talk to her mother about how she has learned to handle conflict in the family. The purpose of this conversation is to help Ellen understand how her mother thinks about family conflict and then to examine her own beliefs in the light of those she has absorbed unquestioningly as she grew up. In this conversation, Ellen's mother might reveal some of her own frustrations and some things she has learned during the course of her marriage. In addition, Ellen may have been interpreting some of her mother's behavior erroneously, as children often do. Such a conversation would provide an opportunity to clear up some of Ellen's childhood misconceptions and generally improve communication between herself and her mother. The therapist also might invite Ellen to bring her mother to one or more sessions so that Ellen can ask questions she might not have the courage to ask alone. During the conversation, the therapist might evoke information about the different areas in which the two women were

raised and the different messages each absorbed about male-female relationships and women's role in marriage. The process could demonstrate
how social categories are constructed and empower both women to
change their ideas about behavior in intimate relationships.

Third, the therapist might explore Ellen's pattern of covering up
conflict and help her talk about her fears of becoming socially unacceptable to her friends. In addition to achieving some personal insight, she
might suggest that Ellen talk to her friends about how they handle
conflict in their intimate relationships. From these discussions, Ellen
could learn that she is not the only one who has the problem, that there
are a range of approaches to addressing it, and that she can seek advice
and support from her friends even when she is not sure that they will
approve of how she is handling the situation.

Fourth, the therapist also will talk with Ellen about patterns of male
and female socialization in the United States and explore from where her
beliefs come. This will help Ellen to place herself in a larger social
context and realize that her acceptance of an abusive situation does not
necessarily constitute a personal failure. Rather, it is a manifestation of a
very deeply held set of U.S. beliefs that she absorbed unconsciously as
she was growing up. She may point Ellen's attention to commercials on
television or in magazines, images of women in movies and popular
novels, and so forth. She may even ask Ellen to do a little pop culture
research and bring the ideas in to discuss or suggest that Ellen view some
films that present strong and loving heroines. Finally, she might bring to
Ellen's awareness U.S. historical and legal precedents that give men the
right to dominate women, manage their property, expect that they change
their names to men's after marriage, and so forth.

Fifth, the therapist would also attribute attention to the environment in
which this abuse is occurring. She would review the records of presenting problems in the counseling center and discuss the issue with the
women's center staff, the health center or rape crisis center staff, the
campus ombudsperson, sorority advisors, and the residence life staff in
an effort to get an informational assessment of the scope of the problem
on this particular campus. She also might speak with some of the coaches
of male teams to find out if they are training their athletes in responsible
management of frustration and stress or discussing relationship abuse,
acquaintance rape, or substance abuse with them. Assuming that the
problem is fairly significant, the therapist would present her findings to
the director of counseling, the dean of students, the athletic director, or
the advisor of the Pan Hellenic Council. The goal of these conversations
would be to begin to develop campus-wide programming efforts that

focus campus attention on interpersonal violence and alternate conflict reduction methods.

In addition to training programs that focus on violence reduction, the counselor might encourage the creation of a campus-wide committee whose role is to examine the aspirations and self-images of women on campus. Their work would be educational rather than remedial and might result in the creation of career planning workshops for women only and discussions with campus clubs and organizations about their ideas of male and female roles within their groups and in the rest of their personal lives. Faculty development workshops also might be created to sensitize faculty members to some of the gender dynamics that occur in the classroom (Sandler, 1993). The goals for these programs would be to create an arena for experimental education in which students could examine the assumptions about gender and power in their current experiences and the lives they anticipate so that stereotypic notions of male and female sex roles would no longer be taken for granted on campus and inequalities would be identified as they were observed.

Additional actions might include reviewing campus policies to be sure they address the problems of interpersonal respect and nonviolent conflict management as part of institutional values. Typical campus mission statements include comments about tolerance of difference, respect for different viewpoints, and the maintenance of a safe and welcoming campus environment. A final piece of the ecological intervention would be to review the campus discipline system. How does the system view relationship violence? Is it considered a serious violation of campus judicial codes? How does the system protect the victim of violence if that person chooses to come forward and name her abuser? Does the system protect confidentiality and balance the needs of the abuser and the abused? Is the focus of the system on problem solving and conflict reduction or on punishment, which might lead to further abuse?

The overall goal of ecological intervention is to address individual problems in their social, cultural, economic, and political contexts. Women and men would be encouraged to see themselves as members of a society that has given them certain messages about sex role behavior. Rather than taking the social messages for granted, the students would be encouraged to examine, discuss, and express their feelings about them. Ecological approaches assume that the person is embedded in a context and that the context is a powerful force in shaping the problem, the per-son's experience of the problem, and the resources available to address the problem. Individual counseling focuses first on pain reduction and then on finding the underlying sources of problems.

Ecological counseling uses the same approach but assumes that underlying causes exist in the environment as well as the individual and that this causes a shift in salience and relative power in an interactive manner. When an intervention improves one dimension of a problem, it will affect other elements of the system and may bring to light other issues that were previously hidden. In this case, encouraging Ellen to speak to her mother may provoke her mother into thinking about divorcing her father, which may lead to economic problems in the family and difficulties for Ellen in staying in school. Ecological approaches generally have ripple effects and rarely are tidy.

The example above describes an ecological intervention with people who are white, economically stable, and relatively privileged in this culture. Similar approaches are effective with people of color and those in less advantaged situations. The major differences in approach are generally a result of the different environments in which the problems occur; different levels of economic resources; different age, race, or culture of those affected by the problem; and so forth. Ecological interventions must be tailored to the person in context and created by therapists who understand the role of context in shaping behavior, attitudes, values, and feelings.

HISTORY AND THEORY OF ECOLOGICAL PSYCHOLOGY

Ecological psychology traces its origin to the theoretical work in the 1930s of Kurt Lewin, who articulated a model of person-environment interaction and an integrated field of study. Lewin is well-known for the $B = f (P \times E)$ formula, which describes behavior (B) as a function (f) of the interaction between person (P) and environment (E). In the field of community psychology, Stokols (1992), Rappaport (1977, 1987), Bronfenbrenner (1979), Kelly (1990; 1987), and Conyne (1985), among many others, are his theoretical and pragmatic heirs.

The social values and priorities of the 1960s gave strong impetus to the ecological approach. During this period, psychologists and other social scientists began to believe that many mental health problems were spawned by larger social and economic problems like racism, sexism, ageism, and chronic exclusion from economic opportunity in the United States. Many Americans began to believe that social rights, civil rights, environmental quality, global peace, economic opportunity, and social policy were all interrelated and that intervention in one sphere inevitably affected other spheres of human life (Kelly, 1990).

Individual mental health problems began to be examined in their social context. Mental illness was described in a contextual manner that included descriptions of intrapsychic issues as well as external stressors and resources available to cope with stress (Albee, 1980). Education and social policy change began to be considered part of an overall effort at preventing mental illness. Community psychologists adopted and adapted public health approaches in rethinking mental health (Stokols, 1992; Kelly, 1987). They emphasized prevention and the role of nonpsychologically oriented systems in helping the residents of specific communities maintain higher levels of mental health (Albee & Ryan-Finn, 1993; Heller, 1993; Werner & Tyler, 1993). They tried to understand "how persons created support systems to cope with everyday hassles, developmental crises and community catastrophes" (Kelly, 1990, p. 770). They discovered that income and opportunity for social and economic mobility were among the best predictors of mental health. They became suspicious of the overlap between social values and definitions of mental health when Gibbs (1980) discovered that typical criteria for describing social class status, occupation, income, level of education, and type of housing were correlated with levels of mental health. These data support early hypotheses that many mental health problems required social as well as individual solutions.

Although not ignoring mental illnesses that have organic, or medical, origins, ecological psychologists have created a much broader set of health promoting interventions, including advocacy on behalf of clients with relevant social services agencies, promoting client competence and empowerment, preventing psychopathology, and integrating social support agencies so that clients receive optimal care (Mowbray, 1990). They have created new models for understanding the components of mental health as well as new research paradigms for assessing the effectiveness of their interventions.

This approach can be represented by the formula:

Incidence of mental illness = organic causes + stress / esteem + social support system

(Albee, 1980, p. 217).

Ecological approaches to counseling are necessarily multidisciplinary, because efforts are made to understand problems in their complex environmental context and to intervene on several levels simultaneously. Areas of study have been divided roughly into biopsychobehavioral factors and sociophysical environmental factors. These two groups of factors in any population would potentially involve the study of age;

exposure to pathogens and environmental stressors; organic neurological or biochemical problems; self-esteem; optimism; depression; anxiety; diet and alcohol consumption; participation in health maintenance activities like exercise or meditation; safety practices; place and type of residence and work; level of economic achievement; range of job-related skills; social climate at home and at work; cultural values and beliefs related to personal health, family, and work; availability of health care and health insurance; and so on ad infinitum. In order to draw a complete picture of the mental health needs of individuals in a particular area or community, a multidisciplinary team would be the most effective means of assessing the situation. To analyze key variables and address specific mental health problems, one might need physicians, an epidemiologist, sociologists, health educators, career development specialists, safety specialists, architects, alcohol/substance abuse counselors, nutritionists, anthropologists, urban planners, policy specialists, individually oriented counselors, and any number of other specialists whose area of study was relevant to issues under discussion. The role of multidisciplinary assessment teams is to identify mental health problems and trace their sources in a way that permits an accurate understanding of their etiology, provides valid guidance in the design of preventive interventions, and clearly suggests methods for evaluating outcomes (Stokols, 1992).

APPROPRIATE USE OF ECOLOGICAL APPROACHES

From one perspective, all counseling is ecological. Even existential psychotherapy examines the individual's perspective on his or her world, the meaning he or she makes of it, and the role that he or she wishes to play in terms of relationships, work, and other significant life choices. No individual exists in a vacuum, even though traditional Anglo-American values often convince people that they alone are responsible for their problems and for finding solutions. Ecological approaches generally are appropriate at some point in the counseling process, depending on the counselor's understanding of client variables and the other counseling strategies and theories in use.

In the relationship-building stage of counseling (Okun, 1987), the environment often is limited to the relationship between the client and the counselor, including expectations each has for the outcome of the process, including training, preconceived ideas, cultural expectations, and so forth. An ecological approach would mandate counselor efforts to empower the client to take charge of the presenting problem at some stage in the process. However, taking charge could cover a range of responses from achieving insight and a level of acceptance to hiring a lawyer, confronting a person, changing jobs, or going back to school, to use a few possible examples. In client centered approaches, any counselor effort to intervene in the wider environment too early in the process might result in increasing the client's dependence on the counselor. This is an undesirable outcome in client centered therapy with Anglo-American clients but is often considered culturally appropriate by Asian-Americans and members of other nondominant U.S. groups. In addition, some clients may seek help for addressing problems that are caused by external sources that an Anglo counselor can remediate efficiently and effectively because of greater familiarity with the dominant culture (Sue & Sue, 1990).

In deciding whether or when to use ecological intervention, the counselor can ask himself or herself a few guiding questions:

How is the problem defined? Is it intrapsychic, physiological, interpersonal, conceptual? Does it have multiple components?

Is this an individual problem, or does it affect more than one person?

Would an environmental or ecological intervention prevent additional occurrences of this problem?

If the counselor intervenes in the environment, will the client consider the counselor a role model and take responsibility for future interventions, or will the client return for help each time the problem recurs?

Is this problem related to historical oppression of the client's culture by the dominant U.S. culture?

If the answers to these questions indicate that the problem derives from conditions that are much larger than the individual life of the specific client, some level of ecological intervention is appropriate.

Ecological approaches to treatment are more a matter of perspective and process than predefined method. Most problems that individuals experience have some connection to the environment and, therefore, can benefit from ecological intervention. People who suffer from organic or biochemically induced problems benefit from low stress environments, because these environments minimize the physiological fluctuations that high stress environments tend to induce (Brown, 1980; Meichenbaum & Jaremko, 1983). People who have unusually intense reactions to stress benefit from biofeedback techniques in addition to intrapsychic insight about the reasons for their reactions. People whose problems are more heavily due to environmental stress benefit even more from ecological approaches. People who are trapped in poverty because of poor education, lack of opportunity, or the structure of the welfare system benefit from a combination of insight therapy and ecological intervention in the systems that induce much of their stress. People whose lives are aggravated by racism, sexism, harassment, environmental violence, or pollution presumably would find their lives more manageable and their mental health more stable if they were less subject to destructive intrusion from external forces. The greater the environmental stress, the more individual resources become necessary to cope. People who seem to have fewer personal resources seem to be more vulnerable to environmental stress. A wealthy person, for example, can live in an apartment building with excellent security, comfortable living space, and enough technology to keep him or her well-fed and well-entertained. A poorer person in an urban environment has fewer material protections and, therefore, must have intrapsychic resources to cope with urban stressors.

A significant difficulty in choosing ecological interventions is that they extend well beyond conversations with the client. Counseling a woman who is experiencing sexual harassment on the job can lead easily to lawsuits, increases in harassment aimed toward her, loss of employment, and the resulting family problems that accompany loss of income. Helping a gay or lesbian person learn to speak up for himself or herself when insulting comments are made about gay people can lead to an increase in self-esteem, but it also can lead to assaults on the person and serious injury or death.

Ecological interventions are multilevel and often require efforts from people who are outside the counselor's normal area of influence or control. For example, if a child is demonstrating aggressive behavior in school, efforts are made to understand the child's frame of mind by talking with him or her or engaging in play therapy, investigating the home situation for evidence of abuse or neglect, and looking at the child's environment in school for evidence of harassment or bullying, the presence of weapons, and so forth. In this case, the counselor serves as the primary investigator, the person who has a trusting relationship with the child, who helps people from a variety of service agencies identify the source or sources of the problem. If many children and adolescents are demonstrating high levels of aggression, are distracted from learning, and are living in unstable home environments with minimal adult supervision, efforts to improve the academic performance of these children might involve some individual counseling for some of them. It might also involve community service agencies, police, tutorial services, school feeding programs, afterschool activities, big brother and big sister programs, and church support programs. The particular intervention(s) that might be most helpful to a specific child could as easily come from a next-door neighbor or an adult tutor as from a traditionally trained counselor or member of the clergy.

Another area of concern in the use of ecological interventions is that they often are disruptive to other persons in the client's life, to the employer, to the local government, and to the belief system of the community. It is one issue to help an individual voluntarily stop smoking. It is a much broader issue to create a smoke-free workplace or to get a parent to stop smoking as a condition of custody with a child who has asthma. An extremely broad example of an ecological intervention that has been helpful and disruptive simultaneously is the women's movement in the United States. Many women have been released from negative self-images, fear of independence, and the general belief that women are not as competent as men (Broverman, Broverman, Clarkson, Rosenkrantz, & Vogel, 1970). On the other hand, the women's movement has provoked all sorts of changes in affirmative action law, sexual harassment law, private male/female relationships, and poverty levels among divorced mothers.

Applications of ethical principles are extremely important in ecological counseling. Respective autonomy, doing no harm, benefiting others, being just, and being faithful (Kitchener, 1985) are the basic principles that undergird the ethical codes of most counseling organizations. It generally is impossible to consider one of these principles without reference to at least one other, because they interact in real life and must be balanced as decisions are made. When thinking about the use of complex ecological interventions whose outcomes cannot be known in advance, it is necessary to advise the client of the possibilities and think together about possible outcomes, both positive and negative. Given the power of the therapist in any counseling relationship, the therapist must take responsibility for outlining his or her hopes for improvement and concerns about negative consequences and let the client choose the course. To do otherwise is to assume the role of social engineer and manipulator, a paternalistic abuse of power that cannot be justified in this culture at the end of the twentieth century. When the client is a minor or is otherwise unable to be responsible for himself or herself, the therapist should discuss interventions with the responsible party. If the client makes choices that conflict irreconcilably with the therapist's values, the normal procedures for referral or termination should be followed. Because of the complexity of ecological interventions, the therapist occasionally may have to consider who his or her client is in the situation

— the individual, the school system, the community agency, or the local government (O'Neill, 1989). When a minor female tells her high school guidance counselor that she is pregnant, the counselor is responsible in varying degrees to the student, her parents, the father and his parents, the school system, the local community, and the state department of child welfare. The student may be considered the client, but the school pays the counselor's salary, and the citizens of the state and the local community determine the rules of reporting in this situation. Who is the counselor's primary client?

RESEARCH ISSUES AND AREAS TO BE EXPLORED

An "ecological definition of mental health [involves] the opportunity to acquire competencies for self-development in the presence of social support" (Kelly, 1987, p. 4). This definition assumes a focus on people-environment transactions that must be understood in a multiple-level, multidisciplinary process. This requires the disciplinary approaches derived from anthropology, sociology, medicine, education, and individual behavior change as well as cost-benefit techniques associated with business and public administration. Stokols (1992) suggests designing assessment and evaluation procedures by splitting the area of study into three segments: physical health, mental and emotional well-being, and social cohesion at organizational and community levels. Interdisciplinary approaches require the development of new research paradigms. Research into the ecology of mental health maintenance relies heavily on constructs from systems theory such as interdependence, positive and negative feedback, and amplification. It attempts to understand and describe dynamic interactions between people and their environments that are "characterized by cycles of mutual influences" (Stokols, 1992, pp. 7–8). Ultimately, research in the ecology of mental health must also investigate the "mesosystem" (Doe, 1990) or the interaction of the subsystems as well as each system separately. This is extremely complex research that involves unknowable numbers of variables, many of which interact in unpredictable ways and might best be understood through the evolving use of chaos theory (Jantsch, 1981; Newton & Caple, 1985; Prigogine & Allen, 1982) rather than any of the more traditional models of social science research. Chaos theory describes change as a process of disorderly evolution in which order masquerades as randomness and change is multidirectional, irreversible, and relatively unpredictable (Gleick, 1987). In this approach, "The material universe is seen as a dynamic web of interrelated events. None of the properties of any part of this web is fundamental; they all follow from the properties of the other parts and overall consistency of their interrelations determines the structure of the entire web" (Capra, 1987, p. 51). This type of research is in its infancy in the social and behavioral sciences and is far more advanced in the physical sciences.

In an invited address to the American Psychological Society, James Kelly (1990) called for new approaches to research in the area of ecological psychology and stated that new paradigms were required because of the complex, interactive, multidisciplinary nature of the phenomena under investigation. He suggested that traditional, positivist approaches to psychological research had become self-contained and restricted and that "multiple, and alternative approaches to inquiry" (p. 776) needed to be developed to create greater understanding. Kelly stated that ecological psychology requires long-term, multiple interventions and that the research processes that evaluate their effectiveness needed to be reconceptualized along qualitative lines. Ultimately, the most effective research models for use in this area will involve both quantitative and qualitative methods derived from all the disciplines identified earlier in this chapter. It will expand to include "action research," which is basically a form of formative evaluation that involves ongoing, self-correcting feedback to monitor the multiple, often unanticipated outcomes of interventions.

Recent research has focused on creating in-depth understanding of the particular interventions in limited locations. There has been a great interest in problems of violence and abuse in such areas as adolescent suicide (LaFromboise & Bigfoot, 1988), juvenile problem behavior (Scholte, 1992), abuse of disabled persons (Doe, 1990), spouse abuse (Sullivan, Tan, Basta, Rumptz, & Davidson, 1992), and abuse of drugs by adolescents (Farrell, Danish, & Howard, 1992). The effectiveness of community based interventions with chronically ill populations has been another area of inquiry (Mowbray, 1990; Bond, Withridge, Dincin, Wasmer, Webb, & DeGraaf-Kaser, 1990; Toro, 1990). The effect of various types of interventions in ethnic communities has been a subject of research, particularly because of the concern of ecological psychology to understand how cultural perspectives shape problem definition and contribute to the creation of culturally acceptable solutions (Levine, 1989; Vega, 1992; Marin, Marin, Perez-Stable, Sabogal, & Otero-Sabogal, 1990). Finally, there has been a great deal of discussion about research paradigms and methodologies because of the challenges articulated by Kelly and others. Little or no research in this area has been done to evaluate the impact of a particular intervention with specific individuals. By virtue of its person/environment assumptions, research will tend and has tended toward ethnographic approaches with groups who share common life circumstances. From this perspective, ecological counseling approaches challenge the very basis of the individual-as-separate-person and, thus, the paradigm that shapes most counseling research and practice. Thus, the effectiveness of the interventions use question is reframed but no less important.

It appears that future approaches to research in this area must be dictated by the topics to be investigated. A single, positivistic paradigm based on the assumptions of Western science and Newtonian mechanics is not relevant to the study of dynamic systems. Rather than permitting research methods to dictate the types of problems that can be studied, ecological and community psychology are committed to developing new approaches that can investigate subjects that are important to the human community and to exercise the creativity and interdisciplinary cooperation necessary to achieve those ends.

REFERENCES

Albee, G. (1980). A competency model to replace the defect model. In M. Gibbs, J. Lachenmeyer, & J. Sigal (Eds.), *Community psychology: Theoretical and empirical approaches* (pp. 213–238). New York: Gardner.

Albee, G., & Ryan-Finn, K. (1993). An overview of primary prevention. *Journal of Counseling and Development, 72*, 115–123.

Bem, S., Martyna, W., & Watson, C. (1976). Sex-typing and androgyny: Further explorations of the expressive domain. *Journal of Personality and Social Psychology, 34*, 1016–1023.

Block, J. (1973). Conceptions of sex-role: Some cross-cultural and longitudinal perspectives. *American Psychologist, 28*, 512–526.

Bond, G., Withridge, T., Dincin, J., Wasmer, D., Webb, J., & DeGraaf-Kaser, R. (1990). Assertive community treatment for frequent users of psychiatric hospitals in a large city: A controlled study. *American Journal of Community Psychology, 18*, 865–891.

Bronfenbrenner, U. (1979). *The ecology of human development.* Cambridge, MA: Harvard University Press.

Broverman, I., Broverman, D., Clarkson, F., Rosenkrantz, P., & Vogel, S. (1970). Sex-role stereotypes and clinical judgments of mental health. *Journal of Consulting and Clinical Psychology, 34*, 1–7.

Broverman, I., Vogel, S., Broverman, D., Clarkson, F., & Rosenkrantz, P. (1972). Sex-role stereotypes: A current appraisal. *Journal of Social Issues, 28*, 59–78.

Brown, B. (1980). *Supermind.* New York: Harper & Row.

Capra, F. (1987). *Uncommon wisdom.* New York: Bantam Books.

Chickering, A., & Reisser, L. (1993). *Education and identity* (2d ed.). San Francisco, CA: Jossey-Bass.

Conyne, R. (1985). The counseling psychologist: Helping people in environments. *Counseling and Human Development, 18*(2), 1–11.

Doe, T. (1990). Towards an understanding: An ecological model of abuse. *Developmental Disabilities Bulletin, 18*(2), 13–20.

Farrell, A., Danish, S., & Howard, C. (1992). Risk factors for drug use in urban adolescents: Identification and cross-validation. *American Journal of Community Psychology, 20,* 263–286.

Gibbs, M. (1980). Social class, mental disorder and their implications for community psychology. In M. Gibbs, J. Lachenmeyer, & J. Sigal (eds.), *Community psychology: Theoretical and empirical approaches* (pp. 173–205). New York: Gardner.

Gilligan, C. (1982). *In a different voice.* Cambridge, MA: Harvard University Press.

Gilligan, C., Lyons, N., & Hanmer, T. (Eds.). (1990). *Making connections.* Cambridge, MA: Harvard University Press.

Gleick, J. (1987). *Chaos: Making a new science.* New York: Penguin.

Heller, K. (1993). Prevention activities for older adults: Social structures and personal competencies that maintain useful roles. *Journal of Counseling and Development, 72,* 124–130.

Howe, N., & Strauss, W. (1993). *13th gen.* New York: Random House.

Jantsch, E. (Ed.). (1981). *The evolutionary vision: Toward a unifying paradigm of physical, biological and sociocultural evolution.* Boulder, CO: Westview.

Kelly, J. (1990). Changing contexts and the field of community psychology. *American Journal of Community Psychology, 18,* 769–792.

Kelly, J. (1987). An ecological paradigm: Defining mental health consultations as a preventative service. *Prevention in Human Services, 4*(3/4), 1–36.

Kitchener, K. (1985). Ethical principles and ethical decisions in student affairs. In H. Canon & R. Brown, (Eds.), *Applied ethics in student service* (New directions in student service 15) (pp. 17–30). San Francisco, CA: Jossey-Bass.

LaFromboise, T., & Bigfoot, D. (1988). Cultural and cognitive considerations in the preventions of American Indian adolescent suicide. *Journal of Adolescence, 11,* 139–153.

Levine, M. (Ed.). (1989). Community psychology in Asia. *American Journal of Community Psychology* (Special issue), *17.*

Levine, M., & Perkins, D. (1987). *Principles of community psychology.* New York: Oxford University Press.

Marin, G., Marin, B., Perez-Stable, J., Sabogal, F., & Otero-Sabogal, R. (1990). Changes in information as a function of a culturally appropriate smoking cessation community interventions for Hispanics. *American Journal of Community Psychology, 18,* 847–864.

Meichenbaum, D., & Jaremko, M. (Eds.). (1983). *Stress reduction and prevention.* New York: Plenum.

Mowbray, C. (1990). Community treatment for the seriously mentally ill: Is this community psychology? *American Journal of Community Psychology, 18,* 893–902.

Newton, F., & Caple, R. (Eds.). (1985). Paradigm shifts: Considerations for practice. *Journal of Counseling and Development* (Special issue), *64*(3).

Okun, B. (1987). *Effective helping* (3rd ed.). Monterey, CA: Brooks/Cole.

O'Neill, P. (1989). Responsible to whom? Responsible for what? Some ethical issues in community intervention. *American Journal of Community Psychology, 17,* 323–341.

Prigogine, I., & Allen, P. (1982). The challenge of complexity. In W. Schieve & P. Allen (Eds.), *Self-organization and dissipative structures* (pp. 4–39). Austin: University of Texas Press.

Rappaport, J. (1987). Terms of empowerment/exemplars of prevention: Toward a theory for community psychology. *American Journal of Community Psychology, 15,* 121–148.

Rappaport, J. (1977). *Community psychology: Values, research and action.* New York: Holt, Rinehart and Winston.

Sandler, B. (1993). *Women faculty at work in the classroom, or, why it still hurts to be a woman in labor.* Washington, DC: Center for Women Policy Studies.

Scholte, E. (1992). Prevention and treatment of juvenile problem behavior: A proposal for a socio-ecological approach. *Journal of Abnormal Child Psychology, 20,* 247–261.

Stokols, D. (1992). Establishing and maintaining healthy environments. *American Psychologist, 47,* 6–22.

Sue, D., & Sue, D. (1990). *Counseling the culturally different.* New York: Wiley.

Sullivan, C., Tan, C., Basta, J., Rumptz, M., & Davidson, W. (1992). An advocacy intervention program for women with abusive partners: Initial evaluation. *American Journal of Community Psychology, 20,* 309–332.

Toro, P. (1990). Evaluating professionally oriented self-help programs for the seriously mentally ill. *American Journal of Community Psychology, 18,* 813–828.

Vega, W. (1992). Theoretical and pragmatic implications of cultural diversity for community research. *American Journal of Community Psychology, 20,* 357–392.

Werner, J., & Tyler, M. (1993). Community based interventions. *Journal of Counseling and Development, 71,* 689–692.

14

Conclusion

Mary Ballou

At the conclusion of the many chapters in this handbook, several ending points can now be made. Many strategies, some old, some contemporary, and some developing, have been excluded. In this final chapter, some of these are briefly addressed. Another discussion in this last chapter is a return to the question of evaluation and a proposal that both research and practice have much to offer each other.

ANALYSES

The first group of interventions left out of the text are the various analyses. The goal of analytical interventions is to shift the level of perception from only individual to also social and systemic. These conceptual shifts broadening awareness from exclusively individual to the influencing forces of factors, conditions, and structures in the social/cultural context hold much importance for U.S. psychology and the culture that supports it. With cultural values of individualism supported by a pragmatic ethic, U.S. psychology and its practitioners and users often need reminding of factors beyond the individual. There are very real situations where comprehending the context in its social and structural forces is important to understanding and to healing. Without strategies facilitating cognitive understandings, which include contextual factors and structures, the principle of agency in context becomes impossible. If the larger context — both social and interpersonal — is not considered, the only options are individual choice, will, and responsibility or a passive recipient construction. These analytical strategies, however, help to establish understanding that includes both the context and the person, often a stance appropriate and necessary for recovery and healing, for instance, when, through sex-role analysis, victims of sexual abuse transform guilt and shame to anger at what was done to them through a power/domination dimension implicit within gender roles. The analyses are strategies that facilitate such conceptual shifts because they help to illuminate the context in which the individual grows and functions.

The analyses are different in terms of the category of focus, specific information, and, some would claim, the distance from the privileged normative standards of the dominant group. Gender role analysis, ethnic analysis, class analysis, race analysis, family analysis, and power analysis all share a common pattern. Individual experience is contextualized and, thus, seen as nonisolated and influenced by forces (beliefs, structures, and actions) external to the individual. Individual self-feelings, beliefs, and values are influenced by these external forces and the procedural aspects of them. Attributions, rewards-position, status, money, influence, valuative and devaluative attitudes, and specific actions are seen as related to the focus of analysis. The self-feelings and beliefs of an individual are, in part, resultant from social context and structural forces within a specific culture.

In use, the strategy starts with the telling of individual experience, often (but not necessarily) in a group. The next step is to look at similarities across experience by virtue of the category, for example, gender or race. Individual experience is not denied but is related to the particular categories. For example, the consistent social messages to females that they are relational and not instrumental may decrease their tolerance for interpersonal conflict and for lengthy training periods of technical noninteractive skills. Similarly, these messages and the structures that support them may provide the developmental impetus for valuing periheterosexual relationships over truth telling in adolescence for females.

The value of these analyses is that the category and its evaluation become seen. Their existence is related to, but not the totality of, the individual, and the socially constructed nature of the action, attitudes, and evaluation can be understood. When one's sense of self and the social and structural evaluations are understood as related, then both causation and accountability are expanded, and numerous courses of change become possible. The client sees that no longer is he or she dumb, bad, immoral, weak, abnormal, or misfitting; his or her family, school, or culture has limited and particular definitions and valued actions.

The dominant group approves of and rewards that which maintains and fits its structure. The gay Hispanic child or the black male adolescent in a busing program or the homeless person or a male seeking to become an early childhood educator all face socially or culturally based negative self-feelings and economic and potential administrative discrimination. These particulars are not the truth but are relative to the group. Such insight often has a powerful and liberating effect on clients who formerly struggled with the negative evaluations and limited options available to them — socially constructed messages that often deeply affect one's sense of self, abilities, and will.

The appropriate use of these strategies is still an evolving question. It is quite clear that their use is inappropriate in an acute crisis situation. Their use also is inappropriate in psychiatric disabilities where clients are not able or willing to question themselves or to take responsibility. Their appropriate use requires concomitant cognitive development and psychological intactness as well as fitting timing. Because these strategies are rather new to psychotherapy, the specifics of the analysis are often in neighboring social science disciplines. Important questions for psychotherapy regarding social conformity, social control, and value positions within counselor and client worldviews appear to be the unsettled issues.

These analyses often are embedded within their own areas. For example, sex-role analysis was developed in feminist therapy (Carter & Rawlings, 1977; Ballou & Gabalac, 1985; Worell & Remer, 1992). The strategies are related to the particular orientation — feminist, multicultural, family. Yet, each is also a strategy that can be used, at appropriate points, in a well-developed counseling relationship. Appropriate analyses are especially useful for changing self-understanding; examining attributions, multiple causative factors, and the power of social and structural forces; and challenging individuals to change negative self-images and skill deficits as well as the narrow conceptions of privilege. Evaluation of these strategies awaits research. Empirical studies will be difficult, because the strategies are indistinguishable from the central tenets of the areas from which they come and because they are rather abstract.

ORDINARY THINGS

Another area not addressed in this book is the healing power of naturally occurring human capacities — phenomena like humor, spiritual beliefs and cultural rituals, states of consciousness and their control, and doing community action work. What makes the events in this list similar is that they occur naturally in some people's lives, and for some people, they are powerful and important to the healing process. Each needs further definition and exploration; yet, each does have interesting accounts of therapeutic use.

Use of spiritual beliefs and cultural rituals are longstanding healing practices in traditions outside of psychotherapy. An aware and respectful learning of these traditions would seem to offer much potential to therapy's strategies. Examples include a variety of events that people do but that are not generally coupled with counseling and therapy. Prayers to dead or absent people are important for grieving, anger, and closure. Religious rituals requesting specific aid and healing practices using particular natural elements (sage for purification) or supernatural phenomena (a deity or force) are other examples. Many people within their own religious and cultural contexts find support, comfort, connection, perspective, and healing from specific rituals. Evaluation of the use of such rituals within or along with psychotherapy has not been published within mainstream mental health literature. Yet, some practitioners are exploring the use of these strategies and communicating about them.

Appropriate uses must include not only existing presence in the client's life but also the counselor's knowledge and willingness to work together with other healers who may be more expert in the particular ritual. Responsible use requires careful consideration of the potential for risk and clients' readiness. Also, the fit of the strategy to the change goal is critical. For example, male clients who need to learn about relationships and relational skills are not best served by vision quests, however in vogue they might be. Culturally specific rituals used out of the cultural context often are disrespectful to the culture and, in fact, model colonialism.

Humor intentionally used in therapy is another promising strategy among the group of naturally occurring strategies. Inviting a client to laugh when an awkward attempt with a new skill is made can be a wonderful communication. When a caring adult warmly smiles or laughs at a child's attempt with a new word or action, the child feels recognized and attended to. Humor can communicate caring, pleasure, perspective, enjoyment, and unity in a common struggle. In addition to affirming the client and joining with her or him, humor can reframe a situation, feelings, or perception.

There is a beginning literature on the use of humor in therapy, but, as yet, it is not developed enough to make judgments. Madanes' (1984) discussion of humor as metaphorical communication and Dimmer, Carroll, and Wyatt's (1990) review of existent studies offer thoughtful treatment of the subject. Yet, there is much caution about the misuse and poorly understood meaning of humor, as well. Hostility and sarcasm are so often communicated through humor that the warnings are serious. In addition, many people, particularly those damaged or in pain, do not relate or respond to humor and laughter. In particular, some may feel further isolated, estranged, or attacked. Yet, how powerful, joining, and transforming humor can be. Its potential seems great while careful exploration, reflection, and evaluation are critical.

Several therapists and authors recommend community involvement for clients at a particular stage of their healing process (for example, Ballou & Gabalac, 1985; Herman, 1992; Miller, 1994). To recover from and then assist with helping others and changing the system that allowed or tolerated the damaging conditions, actions, or attitudes is a solid, integrated, and powerful model for change. Yet, clients' values, abilities, status, and recovery stage must be carefully considered. For instance, in healing from interpersonally or socially precipitated trauma, once the acute intervention is accomplished, it is empowering and reframing for former victims to become helpers and workers for social change. The positive sense of self and of unity with others may be established and heightened through community action. Of course, such involvement suggestion must be explored carefully in a number of ways. Client, readiness, expectation, stage of recovery and health, and motivation are all relevant, as are the resources in the particular community and other demands in the client's life. Again, more experience and evaluation are needed before considered and differential judgments mature, but the potential for clients and for expanding the limits of individual treatment within counseling and therapy are great.

Finally, consciousness and the control of states of consciousness is a developing area of theory and research in psychology. Indeed, some speculate that this arena may be the next major evolution in psychology's development. Consciousness, particularly state-specific consciousness, which includes differing abilities, modes of knowing, processes of perceiving, processing, and remembering, and brain biology, is generating tremendous activity in research and theory and in practice. It is truly an interdisciplinary area.

A list of areas and interests and explorations might include grounding techniques for flashback and somatic memories in trauma treatment; meaning making through value based action in liberation theology; control of autonomic nervous system processes by meditation and biofeedback; stress management for body-wellness, mind-wellness, and relationship-wellness; state-specific consciousness in attention deficit disorder and schizophrenia; altered states of consciousness involved with healing oneself from cancer and other disease as well as learning and memory; healing through physical touch with others; and changes in notions of perspective and values when in balance with nature and natural processes, as in pets for the isolated elderly, regular physical activity, and play. Each of these areas has its advocates and its literature in various stages of development. No doubt, in time, some of the suspected common ground, current inclusion, and excitement will not hold up, but, presently, impressive implications for helping strategies exist in the area of consciousness. Responsible practice requires that professionals move forward into these areas thoughtfully and carefully. Appropriate uses are not established. Sources of information are confusing, widely varied, and presented in different disciplines. Research, evaluation, analysis, and evenly balanced reports have yet to integrate, identify specific factors, or convince. Yet, intuitive connections and clinical experience are leading some to practice these strategies.

The naturally occurring events and processes would seem to hold much potential in the development of strategies for change within therapy. Actually, many are already used through common sense by practicing therapists and clients. For example, the inclusion of religious practices with therapy is something religious clients have been doing since therapy began. Relaxing before making big decisions or a major performance is common and ordinary. Both these examples infer that professional therapy can gain from common and ordinary practices (folk psychology has myth and wisdom). There is, of course, a parallel discussion of academic psychology gaining from practice psychology.

BODY INTERVENTIONS

Another arena of strategies left out of this text is change through interaction with the body. The relationship between or unity of the body and mind have long been troubling to Western intellectual disciplines. The dominant intellectual disciplines in the sciences and social/behavioral sciences chose in the seventeenth century to focus on the material; in the main, that choice is continuing. This material focus led to the development of a powerful science that has enabled tremendous advancement in material and technological understanding and control, but nonmaterial aspects and dimension of reality have not been accorded (much) reality within the choice. Hence, therapeutic interventions aimed at certain dimensions, for example, consciousness, energy, nonphysical healing, are especially nonfitting to the intellectual context of psychology. There are, however, many therapies and notions of body. Some are fairly accepted and heavily researched, like the relationship between diet and psychophysiological functioning or the psychophysical effects of legal and illegal drugs. Healing touch, mentioned before, also has its advocates and supportive studies. Others, however, such as aroma therapy or Rolfing, are more questionable.

There are, however, frequent reports of mind/emotions effects from body based practices. Exercise, yoga, and massage are examples. Also, attention to feeling states shows convincingly that the body is in dynamic relationship to thoughts and feelings. Anger brings body tensing; stress brings hormonal and muscle action; massage, sleep, and orgasm bring relaxation and, often, emotional change. Some kinds of holding communicate protection or comfort; other sorts of holding communicate affection; and still other sorts, ownership or control. Our own human experience tells us that the body and varieties of body actions are connected to other human dimensions. Clinical experience and some research validate both somatic memories and nonverbal behavioral communication.

Behavioral medicine is an exciting area with a large and fast developing literature. It rests upon the interaction between the physical body and psychological states. Body/mind interactions (multicultural psychology) or mediating neurochemical systems (western science) are central to the current developments in both medicine and health psychology. For instance, the relationship between psychological stress and immune system functioning is common knowledge in the 1980s and 1990s. In behavioral medicine, material phenomena like disease, trauma, identifiable neurological based pain, and physiologic effects of drugs affecting both the body and mind are quite acceptable. The ideas present little or no conceptual difficulty. However, nonmaterial interventions, qualities of energy, or states of mind or consciousness affecting the body are more controversial.

Several body therapies, however, take a further step. They posit that the body is a primary part of self and that body sense is a mode of knowing and acting. These claims are so at odds with Western intellectual tradition that they have rarely been taken seriously by mainstream psychology or by practitioners whose knowledge is exclusively tied to mainstream psychology. Nonetheless, body knowledge, sometimes captured in phrases like intuition, gut feeling, emotional sense, and instinct, is not unrelated to human experience. Similarly, several of the "accepted" strategies (imagery, stress management, relaxation response, in vivo flooding, regular exercise, meditation traditions, movement therapy) represent body strategies for mind/emotion change. These interventions, of course, are quite diverse. They have more or less research evaluating their effectiveness and analysis considering the appropriate use. In another volume of interventions, each body based intervention should be separated and considered. Many are quite well-established, as, for example, the relaxation response. Some of the other body techniques are somewhat controversial but are described and supported, for example, healing touch. Others, however, are beyond the limits of contemporary psychology's consideration.

ACTION INTERVENTIONS

Action strategies are another general area where little research exists within psychology. Other than some research supporting the effectiveness of directive therapy, in which the therapist often has the client do something (homework, action plans as in Ellis's Rational Emotive Therapy and Glasser's Reality Therapy), most clinical research has ignored action in therapy and its possible effectiveness for some clients at certain points. There are, however, a range of therapists who practice action in therapy and who are developing models and strategies for action in therapy.

One end of this range is a developing adventure therapy (Gass, 1993), which has evolved out of experiential education and outward-bound programs for troubled youth. It is held to be particularly effective with children, adolescents, and adults who, because of development or primary style, relate better to the concrete and action oriented interventions in a group environment. Often, it is appropriate for those who are cognitively well-defended as well as for people with certain comprehensive, stylistic patterns, as in characterological types. In addition, certain activities have been identified as recommended for particular kinds of recovery, for example, a ropes course for trauma survivors who have established safety and are rebuilding trust (Ewert & Heywood, 1991).

At the other end of the spectrum are practitioners who have adapted to the styles of their clients and may mix walking and talking during therapy. Somewhere in the middle might be those practitioners who encourage their clients at appropriate points to do physical actions to maintain and engage; for example, encouragement to explore joining an activity group (line dancing or nature walking) might be done for human interaction that thwarts isolation and builds relationships. Here, the clients would identify in therapy activities in their community that fit their interests and needs. The client's process of exploring and initiating the activity as well as the actual experience would be brought back for discussion in therapy. Another instance when action interventions are of use would be for a depressed individual. Often, at a certain stage in dealing with depression, action is extremely useful. At first, the action might be merely activity. Later in the process might come a challenge to create meaning in their lives. Taking action that fits one's values and worldview, as, for example, participating in book discussion groups or a big brother program, assisting at a homeless shelter, volunteer training with a crisis service, frequently is important in overcoming depression.

The action strategies are reported to be quite promising for certain clients at certain points in their process. Some initial evaluative research exists about the more organized programs. Yet, for whom, under what conditions, and in which settings are questions awaiting answers.

OTHER AREAS

Many other kinds of strategies could be addressed in this book or, indeed, this chapter. In particular, strategies that are not professionally directed and those stemming from a different time orientation are not contained in the text. Both would be important contributions. Self-help programs and groups are important for many people facing a variety of problems and life conditions. The variety is bewildering and will probably increase with the changes in health care. Although these groups and programs need differentiated, careful, and systematic analysis, they offer enormously important contributions to usual and customary mental health practices.

Time perspective about interventions is a further area. Health can be promoted in development and education. Much like good dental health is promoted by education, training, and occasional professional maintenance, mental health could follow a similar course for individuals. Problem solving, self-esteem, relationship skills, stress management, and conflict resolution could become both school and community programs, much like drivers' education and personal finances are now. Also, the policies and structures in communities and systems could be designed and governed with a commitment to human welfare, much as, now, profit or reelection is a prime motivating factor. If faring well in human mental health were legislated and rewarded, as environmental and physical health is now, there would be far fewer damaged individuals to treat. These are only some of the ideas presented in prevention. Preventive strategy is a hugely important area and one to which much literature is devoted. Some of the literature is topical, focusing on specific content areas (e.g., stress) and some is process oriented (e.g., primary prevention). Both are important to contemporary mental health, and excellent sources of theory, research, and techniques exist within the general literature.

UNANSWERED QUESTIONS, CURRENT DEBATES, AND CLEAR NEEDS

Definitions of health, how to create or increase it, dimensions of import in defining, assessing, and intervening, as well as the essential features of healing are all discussions without consensual agreement. Much is simply unknown about how to help make people well, better, or more suited to or resistant to their environmental conditions. In addition to that which is unknown and obviously complex, certain things are, at base, political. For example, when is it better for a client to cope with and conform to social or dominant standards, and when is it more important to resist them? Who has the power to decide such things, and who gets to name them and, thus, assign relative values to them?

Mental health as social control and therapy as politics are notions that have histories and advocates. Although they are not the entire story, or even particularly descriptive of what most practitioners do, the notions are not entirely inaccurate. Therapy does seek to adjust people to socially set standards. Although often helpful to individuals, it is also conforming to specific standards. This issue is not so much the ability of therapy to facilitate change but the unexamined nature of the change sought. Most therapists seek to help clients better meet their needs. Yet, without examining the underlying values implicit in the goals, defining theory, and interventions, therapists may provide the means to a "health" whose criteria are arbitrary and narrow and, perhaps, in the service of a particular group or ideology. Yet, sometimes, adjustment and social conformance are precisely what a client needs help in. These are not simple issues, but they are important ones.

By now, it should also be clear that appropriateness and effectiveness for intervention strategies are also not simple issues. Appropriateness is not only a clinical issue but also a political one. Similarly, effectiveness raises nonobvious issues.

Since the nineteenth century, Western culture has held tremendous faith in a particular kind of science. A version of empirical logical positivism that acknowledges only material reality has been the guiding force in technological and scientific development. It is no longer clear that this model of science fits applied psychology's needs for evaluative investigation. The growing debate about the kind(s) of systematic investigations needed and fitting for applied psychology exist in detail elsewhere. Here, the importance is the derivative need for clinically useful evaluative information in the service of appropriate, effective, and fitting selection of strategies.

So far, customary research practices have not been especially useful to practitioners in providing them with accurate conclusions about complex interactive and nonobservable factors for clinical practice. Major research projects investigating comparative use of treatment orientations for specific disorders have been useful in providing some answers. The funded and programmatic research undertakings, as, for example, the Weissman depression studies, are yielding meaningful information about effective approaches for particular disorders. Repetitions of smaller studies on specific strategies reveal a pattern of narrowing claims for effectiveness over time and across different researchers, for example, systematic desensitization for phobia. Certain areas are not researched at all.

Evaluative studies of discriminate uses of specific intervention strategies for particular change are not often found. As the chapters here indicate, problems exist with design, consistence, measurement, sample, and specificity of intervention. Often, there is too little research available; when it does exist, it is not credible; and alternate forms of research have not yet made their ways into training programs, funding, and publication approval criteria.

As yet, there is no robust endorsement or even general acceptance of these other methods of systematic investigation. Therefore, the evaluation is not convincing or, worse, left undone. When alternative forms of evaluation are presented, their validity often is questioned and publication denied in many journals. Case studies, other naturalistic accounts, accumulated experience (whether client experience or reflected-upon experience), and professional judgment are often considered not acceptable methodology.

It seems that multiple interventions or changes in certain human dimensions perhaps do not fit the dominant research methodology in psychology. This state of affairs probably has added to the lack of effectiveness research and the lack of respect and collaboration between practitioners and researchers. Practitioners would certainly benefit by solid evaluation of particular strategies for specific changes by distinct clients in identified contexts. Many claims of effectiveness have not held up over time or across experience. Interprofessional communication at staff meetings and conferences, in trade books, and through supervision are major ways in which strategies get shared. Although important, these avenues are probably not systematic enough. Sharing of experience and reflection upon it is strengthened by additional evaluation.

Moreover, it is also clear that researchers would benefit by attending to the full range of human experience and complexity. Practice needs evaluation of its effectiveness, and research needs expansion of content and methods. It seems quite a compelling case for collaboration, each attending to the other.

REFERENCES

Ballou, M., & Gabalac, N. (1985). *A feminist position on mental health*. Springfield, IL: Charles C. Thomas.

Carter, D., & Rawlings, E. (1977). *Psychotherapy for women*. Springfield, IL: Charles C. Thomas.

Dimmer, S., Carroll, J., & Wyatt, G. (1990). Uses of humor in psychotherapy. *Psychological Reports, 66*, 795–801.

Ewert, A., & Heywood, J. (1991). Group development in the natural environment. *Environment and Behavior, 23*, 592–615.

Gass, M. (1993). *Adventure therapy*. Dubuque, IA: Kendall/Hunt.

Herman, J. (1992). *Trauma and recovery*. New York: Basic Books.

Madanes, C. (1984). *Behind the one-way mirror*. San Francisco, CA: Jossey-Bass.

Miller, D. (1994). *Women who hunt themselves*. New York: Basic Books.

Worell, J., & Remer, P. (1992). *Feminist perspectives in therapy*. New York: Wiley.

Index

Achterberg, J., 92–93
Action interventions, 202–3
Activity, and passivity, 121
Adler, A., 8
Adolescents, cognitive restructuring for, 45
Aggression, 126
Agras, W., 96
Ahsen, Akhter, 86–87
Alberti, R. E., 128, 131
Allender, J. S., 92
Allport, Gordon, 22
Analytical interventions, 195–97
Andrews, G., 107
Anton, W., 97
Anxiety, 8; baseline measurement of, 99; decision-making training in, 44; free-floating, 15, 98, 107; hierarchy construction for, 103–5; origins of, 95–96, 112; paradoxical strategies for, 2; ratings for, 99; responses for, 96–97
Arbitration and mediation, 154
Art therapy: case studies in, 72–73; color in, 71–72; family, 71; implementation of, 69–72; theoretical background of, 68–69
Assagioli, Roberto, 85, 89

Assertiveness, defined, 125
Assertiveness training (AT): appropriate use of, 131–32; bicultural, 129–31; components of, 125–26; effectiveness research into, 132–33; goals of, 126; group program for, 128–29; inappropriate use of, 132; need assessment in, 126–29
Assessment: biopsychosocial, 98–99; in ecological intervention, 178–80; of imagery, 104
At a Journal Workshop (Progoff), 139
Authority, frustration with, 8
Awareness, 117–18

Baggs, K., 132–33
Ballou, M., 31
Bandura, Albert, 22, 23, 28, 30, 32–33
Bargaining, 157
Barrera, M., 97
Bassoff, E. S., 121, 123
Battering, 131–32; community intervention in, 168–72; ecological intervention for, 177–83; mediation in, 159–60
Baucom, D. H., 47
Beall, S. K., 148–49
Beck, Aaron T., 38, 40, 42–43, 47

Behaviorism, imagery use in, 84
Beliefs, spiritual, 198, 200
Bennett, S. M., 45
Benson, H., 97
Beutler, L., 46–47
Bibliotherapy: appropriate use of, 61–63; for children, 58, 59–60, 62; effectiveness research into, 63–64; general procedures in, 56–59; group, 60; historical background of, 55–56; levels of, 56–57; stages in, 57–58
Biofeedback, 186
Body, and awareness, 118
Body interventions, 200–202
Body-mind interaction, 87–88, 201
Body sense, 201–2
Bogolub, E. B., 43
Bornstein, P., 45
Bowen, M., 167
Bowman, J. T., 39
Brady, J., 107–8
Breathing, in imagery, 85
Brief Therapy Center, 13–14
Brown, E. F., 59, 60
Buckelew, G. P., 44
Bulimia nervosa, 45
Burns, Robert, 71
Burt, Helene, 71–72

Cancer, imagery in, 92–93
Carranza, V., 79
Carroll, J., 199
Case, C., 73
Centering, 85
Chace, Marian, 73, 76, 77
Chaisson, M., 46–47
Chambliss, D., 97
Change: ambivalence toward, 9; client motivation for, 42; deadlines for, 10; as frightening, 2, 7; resistance to, 7–10; social, 166–67, 199
Chaos theory, 30, 189–90
Chebra, J., 44
Child abuse, 73, 170; mediation in, 159–60
Children: anxiety-incompatible responses for, 97; art therapy for, 69, 71, 73; bibliotherapy for, 58, 59–60,

62; cognitive restructuring for, 45; dance/movement therapy for, 78, 79; modeling for, 28
Civil rights movement, 31, 166–67
Clarke, C., 131–32
Client, characteristics of, 28
Coercion, 31, 49, 50
Cognitions, 37, 38
Cognitive behaviorism, worldview of, 32
Cognitive restructuring: appropriate use of, 41–47; criticism of, 50; defined, 37; effectiveness research into, 41–47; evaluation of, 48–50; feminist analysis in, 40; homework in, 41; as pragmatic, 42; process of, 39–41; theoretical background of, 37–38
Color, in art therapy, 71–72
Community intervention, x–xi, 199; approaches to, 164, 167–68; appropriate use of, 173; effectiveness research into, 173; inappropriate use of, 172–73; origins of, 165; and value systems, 163, 165; variables in, 165–67
Conditioned Reflex Therapy (Salter), 126
Conditioning, Pavlovian, 96
Consciousness, 199–200
Consciousness-raising, 40
Constructive theory, 31
Control: origin of, 8; and psychological problems, 164; through writing, 146, 147
Coping, 39, 97
Coping modeling, 24
Corey, G., 46
Cormier, L. S., 39, 61, 107, 110, 123, 131
Cormier, W. H., 39, 107, 110
Cottone, R., 122–23
Counterconditioning, 96; alternative responses in, 108; first use of, 95; relaxation training in, 100–105
Cox, J., 132
Cox, R. H., 91–92
Craighead, E., 47
Craighead, J., 56
Crampton, Martha, 88, 90
Curley, A., 131–32

Dalley, T., 73

Dance/movement therapy: appropriate use of, 77–78; background of, 73–75; effectiveness research into, 79; goals in, 74; implementation of, 75–77; inappropriate use of, 78–79

Darwin, Charles, *The Expression of Emotions in Man and Animals*, 73

Davis, C. J., 45

Davis, M., 5

Davis, R. C., 45

Debord, J. B., 17

Decision making, 44

Dellmann-Jenkins, M., 43–44

Delongis, A., 47

Depression, unipolar, 44, 47

Diary (Pepys), 137–38

Dimmer, S., 199

Disease, mind-body connection in, 87–88

Divorce, impact of, 153

Divorce mediation: appropriate use of, 159–60; benefits from 162; defined, 153–54; effectiveness research into, 160–61; goal of, 154–59; homework in, 157; inappropriate use of, 159, 160

Doe, T., 175–76

Dowd, E. T., 16, 17

Ecological intervention: approaches in, 180–83, 184–85, 187–88; appropriate use of, 185–89; assumptions of, 176–77; ethics in, 188; goal of, 182–83; research issues for, 189–91; scenario for, 177–83

Ecological psychology, background of, 183–85

Effort/Shape system, 75

Ellis, Albert, 23, 37–38

Emery, R., 160–61

Emilio, R. F., 79

Emmons, M. L., 128, 131

Environmental, change in, x; and individual, xi; levels of, 175–76

Erickson, S., 157

Espanek, Liljan, 73

Ethnicity, 166

Exercise, 201

Existentialism, 3–4

Experiencing Scale, 123

Expression of Emotions in Man and Animals, The (Darwin), 73

Expressive therapies, goals of, 67–68. *See also* Art therapy; Dance/movement therapy

Family therapy, 167

Fanning, P., 5

Fantasy, guided, 89

Feather, B., 112

Feder, B., 69

Feder, E., 69

Feeling states, 201

Felt sense, 118–19

Felt shift, 121

Femininity, images of, 179–80

Feminist movement, 166–67

Feminists, and external reality, 38

Feminist theory, 31

Feminist therapy: appropriate use of, 173; for battering victims, 168–72; components of, 163–64; effectiveness research into, 173; inappropriate use of, 173; model for, 167–68

Fenwick, C. R., 133

Fisch, R., 13–14

Fleshman, B., 79

Flooding, 96

Foa, E., 105

Focusing: appropriate use of, 122–23; bases of, 117; development of, 118–19; effectiveness research into, 123–24; implementation of, 119–22; inappropriate use of, 123

Fodor, I., 110

Foldberg, J., 156, 161

Fowler, Gene, 142

Frankl, Viktor, 3–4, 6–7

Freud, Sigmund, 69; imagery use by, 84

Fryear, J. L., 79

Gallagher, D., 46

Galt, John Minson, II, 55

Gender, 40–41, 167

Gender roles, 179–80, 197

Gendlin, Eugene: on felt sense, 118–19; on felt shift, 121; focusing manual of, 119–21
Gershaw, J., 28
Gestalt psychology, assumption of, 23, 117–18
Gilliland, B. E., 39
Glasgow, R., 97
Glass, C. V., 107
Glerck, J., 30
Goals, cooperation in, 9–10
Goldstein, A., 27–28
Goldsteing, A., 97
Goldfried, M., 97
Goodill, S. W., 78
Gould, P., 69
Graduated modeling, 24
Greenberg, R., 13
Grenier, C. E., 45
Gripton, J., 43
Grounding, 85

Hackney, H., 61, 123, 131
Haley, 7, 15
Hall, D. W., 132
Hanson, S., 44
Harrell, R., 132
Harvey, R., 107
Heber, L., 77
Hecker, J., 106–7
Hergenhahn, B., 24
Hewett, J., 44
Hill, H. J., 17
Hofer, K. V., 43–44
Holistic therapy, 87–88
Hopper, V., 142
Horan, P., 56
Human Figure Drawing Test, 71
Human Mind, The (Menninger), 55–56
Humor, 4, 198–99
Hurwitz, A. J., 79
Hynes, A., 63
Hynes-Berry, M., 63

Imagery: appropriate use of, 87–89; assessment of, 104; effectiveness research into, 91–93; historical background of, 83–85;

impelmentation of, 85–87; inappropriate use of, 89–90; and thought specificity, 40; timing of, 90; transpersonal phase of, 85; variations of, 86
Imaginal modeling, 24–25
Immune system, and imagery, 92
Improvisation, 76–77
Individualism, and social/systemic perception, 195–96
Insomnia, 6–7
Interventions: indentification of, ix; as individualistic, x–xi; standards of, xi, xii. See also specific interventions
Ivey, A., 122

Jabichuk, A., 45
Jacobson, E., 96
Jakab, Irene, 69
James, R. K., 39
Jillings, C. R., 133
Jones, Mary Cover, 95
Journal writing: appropriate use of, 140–42; benefits from, 146–48; cautions for, 142–43; dialogue approach to, 145; effectiveness research into, 148–49; history of, 137–38; in imagery, 86; private approach to, 143–44; use of, 138–40
Jung, Carl, 85; imagery use by, 84

Kanfer, F., 27–28
Kantrowitz, R., 31
Kashack, Ellyn, 169
Kaufman, Harvard, 71
Kaufman, M. E., 131
Kaufmann, J., 170
Kazdin, A., 22–23, 24, 96, 105
Kelly, James, 190
Kinetic Family Drawing, 71
Koppitz, Elizabeth, 71
Kramer, Edith, 69
Kreuger, D. W., 78
Krumboltz, J. D., 44
Kubie, L. S., 84–85
Kwiatkowska, Hanna, 71

Labanotation, 75

Language, 22
Lazarus, A. A., 97, 107, 132
Lazarus, R. S., 47
Learning: from modeling, 26–28; observational/rehearsal, 30–31
Lester, G. W., 47
Lewin, Kurt, 183
Live modeling, 24
Logotherapy, 3, 4
Lopez, G., 13
Lustman, P. J., 44

Mcguire, K., 121, 122
McInnis, K. M., 59, 61
McKay, M., 5–6
McKnight Erickson, M., 157
McNamara, N., 56
Madanes, C., 199
Mallinckrodt, B., 130
Mandala, 70–71
Manipulation, 17
Marital therapy, 47
Martinez-Taboas, A., 14
Masculinity, images of, 179–80
Massage, 201
Masters, J., 105
Mastery modeling, 24
Mediation, and arbitration, 154. *See also* Divorce mediation
Mediator: conceptual framework of, 156–57; defined, 156; professional background of, 155; responsibility of, 154, 156, 157–59
Medicine, behavioral, 201
Meditation, 97
Meichenbaum, Donald, 23, 26, 38
Men, aggression of, 129
Menninger, Karl A., *The Human Mind*, 55–56
Menninger, William C., 55–56
Mental health: education in, 203–4; factors in, x; responsibility for, 3, 32, 42, 48; social context of, 183; as social control, 204; and stereotyping, 179; studies into, 205–6
Mental health training, individualistic views in, x
Mental illness, ix–x; contextual

description of, 183–84
Milby, J., 105
Milne, A., 156, 161
Milne, C. R., 16
Mind-body connection, and disease, 87–88
Minority population, assertiveness of, 130
Mitchell, L. K., 44
MMPI Depression Scale, 46
Modeling: acquisition phase of, 25–26; application of, 24, 28–30; in assertiveness training, 125–26; and client characteristics, 28; in cognitive restructuring, 40; defined, 21; learning enhancement from, 26–28; misapplication of, 30–34; origins of, 22–23; performance phase of, 26; types of, 24–25
Moreno, Jacob, 23
Morris, R., 100
Murphy, G. F., 44
Mutuality, 156–57

Naumburg, Margaret, 69
Nichols, M. P., 43
Nonassertiveness, 126
Normative behavior, defining of, 31–32

Okun, B. F., 29, 43
O'Leary, K. D., 131–32
Olson, M., 24
O'Neal, G., 44
Operant conditioning, 22
Optimism, 48
Oster, G. D., 69

Paradoxical intervention: application of, 2, 5–10; appropriate use of, 15–16, 18; characteristics of, 2–3; complaint-based directive in, 7, 8; criticism of, 17; defiance-based directive in, 7–8; defined, 1; effectiveness research into, 13–15; ethics of, 17; goal of, 12; inappropriate use of, 16; joining/mirroring technique in, 7, 9; long-term effects of, 16–17; origins of, 3–5; presentation of, 18; principles in,

5–6; reframing in, 11–12; as risk free, 14; symptom prescribing in, 10–11; theoretical approach to, 4–5

"Paradoxical Intervention in the Treatment of Chronic Anorexia Nervosa," 14

Pardeck, J. T., 55, 62

Participant modeling, 24

Passivity, and activity, 121

Pearson, J., 160, 161

Penfield, W., 84

Pennebaker, J. W., 148–49

Pepys, S., *Diary*, 137–38

Peris, Fritz, 23

Personality theory, and human subsystems, xiv

Phillips, D., 97

Phobia, conception of, 112

Pie, R., 13

Positivism, xiii, 205

Posttraumatic stress disorder, 97

Power, 164

Prather, R. C., 45

Procrastination, 13

Progoff, Ira, *At a Journal Workshop*, 139

Psychotherapy: goal of, 12; success factors in, 96

Quevillion, R., 45

Race, 166

Rachman, S., 96

Rational-emotive therapy model, 23, 38

Reality, 110; and experience perception, 117; feminist view of, 38

Reciprocal inhibition, 95–96

Reframing, 176, 199; function of, 11–12

Reiland, J. D., 78

Relapse, 12, 107

Relaxation: and hierarchy imagery, 104–5; in imagery, 85, 88; and imaging, 95; impact of, 112; metronome-conditioned, 97; progressive muscle exercise in, 96; training in, 100–105, 111

Religion, 198, 200

Renneberg, B., 97

Resistance: to change, 7–10; and

symptom prescribing, 10–11

Responsibility, for mental health, 3, 32, 42, 48

Rhoads, J., 112

Riedel, H. P., 133

Rimm, D., 105

Rituals, cultural, 198

Roberts, G. T., 39

Role-playing: application of, 21–22, 28–30; in assertiveness training, 125; in bibliotherapy, 58; in bicultural AT group, 130; and client characteristics, 28; in cognitive restructuring, 40; defined, 21; misapplication of, 30–34; in modeling, 26; origins of, 23; types of, 24

Rosen, G., 97

Rosenbaum, A., 131–32

Rosenfield, A., 13

Rosenthal, R., 13

Rush, Benjamin, 55

Salomon, G., 28

Salter, Andrew, *Conditioned Reflex Therapy*, 126

Sand, George, 138

Sargent, K. L., 59

Schaub, B., 85, 90

Schaub, R., 85, 90

Schizophrenia, 148

Schofield, E., 78

Schoop, Trudy, 73

Schwartz, R. C., 43

Schwarzen, R., 33

Science, 30, 205

Self, and body, 201–2

Self-absorption, 3

Self-blame, 32

Self-concept, 39

Self-efficacy theory, 23, 28, 30; debate over, 32–33

Self-esteem, from journal writing, 147

Self-help programs, 203

Self-statements, 41

Self-transcendence, 3–4

Seltzer, Leon, 13

Shaffer, W., 98–99

Shea, J., 123

Sheehan, P. W., 83
Shoham-Salomon, V., 13
Sibbison, W., 153
Simkin, J., 123
Simons, A. D., 44
Singer, J. L., 83, 91
Singer, Jerome, 84
Smerigilio, U., 45
Smith, M. L., 107
Social class, 165–66
Socialization, 181
Social learning theory, 22
Social skill training, 126
Sourkes, B. M., 70
Spence, S. H., 132–33
Spiritualism, 198, 200
Spouse abuse, 131–32, 159–60
Sprafkin, R., 28
Starke, M. C., 132
Steketee, G., 105
Stokols, D., 189
Stoltenberg, C., 132
Strauss, F., 132
Stress, and biofeedback, 186
Stress management, x
Subjective distress scale (suds), 99, 100, 103, 104–5, 108
Subjective Units of Discomfort Scale, 128
Sympton, prescribing of, 8, 10–11
Symptom-solution cycle, 6
Systematic desensitization, x; coping, 97; defined, 95; effectiveness research into, 105–6; limitations of, 106–8; mechanisms of, 96–97; paradigm/strategems for, 98–105; problems in, 108; procedure modification in, 112; research into, 108–13; self-administered, 97–98; success factors in, 96–97

Telch, C. F., 46
Telch, M. J., 46
Therapeutic relationship: coercion in, 31, 49, 50; in cognitive restructuring, 48–49; manipulation in, 17; in paradoxical intervention, 5; relationship-building stage of,

185–86; requirements of, xiii–xiv
Therapist, dual role of, 1, 15
Therapy: central paradox of, 1–2; coercion in, 31, 49, 50; as politics, 204; solution focused, 139
Thoennes, N., 160, 161
Thorpe, G., 106–7
Treatment, as theory driven, x, xi, xii
Trust, 156–57

Valentich, M., 43
Values, 163, 195–96
Value systems, 165
Victim, blaming of, 32
Violence: community intervention in, 168–72; ecological intervention for, 177–83; increase in, 33
Visualization, training in, 104

Wachtel, P., 96, 97, 109, 110
Walker, S., 43
Watkins, P. C., 45
Watzlawick, P., 13–14
Weakland, J., 13–14
Wehr, S. H., 131
Weishaar, M. E., 42–43
Wetzel, R. D., 44
Whitehouse, Mary, 73
Williams, J. M., 132
Williamson, D. A., 45
Willoughby Neuroticism and Fear Survey Questionnaires, 99
Wilson, G., 96, 105
Wolpe, Joseph, 100; on assertive behavior, 126; on reciprocal inhibition, 95–96; on subjective distress scale, 99; on systematic desensitization, 108–9
Wombach, C. A., 13
Women: AT study on, 132–33; battered, 131–32; and divorce, 153; journal writing by, 147; as nonassertive, 129; voices of, 138
Wood, P., 130
Wyatt, G., 199
Wyer, M., 161

Yalom, J. D., 43   Yost, E., 47
Yoga, 201
Yontef, G., 123   Zigler, E., 170

About the Contributors

MARY BALLOU is an associate professor of counseling psychology and provides psychotherapy in a medical group. She is widely published, including three earlier texts — *Health Counseling, Mental Health: A Feminist Perspective*, and *Personality and Psychotherapy Feminist Reappraisals*.

JANE FRIED is an assistant professor and coordinator of counseling and student services programs at Northeastern University. She has published articles and a monograph and is currently focusing on diversity within student services.

ROUEIDA GHADBAN is a third-year doctoral student in clinical psychology at the New School of Social Research in New York. This is her first professional publication.

ELAINE LEEDER is an associate professor in the sociology department at Ithaca College. She has published numerous articles and two books, including *Treating Abuse in Families: A Feminist and Community Approach*.

LAWRENCE LITWACK is professor and department chair at Northeastern University. He has taught at several universities and has published extensively.

LUCIA MATTHEWS is a first-year doctoral student in counseling psychology at Northeastern University. This is her first professional publication.

SUZANNE ST ONGE is a psychiatric nurse practitioner and a doctoral student in counseling psychology at Northeastern University. This is her first professional publication.

JAN YOUGA is an associate professor of writing at Keene State College. She served as director of writing at Gordon College and director of English education at Illinois State University. She has authored *The Elements of Audience Analysis* and *Writing Are Readings*.

ISBN 0-275-94851-X

9 780275 948511

HARDCOVER BAR CODE